New York Painting and Sculpture: 1940–1970

New York Painting and Sculpture: 1940–1970

BY HENRY GELDZAHLER

Curator of Contemporary Arts,
The Metropolitan Museum of Art

Foreword by Thomas P. F. Hoving

Director, The Metropolitan Museum of Art

E. P. Dutton & Co., Inc. New York

in association with The Metropolitan Museum of Art

To the memory of two museum men:
James J. Rorimer
and René d'Harnoncourt

Published simultaneously in Canada by Clarke, Irwin & Company Limited, Toronto and Vancouver.

Library of Congress Catalog Card Number: 71–87179

Bonnie Burnham (handwritten signature)

Contents

Acknowledgments

A generous grant from the Xerox Corporation helped make this exhibition possible.

Without the help of Kay Bearman, Consultant to this exhibition, and without the encouragement of George Trescher, Secretary to the Museum's Centennial, this exhibition and its book would not have materialized.

I would like to thank Christopher Scott and Allen Rosenbaum for assistance with the introduction, Stuart Silver for his flexible ideas about installation, and Clifford La Fontaine for his maquettes.

I am grateful to Walter Hopps for securing and installing the Joseph Cornells.

Conversations with Philip Leider, Clement Greenberg, Michael Fried, John J. McKendry, and many of the lenders to the exhibition have been of great help and interest.

I would also like to mention the following people for their special cooperation in supplying material for this publication: Barbara Adler, Elita Agee, Martha Baer, Leslie Feely, Manuel E. Gonzalez, Bruce Jones, Alkis Klonaridis, Phyllis Lester, Cintra Lofting, Linda Loving, Margaret McConnell, Audrey McCowin, April McMenamin, Eric Pollitzer, Jane Salzfass, David Spangler, Jock Truman, Diane Waldman, Joan Washburn, David White, David Whitney, and Barbara Wool.

The members of my office staff worked unstintingly: Kay Bearman provided the catalogue information and the biographies; Jacquelyn Serwer the bibliography; and James Wood, Assistant Curator of the Department, has been responsible for overseeing the countless details of shipping and insurance. Karen Asakawa has been a valuable secretary.

Finally, I would like to thank Thomas P. F. Hoving and the Trustees of the Metropolitan Museum for their confidence; and the artists in the exhibition and their families for their generosity and encouragement.

Private Collectors

Harry N. Abrams Family Collection, New York
Josef Albers, New Haven, Connecticut
Mr. and Mrs. Harry W. Anderson, Atherton, California
Mr. and Mrs. Lester Francis Avnet, New York
Mr. and Mrs. E. A. Bergman, Chicago, Illinois
Mr. and Mrs. Jacob Berman, Sherman Oaks, California
Mr. and Mrs. Donald Blinken, New York
Irving Blum, Los Angeles, California
Jason Ferus Blum, Los Angeles, California
Peter Brant, New York
Mrs. Abner Brenner, Washington, D.C.
Dr. and Mrs. Bernard Brodsky, New York
Leonard M. Brown, Springfield, Massachusetts
Carter Burden, New York
Edward Carey, New York
Mr. and Mrs. Leo Castelli, New York
Mr. and Mrs. Louis D. Cohen, Great Neck, New York
Joseph Cornell, Flushing, New York
Mrs. Stuart Davis, New York
Jaime C. del Amo, Madrid, Spain
Mr. and Mrs. Edward L. Diehl, Cambridge, Massachusetts
Mrs. Elise C. Dixon, Scottsdale, Arizona
Mrs. Marcel Duchamp, New York
Mrs. Julius Epstein, Northfield, Illinois
Estate of Hans Hofmann
Estate of Franz Kline
Estate of David Smith
Mr. and Mrs. Richard L. Feigen, New York
Morton Feldman, New York
Helen Frankenthaler, New York
Mr. and Mrs. Allan Frumkin, New York
Mr. and Mrs. Victor W. Ganz, New York
Mr. and Mrs. Maurice Geller, New York
Mr. and Mrs. Milton A. Gordon, New York
Adolph Gottlieb, New York
Mrs. Esther Gottlieb, New York
Mr. and Mrs. Clement Greenberg, New York
Mrs. Albert M. Greenfield, Sr., Philadelphia, Pennsylvania
Robert Halff, Beverly Hills, California

Joseph H. Hazen, New York

Mr. and Mrs. Ben Heller, New York

Dr. and Mrs. Charles Hendrickson, Newport Beach, California

Joseph H. Hirshhorn Collection

Joseph H. Hirshhorn Foundation

Mr. and Mrs. Richard Hokin, New York

Mr. and Mrs. Norman Ives, Woodbridge, Connecticut

Mrs. Martha K. Jackson, New York

Jasper Johns, New York

Carl W. Johnson, Beverly Hills, California

Philip Johnson, New Canaan, Connecticut

Mrs. Julie Judd, New York

Dr. and Mrs. Ernest Kafka, New York

The Kleiner Foundation

Mr. J. Patrick Lannan, Palm Beach, Florida

The Lannan Foundation

Mr. and Mrs. Julien Levy, Bridgewater, Connecticut

The Albert A. List Family Collection

Mrs. H. Gates Lloyd, Haverford, Pennsylvania

Miss Lois Long, New York

Dr. Peter Ludwig, Cologne, Germany

Lewis Manilow, Chicago, Illinois

Dr. and Mrs. Edward Massie, St. Louis, Missouri

Mr. and Mrs. Robert B. Mayer, Winnetka, Illinois

Richard Meier, New York

Mr. and Mrs. David Mirvish, Toronto, Canada

Robert Motherwell, New York

Mr. and Mrs. Morton Neumann, Chicago, Illinois

S. I. Newhouse, Jr., New York

Mrs. Albert H. Newman, Chicago, Illinois

Mrs. Annalee Newman, New York

Mr. and Mrs. Kenneth Noland, New York

Mrs. Claes Oldenburg, New York

Jules Olitski, New York

Mr. and Mrs. David I. Orr, New York

Mr. and Mrs. Stephen D. Paine, Boston, Massachusetts

Dott. Giuseppe Panza di Buomo, Milan, Italy

Mrs. Betty Parsons, New York

Mrs. Barbara Reis Poe, New York

Alan Power, London, England

Mr. and Mrs. John Powers, Aspen, Colorado

Robert Rauschenberg, New York

Miss Anna Reinhardt, New York

Mrs. Rita Reinhardt, New York

Mr. and Mrs. Bernard J. Reis, New York

Dustin Rice, New York
Robert Rosenblum, New York
Mr. and Mrs. Robert A. Rowan, Pasadena, California
Lawrence Rubin, New York
William S. Rubin, New York
Steve Schapiro, New York
Mr. and Mrs. Eugene M. Schwartz, New York
Mr. and Mrs. Robert C. Scull, New York
Mr. and Mrs. Stanley K. Sheinbaum, Santa Barbara, California
Mr. and Mrs. Robert E. Simon, Jr., New York
Mr. and Mrs. Joseph Slifka, New York
Mr. and Mrs. Sonnabend, Paris, France
Mrs. Doris Starrels, Los Angeles, California
Frank Stella, New York
Mr. and Mrs. Robert A. M. Stern, New York
Mr. and Mrs. Frank M. Titelman, Altoona, Pennsylvania
Mr. and Mrs. Burton Tremaine, Meriden, Connecticut
Miss Ondine Vaughn, New York
Samuel Wagstaff, Jr., Detroit, Michigan
Mrs. Eleanor Ward, New York
Andy Warhol, New York
Albert F. Weis, Savannah, Georgia
William M. White, Jr., New York
David Whitney, New York
Donald Windham, New York
Mr. and Mrs. Lewis V. Winter, New York
The Woodward Foundation of Washington, D.C.
Mr. and Mrs. C. B. Wright, Seattle, Washington
and, in addition, several lenders who prefer to remain anonymous

Museums
Albright-Knox Art Gallery, Buffalo, New York
Allen Memorial Art Museum, Oberlin College, Oberlin, Ohio
Art Gallery of Ontario, Toronto, Canada
The Art Institute of Chicago, Chicago, Illinois
The Baltimore Museum of Art, Baltimore, Maryland
The Brooklyn Museum, Brooklyn, New York
California State College, Long Beach, California
The Cleveland Museum of Art, Cleveland, Ohio
The Connecticut Bank and Trust Company, Hartford, Connecticut
Dallas Museum of Fine Arts, Dallas, Texas
Isaac Delgado Museum of Art, New Orleans, Louisiana
The Detroit Institute of Arts, Detroit, Michigan
Everson Museum of Art, Syracuse, New York
The Solomon R. Guggenheim Museum, New York

The Israel Museum, Jerusalem, Israel
Los Angeles County Museum of Art, Los Angeles, California
Fondation Maeght, Saint Paul, France
Munson-Williams-Proctor Institute, Utica, New York
Museum of Art, Carnegie Institute, Pittsburgh, Pennsylvania
The Museum of Contemporary Art, Nagaoka, Japan
The Museum of Modern Art, New York
The National Gallery of Canada, Ottawa, Canada
Pasadena Art Museum, Pasadena, California
The San Francisco Museum of Art, San Francisco, California
Seattle-First National Bank, Seattle, Washington
University Art Museum, Berkeley, California
Victoria & Albert Museum, London, England
Wadsworth Atheneum, Hartford, Connecticut
The Walker Art Center, Minneapolis, Minnesota
Wallraf-Richartz Museum, Cologne, Germany
The Whitney Museum of American Art, New York
Yale University Art Gallery, New Haven, Connecticut

Art Galleries

Richard Bellamy, New York
Grace Borgenicht Gallery, New York
Leo Castelli Gallery, New York
Cordier & Ekstrom, Inc., New York
The Downtown Gallery, New York
Dwan Gallery, New York
Fischbach Gallery, New York
Noah Goldowsky, New York
Sidney Janis Gallery, New York
Tirca Karlis Gallery, Provincetown, Massachusetts
M. Knoedler & Company, Inc., New York
Gordon Locksley Gallery, Minneapolis, Minnesota
Lo Giudice Gallery, Chicago, Illinois
Marlborough-Gerson Gallery, New York
The David Mirvish Gallery, Toronto, Canada
Betty Parsons Gallery, New York
Perls Galleries, New York

The Metropolitan Museum of Art has been called "the most extraordinary visual encyclopedia in the Western Hemisphere." And that is what it is—stuffed with treasures, splendid with the myriad designs of all facets of art history. The treasures of the Metropolitan reach as far back in time as we can see, into all the places of the world where man has been turning his visual experience into concrete form. Man continues to bring forth visual treasures today. He will never stop.

An encyclopedia like the Metropolitan Museum is therefore never complete. It has a constant growth process and is continually being reedited and refined. Whole volumes are being added to the encyclopedia, for the Metropolitan is, for those who know it, not one museum but eighteen encompassing a span of fifty centuries of creativity.

One of the newest volumes, the most recent museum within the Metropolitan, is the Department of Contemporary Arts, instituted barely two years ago and given the duties of collecting, preserving, and exhibiting not only paintings and sculpture, but drawings, prints, furniture, period rooms, and decorative arts of the twentieth century. This department has even recently been granted the additional charge of presenting one-man shows of living artists. This was an extremely important decision by the Museum's Board of Trustees because it puts us on our mettle not to become purely academic and safe, and it ensures a continuing vitality by forcing us to keep our doors open to any style of painting and sculpture of any period that presents artistic excellence.

This extraordinary exhibition, "New York Painting and Sculpture: 1940–1970," consists of 408 works of art by forty-three gifted creators loaned from museums and private collections around the world. It is a landmark for the new Department of Contemporary Arts, being its first major effort to investigate that moment fully and deeply in a way that has never been done before. Many of these works come back to New York for the first time since they were created. The unique nature of this historical view of the New York School—the first ever undertaken on this scale—makes it imperative that this exhibition appear during our Centennial year. It is also the first exhibition of a distinguished series that will be held in a five-year period starting with the Centennial year. Through this series the Museum will attempt to illuminate for its visitors some of the key moments of five millennia of the visual arts.

"New York Painting and Sculpture: 1940–1970" has been a difficult and creative endeavor. It has been difficult because we have not had the luxury of looking back over a long period of time. The works of art of 1940–1970 are around us in profusion. Most of the artists who worked in the period are still alive and vocal. The show is creative in the curatorial sense because one man, Henry Geldzahler, endowed with a formidable visual talent has chosen 408 paintings, sculptures, and drawings of the highest character, each the most important statement in a particular moment of an artist's career. The choices have been made from literally thousands of possibilities.

Although it is conceivable that no two people would have picked anywhere near the same works of art from the New York School, 1940–1970, it is highly unlikely. Quality in any period, if it is sought after with diligence and determination, is sure to come out. Anyone who sees this show will be convinced, I believe, that the highest quality of this exciting time has been fully captured.

The exhibition, the book, and the program of lectures and concerts relating to the exhibition have been made possible through a generous grant from the Xerox Corporation. It is particularly appropriate that Xerox chose to underwrite "New York Painting and Sculpture: 1940–1970"; the corporation's own growth and success parallels exactly the period that this exhibition celebrates, and the graphic image of Xerox has always reflected the best in contemporary design. Through its generosity and enthusiasm, Xerox sets an example for other United States corporations to follow as enlightened patrons of the arts.

I know that Arthur A. Houghton, Jr., President, and Roswell L. Gilpatric, Chairman of the 100th Anniversary Committee, join me in thanking Xerox and the 165 lenders to the exhibition. Without the generosity of collectors and museums as far away as Japan and Israel, it would not have been possible to build such a comprehensive exhibition. John Macrae III and Cyril Nelson of E. P. Dutton & Co. have contributed enormously to the preparation of this book.

Finally, I want to thank Henry Geldzahler and the members of his staff of the Department of Contemporary Arts and Stuart Silver and the members of his staff of the Department of Exhibition Design for conceiving and executing the exhibition and its installation as the opening event of the Museum's Centennial celebration.

THOMAS P. F. HOVING
Director

July, 1969

12

New York Painting and Sculpture: 1940–1970

New York Painting and Sculpture: 1940–1970

Almost thirty years have passed since Arshile Gorky and Jackson Pollock announced in their painting that a new era was breaking in American art. The augury was correct. By reason of its own achievement and the clear and indisputable effect it has had throughout the world, the art of the New York School stands as the most recent in the grand succession of modern movements from Impressionism through Cubism and Surrealism.

Much has been said about the achievement of the New York School in the past several decades. National pride and international acclaim recognize that something magnificent has happened. On the occasion of its Centennial, The Metropolitan Museum of Art celebrates this achievement with the exhibition "New York Painting and Sculpture: 1940–1970." For the first time, admirers of modern art will be able to see in this book, which is an extension of the Museum's exhibition, paintings and sculptures in large numbers by the major figures who have produced the vital sequence of moments that make the New York School the historical successor to the School of Paris, the two generations of artists who have so successfully perpetuated the vitality and innovative energy that is the hallmark of any major movement.

The limitation to New York art in this exhibition is not parochial. The term "New York art," in fact, includes most of the significant American art produced in the past three decades. The School of Paris was an umbrella that covered Russia as well as Spain. Regardless of where a work is made, unless it is primitive, anachronistic, or truly eccentric, it becomes associated with the center of its day, the city whose style it reflects. Thus we unblushingly include Morris Louis and Kenneth Noland, the acknowledged leaders of what Washington likes to call its School of Color Painters, because their exhibiting history, the sources of their art, and their most cogent influence have all been located in New York.

The fact that New York has followed Paris as the dominant center of world art does not preclude the possibility of another, even several other cities, being the loci for important art. It seems clear at this writing, as it has been for a decade, that London and Los Angeles provide the two most fertile alternatives to New York.

The New York School includes Americans born in Armenia (Arshile Gorky), Holland (Willem de Kooning), Germany (Josef Albers and Hans Hofmann), Russia (Mark Rothko), and Sweden (Claes Oldenburg), as well as three men who grew up in California (Jackson Pollock, Philip Guston, and Robert Motherwell), a Texan (Robert Rauschenberg), and a Georgian

(Jasper Johns). Except for Albers and Hofmann, who spent their formative years in Europe, all those named came as young men to paint or sculpt in New York.

Artists, both American and foreign, have looked to New York for much the same reasons that have always caused ambitious artists to gravitate toward contemporary cultural centers. The climate of discussion, theory, and technical advance at the center offers the opportunity for learning, testing, and growing. The teachers and schools are here, as are the accomplished artists whom they want to emulate and measure themselves against. Economic factors make New York (Paris, London, or Los Angeles) a center as well. The connoisseurs, collectors, critics, and commissioners are here, as are the art dealers, architects, and the private foundations that grant awards to artists. And perhaps most important of all, the museums and continuing gallery exhibitions that make possible the dialogue out of which significant art is produced are present in New York to an unprecedented degree.

New York stands for a style of life to the artist, a reference point, and a base of operations. Even if he is in no way associated with New York, except as one of the places he exhibits (one thinks of Mark Tobey, Sam Francis, Richard Diebenkorn, Larry Bell, and Robert Irwin, all West Coast artists), he makes the occasional talismanic visit to the city, most often simply to see what is happening. Artists of fully mature and personal styles, while their work remains largely untouched by the new, often are curious to see it just the same, for while they are passionately committed to their vision and expression, they are also disinterestedly committed to and fascinated by all art.

It is quite possible to produce great mainstream art at a distance from the center. But this is only possible (except in the rare case of the primitive) after the artist has first steeped himself in the continuous and evolving traditions which can only be absorbed in the sophisticated centers. Later, it is possible to move away, as did Georgia O'Keeffe to New Mexico and David Smith to Bolton's Landing, and continue to produce art in touch with the vital forces of the day. It is during the period of development, of formation of outlook and style, that the immediate contact with the sources of energy is necessary. These, in time, came to be built into the fiber and character of the artist, and he can, when mature, move wherever he will and carry his interiorized contemporary world with him.

Thus the true school for the young artist, once he has gained the confidence and passionate certainty to know that he wants to be a painter or a sculptor, is the ferment and activity of the center, its multiplicity of styles and its complex traditions. Over and over again in repeated studio visits over the past ten years and in many days spent in viewing students' work in provincial art schools, I have found that nothing can replace the firsthand knowledge of the great works on view in New York's museums and the turmoil that follows the exhibition of new work by contemporaries and older colleagues.

In 1929, when in the face of the Metropolitan Museum's conservatism the founders of The Museum of Modern Art had the excellent idea of making advanced European art available to an American public that had been tantalized and scandalized sixteen years earlier by the Armory show, they moved with courage and energy into an educational project of great importance. History records that the job was done superbly. In fact, the Modern's educational program helped make it possible for a generation of New York-based painters and sculptors to inherit the European Modernist tradition.

In his article, "Arshile Gorky, Surrealism, and the New American Painting" (reprinted in this book), William Rubin provides a specific example of the American painter's dependence on firsthand knowledge of works of art in New York's public collections. Professor Rubin posits Gorky's knowledge of a specific Miró, the *Dutch Interior* of 1928, "a picture that was constantly on view in the permanent collection of The Museum of Modern Art and was probably a major influence on Gorky's *Garden in Sochi*," and then goes on to say that it was in the 1941 Miró retrospective held at the museum that "Gorky could observe in detail Miró's conversion from Cubism to Surrealism."

In the forties and early fifties The Museum of Modern Art and The Solomon R. Guggenheim Museum, with its excellent collection of nonobjective art, were among the daily meeting places and discussion centers for the serious artist and student who had to come to grips with Cubism and its aftermath if they were to paint in the Modernist tradition. Two factors, in addition to The Museum of Modern Art's persuasive permanent collection of modern European art, are generally recognized as having helped make New York a major international center for painting and sculpture after 1940. One was the Works Progress Administration; the other was the presence of European artists in New York during the years of World War II. W.P.A., with its various programs, was designed by the Roosevelt Administration during the years of the Depression to assist artists in surviving an economic catastrophe that had cut to virtually nothing private support of the arts. The W.P.A. programs gave artists a sense of community, shared problems, and styles of life. Out of this grew friendships and alliances, discussion groups, and several short-lived schools. W.P.A., with its resemblance to an artists' union, provided a common ground for the largely isolated American painter and sculptor. Discussions became fruitful and engaging; they developed from the artists' position in society to artists' rights, to questioning Marxism as the answer, to considerations of style, to admiration of and resistance to Picasso's overwhelming presence. Eventually, a key institution in the development of an artistic community in New York, The Club, was to be the issue and heir of the sense of shared involvement engendered

17

during the difficult years of the Depression, alleviated in some measure by the W.P.A. Among the artists who participated in the program were Jackson Pollock, Willem de Kooning, Burgoyne Diller, Arshile Gorky, Stuart Davis, and David Smith. Something of the mood of the period is revealed in David Smith's memoir:

Our hangouts were Stewart's Cafeteria 7th Ave. near 14 St close to [Stuart] Davis' studio and school and 5¢ coffee was much closer to our standards but on occasion we went to the Dutchman's, McSorley's and Romany Marie's. We followed Romany Marie from 8 St where Gorky once gave a chalk talk on Cubism, to several locations. Her place came closer to being a continental cafe with its varied types of professionals than any other place I knew. It was in Marie's where we once formed a group, [John] Graham, Edgar Levy, Resnikoff, de Kooning, Gorky and myself with Davis being asked to join. This was short lived. We never exhibited and we lasted in union about 30 days. Our only action was to notify the Whitney Museum that we were a group and would only exhibit in the 1935 abstract show if we were all asked. Some of us were, some exhibited, some didn't and that ended our group. But we were all what was then termed abstractionists.[1]

Another factor that liberated the American artist was the transfer of much of the School of Paris's energy to New York through the emigration of several of Europe's most advanced and admired artists. Léger and Mondrian and a sizable contingent of Surrealists—Marcel Duchamp, Matta, Max Ernst, Marc Chagall, Yves Tanguy, Salvador Dali, André Masson, and André Breton—spent the war years in New York and continued to produce important work here. There was something sacrosanct about the presence of these figures in New York, for they made flesh of legend and of recent art history. Mondrian and Léger, especially, continued to develop along lines that were consistent and continuous with their European work but which yet took cognizance of New York as their environment; Mondrian's *Broadway Boogie Woogie* and *Victory Boogie Woogie* are great American works by a European. The American artist, looking at the new and radical art by the Europeans executed in New York, no longer felt it was necessary to go abroad to become an artist, an American prejudice since the days of John Singleton Copley and Benjamin West. Jackson Pollock put the matter succinctly in his answer to a question put to him by an interviewer in 1944:

I accept the fact that the important painting of the last hundred years was done in France. American painters have generally missed the point of modern painting from beginning to end. (The only American master who interests me is Ryder.) Thus the fact that good European moderns are now here is very important, for they bring with them an under-standing of the problems of modern painting. I am particularly impressed with their idea

[1] *David Smith by David Smith* (New York: Holt, Rinehart & Winston, 1968), p. 35.

of the source of art being the unconscious. The idea interests me more than these specific painters do, for the two artists I admire most, Picasso and Miró, are still abroad.[2]

It became clear that great international painting could be executed in New York, that there was nothing talismanic about Paris. American painters understood that artists make art wherever they are, once they have absorbed those elements of tradition they find personally useful.

The familiarity of the young American abstractionists with each other's work in the thirties and forties, fostered in part by the W.P.A.'s role as an artists' union, and gained through studio visits, informal discussions, and group shows in both galleries and museums, created a new resonance and a new level of ambition. Dependence on European models, illustrated by Miró's influence on Gorky and Pollock's frank avowal, constituted invaluable apprenticeships without which they would never have attained the independent mastery that made them the forerunners of the new American painting. These historical examples indicate that future practitioners and supporters of new art must have an opportunity to see what has been so far achieved so that they may come to terms with it and find unique ways to contribute to its perpetuation. One of the reasons French art weakened so considerably after World War II was that the key paintings and sculptures of the first half of the century were not on view in Paris. Thus, in showing the work of the New York School, we do more than honor the artists and do justice to history. That their work is on view, even relatively briefly, helps to ensure the continuation of the tradition.

New York's museums have served our artists and public well by collecting and exhibiting the key works of the Modernist tradition as it evolved in Europe between 1870 and 1940. The Metropolitan Museum's collection of Impressionist and Post-Impressionist pictures, the Modern's unparalleled history of the modern period (illustrated by originals), and the Guggenheim Museum's largely non-Parisian (Russian, Dutch, German) range of nonobjective art, form a more significant collection than that of any city in Europe. Each of these museums and The Whitney Museum of American Art have shown an awareness of the new American art as it has developed, but now, with three decades of clear historical achievement by the New York School, we must meet our responsibility to the continuing process out of which new art develops by showing the best recent art and by presenting it in conjunction with the older and more established work.

At the Metropolitan Museum there have never been funds allocated specifically for the purchase of European modern art. With the limited money

[2] Jackson Pollock, Interview (formulated by Pollock with the help of Howard Putzel), *Arts and Architecture*, Vol. 61 (February, 1944), p. 14. Francis V. O'Connor, *Jackson Pollock* (New York: The Museum of Modern Art, 1967), p. 32.

available, the European Paintings Department has concentrated its energies in fields less well covered in New York than the modern. The most continuous and coherent modern collection at the Metropolitan is of American painting. The reasons for this are twofold and equally important in the history of the collection. The first was the establishment of the George A. Hearn Fund (1906) and the Arthur H. Hearn Fund (1911) that were specifically earmarked for the purchase of American painting (not sculpture). The second was the magnificent Alfred Stieglitz Bequest, made in 1949, coincidentally the year that pressure by New York artists led to the founding of the Department of American Painting and Sculpture. The Stieglitz Bequest gave us an impressive collection of works by American artists who were first exhibited in Stieglitz's galleries, such as Marsden Hartley, Arthur Dove, John Marin, and Georgia O'Keeffe, together with fascinating minor works by Matisse, Picasso, Brancusi, Severini, and other European artists Stieglitz introduced into America.

With the aid of the Hearn Funds, Robert Beverly Hale, the curator of the new department, was able to make such major purchases as Pollock's *Autumn Rhythm* (illustrated page 270), and Gorky's *Water of the Flowery Mill* (illustrated page 76), both in the current exhibition. The pressure on the part of the artists that caused the creation of the department coincided quite naturally with the growth in importance of our native art. It is thus ironic but understandable that as pressure mounted to expend the Hearn Funds, the rise in prices made these funds inadequate for their purpose. Rumor persisted into the sixties that the fabulous Hearn Funds lay idle. If they did, it was so that the money could accumulate long enough to make an important purchase. When major American paintings cost eight hundred or a thousand dollars, it was possible to make many significant acquisitions with the funds' income each year. Today the income cannot purchase the tenth part of a major Pollock. Recently, accumulated income has made it possible to purchase three major paintings in the exhibition, Morris Louis's *Alpha-Pi* (illustrated page 91), Ad Reinhardt's *Red Painting* (illustrated page 102), and Barnett Newman's *Concord* (illustrated page 94), which he exhibited at his first one-man show at the Betty Parsons Gallery in 1950.

While the Metropolitan Museum has not had an extensive collection of contemporary New York art to draw upon, it was often, through the fifties and sixties, the one place in New York where several galleries were consistently devoted to the permanent exhibition of the new American painting. With the founding of the Department of Contemporary Arts in 1967 the Museum, under its new director Thomas P. F. Hoving, further committed itself to collecting and exhibiting American and international painting, sculpture, and the decorative arts of the twentieth century. In three exhibitions mounted in the past two years—James Rosenquist's mammoth *F-111*, a small show of large works by Morris Louis, Kenneth Noland, and the English sculptor Anthony Caro, and five new sculptures by Jules Olitski—the Museum discovered that its size and flexibility, particularly during the current period of renovation, provided a unique opportunity to exhibit new work that has often in recent years grown in size and originality of concept beyond the normal confines of the commercial gallery.

New York's specialized museums have been so locked into complex and far-reaching exhibition schedules, which commit their time and space as much as three years into the future, that they have often been unable to serve the needs of the present. In spite of its concentration of artistic activity, New York does not provide an adequate exhibition hall, spacious, flexible, and available at fairly short notice to survey developments as they occur.

The Jewish Museum performed this essential function when it presented valuable mid-career retrospectives of the work of Helen Frankenthaler (1960), Robert Rauschenberg (1963), Jasper Johns (1964), and Kenneth Noland (1965), as well as the important sculpture exhibition called "Primary Structures" (1966), which revealed the strengths and some of the emptiness of the new Minimal sculpture. But it is clear that The Jewish Museum, with several roles to play in the community and with space that is not really adequate to the task, cannot fulfill the need for timely exhibitions all by itself.

The Metropolitan Museum's Centennial celebration has created the opportunity to see the shape of our recent tradition.

We point with optimism to increased museum attendance figures as an indication of a more interested public, and while this may be true, we should remember that statistics do not make a cultural renaissance. In the past century the increasing privacy of the artist's vocabulary and the decreasing regard for public reaction has attenuated the public for contemporary art to an alert and interested few attuned to the closest scrutiny of formal and philosophical developments that escape the inexperienced. At first, advanced art has meaning only to a small but passionate audience made up of artists and their immediate coterie. But no matter how many or how few people come through each year, the museum must continue to make the best works in the collection available to the public. It must continue to acquire and borrow the finest works of art and to present them intelligently to the real audience, to those of the newly immense public who linger and look.

Nonetheless, as a result of the heroic program of art education which began with the founding of The Museum of Modern Art and has been extended to the art departments of our schools and colleges, newspapers, periodicals, and television, advanced art is gradually being made accessible and comprehensible to the general public. But even though much of the public is unaware of the

21

presuppositions that make modern art fully comprehensible, this does not exclude the possibility of response or enthusiasm. It is only a matter of time before important changes and breakthroughs become clearer, especially as key paintings and sculptures continue to make their way into public collections. We must remember that the Impressionist paintings, which are perhaps the most universally appreciated works of art in the Metropolitan's collection, originally outraged a public goaded by hostile critics.

The second floor galleries of the Museum, usually devoted to the permanent collection of European paintings, are ideal for showing American art of the past three decades (it is in these galleries that "New York Painting and Sculpture: 1940–1970" is being housed). The juxtaposition of grand and intimate spaces provides a setting for works of art of every scale. Contrary to prevalent opinion, paintings by such artists as Jackson Pollock and Morris Louis demand the same natural light in which we are accustomed to seeing Rembrandt and Monet. The original Museum of Modern Art building of 1939 (by Edward Durell Stone and Philip L. Goodwin) and Frank Lloyd Wright's Guggenheim Museum were conceived in the thirties for easel pictures. In both buildings the natural lighting in the architects' original plans has been eliminated for reasons of expansion and taste. At the Modern, the window wall facing 53rd Street has been covered by false interior walls to increase hanging space. At the Guggenheim, Wright's combination clerestory and skylighting was eliminated when James Johnson Sweeney cantilevered paintings off the wall rather than hanging them close to the wall as was intended, necessitating a supplementary artificial lighting system.

In 1947, in his application to the John Simon Guggenheim Foundation, Jackson Pollock heralded an end to the historical situation for which these museums were designed in a prophetic statement:

I intend to paint large movable pictures which will function between the easel and mural . . . I believe the easel picture to be a dying form, and the tendency of modern feeling is toward the wall picture or mural. I believe the time is not yet ripe for a full transition from easel to mural. The pictures I contemplate painting would constitute a halfway state, and an attempt to point out the direction of the future without arriving there completely.[3]

(By 1949 and 1950 Pollock and Barnett Newman were painting their huge, mural-sized pictures.) Philip Johnson's addition to the Modern (1962–64) and Marcel Breuer's new Whitney Museum (1966) accommodate the new large paintings and sculptures. Because of the insistence on artificial lighting in both buildings and the lack of truly generous space at the Modern, it is the Metropolitan that will serve best (until a modern museum is built with a grand,

[3] Francis V. O'Connor, *Jackson Pollock* (New York: The Museum of Modern Art, 1967), pp. 39–40.

rhythmic procession of skylight galleries) as the place in New York in which to see our own monumentally scaled art.

There are other than physical advantages to exhibiting contemporary art at the Metropolitan. The extent to which even the most radical Modern Art is continuous with and dependent upon tradition can be revealed as never before when that new art is exhibited alongside the art of the past. The isolation of Modern Art at the other museums creates an essentially artificial separation between contemporary art and the art of the past. Specialists in Modern Art too easily fall into the trap of measuring contemporary art only against itself, rather than the art of the past, the ultimate test of quality. De Kooning has said it gives him particular joy to see his work (*Easter Monday*, in the Metropolitan's permanent collection) hanging forty feet from the Rembrandts against which he must finally measure himself.

Robert Rosenblum, in his cogent article, "The Abstract Sublime," (reprinted in this book) has suggested revealing and enriching analogies between painting of the Romantic movement and the work of Jackson Pollock, Mark Rothko, Clyfford Still, and Barnett Newman. Clyfford Still is seen as an analogue to the British Romantic painter James Ward; Mark Rothko is compared to Caspar David Friedrich and Joseph Turner; and Jackson Pollock is also viewed in terms of Turner. Barnett Newman may be understood as well to participate in the Sublime, but without a specific predecessor. Such comparisons with the past are not intended to sanction or justify the achievement of these contemporaries; they enlarge our vision and enrich our experience of their work. Rosenblum's thesis demonstrates that these works breathe naturally in the history of art. The way is open to other telling analogies linking our artists with other ideas and epochs, links across history that Henri Focillon saw as families of ideas.

As curator, my guiding principles in deciding which artists to include in the exhibition "New York Painting and Sculpture: 1940–1970" have been the extent to which their work has commanded critical attention or significantly deflected the course of recent art. These "deflectors," as they may be called, are those artists who have been crucial in redirecting the history of painting and sculpture in the past three decades. My aim has been to choose works of quality and stature by those artists who have posited the major problems and solutions of our immediate tradition.

George Kubler in his stunning essay *The Shape of Time*, a work that makes Kubler a natural heir to his teacher, Henri Focillon, writes:

Every important work of art can be regarded both as a historical event and as a hard-won solution to some problem . . . The important clue is that any solution points to the existence of some problem to which there have been other solutions, and that other solutions to this

23

same problem will most likely be invented to follow the one now in view. As the solutions accumulate, the problem alters. The chain of solutions nevertheless discloses the problem.[4]

The innovative artist in his grasp of a new possibility inevitably alters the problem and therefore deflects the tradition through his solution. The current exhibition was conceived as an accumulation of thirty years of solutions to a constantly changing set of problems—problems and solutions that make up a vital tradition.

Forty-three artists are represented in this giant exhibition. Not even at the height of the High Renaissance, Impressionism, or Cubism has anything like this number of artists finally seemed crucial to the development of the art of their time. Arshile Gorky, Jackson Pollock, and David Smith today look like the giants of their epoch, and a safer and more classical show could have been mounted devoted to their work alone. But we are celebrating a fortunate era of plentitude, and it is this sense of plentitude I hope to re-create in the current exhibition.

At a later time, one might well look back to reconsider and reevaluate, to see different clusters and configurations of artists and movements. Many artists of quality have not been included in the exhibition. One thinks of the American Surrealism of William Baziotes and Theodore Stamos; the Abstract Expressionism of Richard Poussette-Dart, James Brooks, Jack Tworkov, Conrad Marca-Relli, Joan Mitchell, and Al Leslie; the abstractions of Rollin Crampton, Robert Goodenough, Jack Youngerman, Cy Twombly, Ray Parker, Al Held, and Friedel Dzubas; the Abstract-Expressionist sculpture of Herbert Ferber, Seymour Lipton, Theodore Roszak, Raoul Hague, and Reuben Nakian; the figuration of Larry Rivers and Alex Katz; and the full Pop Art of Tom Wesselmann, Jim Dine, Marisol, and Robert Indiana. All these artists will be remembered and collected and, like the art in the exhibition, will be reevaluated by each successive generation of artists, critics, museum men, collectors, and the general public in that process in which the history of taste merges indistinctly with the history of art.

"New York Painting and Sculpture: 1940–1970" has been limited to artists whose distinctive styles emerged and were viewed before 1965 in galleries, group shows, and museums. This by no means indicates a lack of interest in subsequent developments. But the making of reputations and the discovery of new talent is not the role of the Metropolitan. Three young artists, Edward Avedisian, Walter Darby Bannard, and the Californian, Ron Davis, for example, have each grown rapidly in accomplishment and stature, but the record of their achievement is not yet clear and they are not included in the current exhibition.

[4] George Kubler, *The Shape of Time* (New Haven: Yale University Press, 1962), p. 33.

It has been the Whitney Museum's function, especially during the fifties and sixties when so much varied work was on view every year in New York's many galleries, to recapitulate the season, impartially, in the mammoth Annuals devoted in alternate years to sculpture and painting. While the Whitney emphasized perhaps too much the provincial and regional aspects of American art, it provided a forum in the thirties and forties for our internationally minded abstract artists before they had an audience to support them. (The Whitney Museum held a show of American abstract art in 1935.) It was at the Whitney Museum, when it was on Eighth Street, that I saw the Arshile Gorky Retrospective in 1951, which convinced me of the emotional power in contemporary abstract art.

From its founding, the Whitney has had a sense of responsibility and fairness to all the styles that at any moment make up the totality of contemporary art. This sense of fairness has always made the annual exhibitions of painting and sculpture at the Whitney anthologies rather than attempts to define styles and emphasize quality. For many of us growing up in New York, the Whitney Annual was always a much-anticipated event, for it allowed us to see in one large exhibition much of the best that was being produced along with the most stagnant, least provocative art imaginable. Thus the viewer was thrown into the healthful turmoil of doing what some consider the museum's job—of deciding, comparing, rejecting, and accepting until he felt, often after several visits to the same Annual, that he was able to find his own way to what constituted quality in contemporary American art.

"New York Painting and Sculpture: 1940–1970" is not a general inventory of the past three decades but an evaluation, a sorting out of major themes and figures. This exhibition represents my view of the historic impulse that produced such continued excitement and high achievement in the past three decades.

The Museum of Modern Art's program is to illustrate art history, applying historical methodology into and through the twentieth century up to the most recent movement which can be dealt with historically, Abstract Expressionism. The Museum of Modern Art was founded in the nineteen twenties to take up the slack left by the Metropolitan Museum whose coverage of the history of art ended with the Impressionists. Alfred Barr and his staff put together the world's finest collection of painting and sculpture of the period from 1870 to 1940, which from one point of view may be seen as a discrete historical entity entitled "The Modern Period." In two exhibitions in 1936, "Cubism and Abstract Art" and "Fantastic Art, Dada and Surrealism," and in the accompanying catalogues, Alfred Barr formulated the sequence of movements and pinpointed the great works of the twentieth century up to that time, setting the

25

standard for subsequent scholars. With "The New American Painting and Sculpture: The First Generation," held in the summer of 1969, William Rubin assembled an exhibition consistent with the policy established by Alfred Barr.

The Museum of Modern Art deals with history as a continually closing system up to the point where there is sufficient data and perspective to tell the story convincingly. Collecting paintings at the Metropolitan in the past century has been geared to the values of the connoisseur-collector rather than to those of the systematic historian. Thus, while the result of what might be termed a century of the leisurely accumulation of works of art has led to a persuasive survey of the history of art, the collection was not formed systematically. This informality makes it possible to bring together works of art from the standpoint of both the historian and the connoisseur.

The current exhibition has been planned in a similarly open spirit. There is a danger that in acceding to the demands of historical processing, we may fail to do justice to the present. Far from closing the books on the Abstract Expressionists, we celebrate the continuing vitality of the New York School. Several of the artists in the exhibition, well known for successful work in an earlier manner, are currently extending their visions and reputations into the present with some of their best work; Robert Motherwell's new "Open" series of 1968 and 1969 will be seen in retrospect as essential to a clear understanding of his achievement as are the well-known Spanish Elegies (three works from his new series are in the current exhibition); Adolph Gottlieb has turned to sculpture for the first time (the two pieces shown here are his first sculptures to be seen publicly in New York); and Barnett Newman has opened new vistas with his recent paintings in triangular format, which relate to his sculptures, *Here I* and *Here III* (both illustrated page 244). Among the younger men, Kenneth Noland's new horizontal stripe paintings and Jules Olitski's low-lying sprayed aluminum sculptures are as subtle and as full of implications for the future as anything in the art of the past decade. Invariably, artists want to feature their most recent work. It is understandable that as they change and develop they naturally feel closest to their most recent styles.

New work by established artists is judged, praised, or faulted with even greater rigor than that of the fledgling. There are no safe reputations in Modern Art. The same dialogue that leads so productively to the constant renewal of tradition makes of each new departure an adventure and a dare. The art of the past seems more orderly; critics and historians have marshaled the facts for us, and our sense of quality is aided by perspective. It is possible to clarify the art of a past, closed historical period. New work is judged qualitatively almost as if it were discontinuous with everything done before. While the critical process in which the new art is dissected, in which rules change as fast as new problems and solutions are set, is exhilarating and rigorous it is also seemingly chaotic and shapeless except to the few who are continually in touch and in sympathy with it.

The art historian and critic, Michael Fried, extends the historical approach beyond Abstract Expressionism to an analysis of the achievements of Morris Louis, Kenneth Noland, Jules Olitski, the English sculptor Anthony Caro, and Frank Stella, and deals convincingly with the sources and achievements of these artists, who continue the Modernist tradition in abstract art (see his essay, "Shape as Form: Frank Stella's New Paintings," reprinted in this book). Pollock and Newman are seen not only as great artists in their own time but as problem setters whose new ideas enriched the possibilities in abstraction. Louis, Noland, Olitski, Caro, and Stella can then be seen as taking the hint, providing solutions to some of the questions raised by the older generation.

Clement Greenberg, whose writings both Rubin and Fried acknowledge, and whose essay is also included in this book, has been the most acutely perceptive observer of and commentator on American painting and sculpture during the years covered by the current exhibition. His greatness has been not only in recognizing the achievement of Pollock and Gorky in the early forties, Newman, Rothko, and Still in the fifties, and Louis, Noland, and Olitski in the late fifties and sixties, but also in locating them in terms both of their uniqueness and their place in a tradition that Greenberg, more than anyone else, has revealed as a continually vital one.

While the process by which journalists come to terms with the art of the past decade has accelerated, many continue to be hostile to most recent art on first consideration. Time and again they lament the choice of artists representing the United States at Venice, São Paulo, or the international world's fairs, never suggesting alternate artists, who would, in their opinion, better represent our culture abroad. We miss the fierce and positive dialogue of the European journalists. In this country one must turn to the art magazines, which presuppose a greater degree of sophistication and commitment than do the dailies and Sunday supplements.

During the period covered by the current exhibition, four art magazines have served as forums in the presentation and interpretation of the new art, thus making it available to a much wider audience than could frequent the studios, galleries, and clubs whose exclusive concern was the new art. *Art News*, under Thomas B. Hess since the mid-forties, has consistently covered the art world, often with relish (Abstract Expressionism), sometimes with disdain (Pop Art), but always fully and with copious illustrations. *Arts Magazine*, under Hilton Kramer in the fifties and early sixties, devoted extensive coverage to the new art with Donald Judd as a regular contributor. James Fitzsimmons' Swiss-based *Art International* has covered both European and American art since

1958. The latest entry into the field, *Artforum,* was founded in California in the early sixties and moved to New York in June, 1967, to observe the scene better in the person of its editor Philip Leider. No clearer record of these decades exists or is likely to exist than the issues of these magazines. Not only are the major figures treated often and in depth, but there is also much to learn about the context in which their art was produced, about fellow artists who struck off in other directions, often personal and eccentric, but fruitful nonetheless. Critical positions are stated with passion and vigor, artists' statements abound, and the rise and fall of minor reputations alongside the constant rise of the major ones make fascinating reading.

Making one's way intelligently through the maze of art produced in our time has been complicated unnecessarily by journalistic simplifications, attempts on the part of the various media to make sense of the new on a popular level. An example of a phrase coined by a journalist in the effort to encapsulate the art of the mid-sixties in New York was the nonsensical and unhistorical impression fostered by *Time* magazine that Op Art followed Pop Art. This is cute, memorable, and untrue. Duchamp, Albers, Max Bill, and Vasarely, among many others, were producing art in the twenties, thirties, and forties, one element of which was a concern with optical effects, as everyone conversant with these developments knows, and as anyone can learn from a casual perusal of the art periodicals of the period.

The mass media with their concern for immediacy and emphasis on the current moment make it imperative that we recall the simple historical truth that it is the total career, not merely the novel moments that matter. Bonnard developed the elements of his style in the 1890s and went on to paint beautiful pictures until his death in 1947. His style changed somewhat over the years, but the changes were gradual and internal, and they had nothing to do with fashion or with contemporary movements (Cubism, then Surrealism) which seemed at the time to be the only styles in which a vital artist could work. When we organize a Bonnard show today, it is not only that first innovative decade of the 1890s we consider, but also the total evolution of a style that encompassed fifty years.

I well remember in the late 1950s being shocked to hear painters, who believed in the primacy of de Kooning's position and who admired him, wondering aloud whether next year's show would repeat his success, whether he could consolidate his lead not by painting a beautiful show but by changing in an unexpected and unpredictable way. Pollock and Kline were also under this kind of pressure, which is cruel and destructive even for the strongest character. Fortunately, the younger generation has had the example of the successful Abstract Expressionists before them and are much less vulnerable than were the artists in the fifties, the first to sit on this particular griddle.

It was not until the nineteenth century that a regular, professional art critic became necessary to interpret current painting to the public. The artist of the Renaissance, the Baroque, and the eighteenth century painted for an educated, enlightened, and enfranchised class of art connoisseurs, the aristocracy and the church hierarchy of the period before the French Revolution. His audience was clearly defined and there was a shared body of knowledge, literary and artistic, that patron and artist took for granted. Thus if a myth were referred to in a painting, or more likely, if a painting were commissioned to illustrate a favorite, personally meaningful myth, no educated viewer found it incomprehensible; at times a complicated literary painting might be an elegant visual puzzle, but there was a correct answer and it could be worked out. With the loss of a literary apparatus we have the beginnings of Modernism which Clement Greenberg defines as ". . . the use of the characteristic methods of a discipline to criticize the discipline itself, not in order to subvert it, but in order to entrench it more firmly in its area of competence."[5] Artistic problems become the subject of art. It is then not surprising that the media and the journalists jumped at the chance to write about Pop Art and Minimal Sculpture, for both these styles are theatrical. The cooler art of Newman, Rothko, Louis, and Noland is undeniably more difficult for the critic who, by his very nature, is reduced to words. An art that is antiexpressionistic and nongeometric, that makes no references to nature or literature and is comprehensible only in the context of Modernist art, is tremendously difficult to write about. This very difficulty may well have contributed to its greater staying power. It has been allowed to remain visual; the impact is still in the works themselves, whereas art that has news value must necessarily run the risk of becoming, in time, stale news.

It seemed for a while that the gallery system, with its biennial exhibitions of each artist's work, was implicated with the media in applying the false urgency of Hollywood to the fine arts. Certain galleries were open to criticism for playing to an audience overeager to spot trends, rising reputations, and falls from favor. It appeared to many that new shows by even the most established artists were conceived more in response to the demands of fashion than art. Before the galleries were discovered by the media, several major artists, David Smith, Barnett Newman, and Clyfford Still, among others, had broken ties with their dealers and started to sell their work privately to individuals and to museums. By breaking away from galleries, these artists freed themselves of confining relationships and commissions often as high as fifty percent. During the sixties the gallery system in itself came to be pictured as sordid and commercial, at best a necessary evil. The idea has grown among a group of radical younger

[5] Clement Greenberg, "Modernist Painting," *Arts Yearbook 4* (1961), p. 103.

men that the system is parasitic and overcommitted to established styles in painting and sculpture. In addition, contemporary art has continued to grow in scale and conception defying the physical limits of the conventional gallery, which, in a sense, reproduces the intimacy of the home. Some new art, such as Frank Stella's forty-foot paintings and Mark di Suvero's huge constructed sculptures, too big for galleries, looks better and can be better viewed in the studio, warehouse, museum, or exhibition hall than in the commercial gallery.

However, looking back over the exhibiting history of the postwar period, it is clear that the art dealers performed an invaluable service in supporting artists and in making art available. In the last twenty years younger artists in search of the inspiration and challenge necessary to their development have had to shift their attention away from the museums to the only place where new and advanced art has been systematically exhibited, the commercial art galleries. The galleries play more than an amusing social role in the history of the period, they have served as school, forum, and news transmitter to the community interested in the complex course art has taken. The dealer who is alert to quality, who has committed himself early and clearly to the new art, has risked ego, prestige, and money, and must finally be considered a minor cultural hero.

In 1942 the gallery became the focal point for the artists and their immediate coterie, which comprised their total audience at the time, when Peggy Guggenheim, encouraged by the presence of the Surrealists in New York, among them her husband Max Ernst, opened her gallery called Art of This Century. She gave one-man shows to Jackson Pollock (1943, 1945, 1947), Hans Hofmann (1944), Robert Motherwell (1944), and Mark Rothko (1945), as well as to such Europeans as Jean Helion, Hans Arp, Max Ernst, Alberto Giacometti, and Theo Van Doesburg, exhibiting the work of these Americans in the more sophisticated context of European art. After the war Art of This Century was closed and Peggy Guggenheim moved to Venice.

The postwar New York market for European Modernist art and the growing challenge of New York's own artists led to the opening of two more galleries in the forties, those of Samuel Kootz in 1945 and Sidney Janis in 1948. Kootz's first triumph was in bringing back recent Picassos from liberated France to an American audience that had been deprived during the war years of the work of an artist they regarded as a hero. By the late forties Kootz was also exhibiting William Baziotes, Robert Motherwell, Hans Hofmann, David Hare, and Adolph Gottlieb. Janis opened with a stable dominated by European Cubists and Surrealists including Léger, Kandinsky, Delaunay, Mondrian, and Henri Rousseau, all of whom were given one-man shows. Collectors whose eyes had been trained by The Museum of Modern Art bought works that later ended up there as gifts or on loan, as did Mr. Janis's own collection. Janis's original list of Europeans was gradually complemented by the addition of a number of American artists who had proved themselves in previous gallery exhibitions; first Josef Albers in 1949, followed by Pollock in 1952, de Kooning and Arshile Gorky in 1953, Rothko in 1955, Philip Guston and Franz Kline in 1956, and Motherwell in 1957. Janis has continued to change with the times. In the sixties, after putting together the first show of Pop Art, which he called, in the French manner, The New Realism, he has shown the work of Claes Oldenburg, George Segal, Jim Dine, and Marisol, as well as such abstractionists as Ellsworth Kelly and Richard Anuszkiewicz. Two other dealers who also contributed to the density and richness of exhibition life in New York in the 1950s were Charles Egan who showed Jack Tworkov, Reuben Nakian, Kline, Guston, Joseph Cornell, and Robert Rauschenberg, all between 1952 and 1955, and Eleanor Ward whose Stable Gallery exhibited Conrad Marca-Relli, Joan Mitchell, Cy Twombly, Larry Rivers, John Graham, Myron Stout, Isamu Noguchi, Joseph Cornell, and James Brooks in the fifties, and Richard Stankiewicz, Andy Warhol, and Robert Indiana in the sixties.

Betty Parsons' first gallery, the Wakefield, was in a bookstore. She opened in 1940 and showed Walter Murch (1941), Alfonso Ossorio (1941, 1943), Joseph Cornell (1942), Saul Steinberg (1943), Constantine Nivola (1943), Theodore Stamos (1943), and Adolph Gottlieb (1944). Between 1944 and 1946, as director of the Mortimer Brandt Gallery, she gave one-man shows to John Graham, Theodore Stamos, Hedda Sterne, Alfonso Ossorio, Hans Hofmann, Mark Rothko, and Ad Reinhardt. In her continuing capacity as director of the Betty Parsons Gallery she has been responsible for presenting the committed art public with some of its most memorable moments, among them Pollock's 1948 exhibition in which he showed pictures such as *Cathedral* (illustrated page 269), a painting that announced his most radically innovative period (Pollock had shows at Parsons in 1948, 1949, 1950, and 1951). She was also responsible for Barnett Newman's two one-man shows of 1950 (which included *Concord* [illustrated page 94] and *Covenant* [illustrated page 239]) and 1951, which introduced a powerful new voice into contemporary art. (He was not to show again in New York until his French and Company exhibit in 1958.) With Rothko, Still, and Reinhardt, Newman offered a viable alternative to the full-blown painterly abstraction that seemed to typify the style of the fifties. The austerity of Newman's work, his refusal to employ tired devices in even their most elemental form, gave him an extremely limited audience through the fifties (Clement Greenberg, Betty Parsons, Tony Smith, and some fellow artists), until another generation of painters, Louis, Noland, and Stella among them, referred to him in their work. His vertical stripe, or "zip" as he prefers to call it, denies both Cubism and geometry, two of the staple props of abstract

31

art before him. Betty Parsons also showed Clyfford Still (1947, 1950, 1951), Ad Reinhardt (twelve times between 1946 and 1965), Bradley Walker Tomlin (1950, 1953), Robert Rauschenberg (1951), and Ellsworth Kelly (five times between 1956 and 1963). The Betty Parsons Gallery continues to provide a forum for both older and younger artists.

Leo Castelli opened his gallery in 1957 with a group show made up largely of European masters, but which included de Kooning, Pollock, and David Smith, thus indicating the possibility of a drift toward the Americans in whom Castelli had been interested since the forties. In 1957–58 Castelli showed Marisol, Jasper Johns, Robert Rauschenberg, and Friedel Dzubas, in 1958–59 Esteban Vicente and Gabriel Kohn, and in 1959–60 he represented Frank Stella, Cy Twombly, John Chamberlain, Lee Bontecou, and Jack Tworkov in group and one-man shows. Since then he has added James Rosenquist, Andy Warhol, Roy Lichtenstein, Larry Poons, Donald Judd, and, most recently, Dan Flavin. Like Janis, Castelli runs a gallery that reflects the growth and change of the American scene.

André Emmerich through the sixties showed the work of Morris Louis, Kenneth Noland, Helen Frankenthaler, and Jules Olitski. (Olitski's history demonstrates the complexity of many artists' gallery associations. Before showing with Emmerich he had been with Iolas, French and Company, and Poindexter. He is now represented by the Lawrence Rubin Gallery.) Two "blue chip" galleries currently represent many of the original generation of the New York School. The Pollock Estate, the David Smith Estate, the Kline Estate, Rothko, Guston, Motherwell, and Gottlieb exhibit at Marlborough-Gerson, while M. Knoedler and Company handles Newman, de Kooning, and the Gorky Estate.

One of the most fascinating galleries of the sixties was Richard Bellamy's Green Gallery. Its greatest strength was in Bellamy's constant search for new talent, a search not enough dealers are willing to undertake. Bellamy made countless tours of studios and subsequently exhibited for the first time James Rosenquist, Larry Poons, Lucas Samaras, Robert Morris, and Donald Judd and gave the first uptown shows to Tom Wesselmann, Claes Oldenburg, and Dan Flavin, the first sculpture show to George Segal, and the first American show to the British painter Richard Smith. He accomplished all this in about five years. The Green Gallery worked, in effect, as a talent scout for the larger and more established dealers. Today, former Green Gallery artists show at Sidney Janis, Leo Castelli, The Pace Gallery, and Richard Feigen. Bellamy has become a private dealer.

The 1964 and 1966 Venice Biennales and the 1965 São Paulo Bienal were the occasions for attacks on the art dealers because nearly all the artists chosen to represent the United States came from four galleries: Leo Castelli, André

32

Emmerich, Sidney Janis, and The Pace Gallery. (Alan Solomon was United States Commissioner in 1964 at Venice; he showed Louis, Noland, Rauschenberg, Johns, Stella, Chamberlain, Oldenburg, and Dine. Walter Hopps chose the artists for the 1965 São Paulo Bienal: Barnett Newman, Larry Poons, Donald Judd, Frank Stella, Larry Bell, Billy Al Bengston, and Robert Irwin. In 1966 I chose Helen Frankenthaler, Jules Olitski, Ellsworth Kelly, and Roy Lichtenstein to represent the United States at the Venice Biennale.) This should have been in no way surprising. In the past hundred years in which advanced art and the gallery system have coexisted there has never been more than a handful of galleries at any one time prepared to show the best, most innovative work of the moment. With the Impressionists and the Post-Impressionists the galleries were Durand Ruel, Bernheim Jeune, and Wildenstein; Kahnweiler was, at first, almost the exclusive dealer for the Cubists; the Abstract Expressionists, as we have seen, were launched by Peggy Guggenheim, then by Charles Egan, Betty Parsons, Samuel Kootz, and Sidney Janis. It is clearly more important to represent the United States at these international exhibitions and world's fairs by the best being done than to be concerned with an equitable distribution among dealers.

While the total self-interest of New York's real-estate industry, for example, is contributing to the destruction of the city, this same self-interest in the economics of the art world may finally benefit the public. A work of art often makes its way from the privacy of the artist's studio, through the gallery, to the collector, and finally to the museum. The general public is excluded from purchasing and living with much of the best art being produced in our society, for it is in short supply in relation to the number of potential owners, and because it is expensive. Ironically enough, these very factors, scarcity and price, inevitably help speed paintings and sculptures into museums and other public situations where they become available to the widest possible audience. Our tax laws make it sensible for the wealthy to give works of art to museums, and our social structure makes it attractive to be associated with a museum. These tax laws are a major factor in the rapidly increasing number of museums in the United States and in the continuing expansion of existing institutions. While works of art are sometimes bought cheap and sold dear, or are accumulated in the drive toward upward social mobility, there are also many collectors who love art, and are willing to share it with others.

We need not turn to ancient times to find knotty problems of precedence, dating, and sequence in art. The years 1948–50 in New York provide them in abundance. Future historians will inherit the task of unraveling the intricacies of these years. What is clear is that Gorky and Pollock opened the way for a generation of abstract artists. Gorky pushed the European biomorphic tradition beyond the influence of Picasso, Miró, and Matta. Pollock's mastery of the controlled accident, his ability to project his style with both gesture and exactitude on a broad, allover surface created a new level of expectation that served as an inspiration to the artists who followed. These steps in large part made it possible to shed the Surrealist preconceptions of small format and multiple elements that were, before 1948, the hallmarks of American abstraction.

David Smith's career spanned three decades, from the Picasso–Gonzalez inspired thirties to the close relationship with the new American abstraction in the sixties, specifically with the work of Kenneth Noland. Smith subsumed and surpassed his sources, as did Gorky, to create a body of work that stands indisputably with the best sculpture of the modern period. The late and glorious "Cubi" and planar pieces in stainless steel, such as *Becca* (illustrated page 107) and "Untitled" (illustrated page 312), have buffered surfaces reminiscent of the activated plane of Pollock's allover painting. The painted pieces of his last years (with endless changes of color in the attempt to get it "right") comment upon and learn from the color painting of the sixties.

His love of materials, the joy with which he contemplated and then extended their possibilities, shines through in his writing:

Steel . . . can be stainless, painted, lacquered, waxed, processed and electroplated with molybdenum. It can be cast. Steel has mural possibilities which have never been used. It has high tensile strength, pinnions can support masses, soft steel can bend cold, both with and across its grain, yet have a tensile strength of 30,000 lbs. to one square inch. It can be drawn, cupped, spun and forged. It can be cut and patterned by acetylene gas and oxygen and welded both electrically and by the acetylene oxygen process. It can be chiseled, ground, filed and polished. It can be welded the seams ground down leaving no evidence. The welds can possess greater strength than the parent metal. It can be formed with various metals by welding, brazing and soldering. Metals fall naturally to my use and [are] useful to my concept.[6]

Language for Smith was another joyous material.

In the mid- and late fifties it looked to many as if de Kooning would dominate painting for a significant time to come. A group of small galleries sprang up on East Tenth Street devoted to artists later called Second Generation Abstract Expressionists; much of their work derived its impulse and borrowed some of its energy from de Kooning's manner in the mid-fifties, the wide, slashing abstractions that look tame and lovely now, but seemed raw and angry then. It was to artists such as Alfred Leslie, Michael Goldberg, Grace Hartigan, and Norman Bluhm that Sam Hunter referred when he wrote in 1958:

[6] *David Smith by David Smith* (New York: Holt, Rinehart & Winston, 1968), p. 53.

There is no single figure who has exerted greater influence on American painting over the past decade [than de Kooning]; he is directly responsible for the general physiognomy of much of the painting of the rising generation.[7]

While de Kooning's personal contribution has been great, the line he fathered, as it turns out, was not the fertile one. De Kooning himself retired from the scene to East Hampton to work almost exclusively on the "Women," a unifying theme in his work since the late thirties.

There was a richer vein to be explored in the implications suggested by the works of Newman, Rothko, Reinhardt, and Diller, which were to engage the cooler sensibilities of the younger abstractionists such as Stella, Judd, Morris, Poons, and Flavin. And in the late fifties another alternative to Abstract Expressionism emerged—first around the Reuben Gallery on the Lower East Side, then uptown at the Green Gallery, Castelli, and the Stable—the Happenings and the new painting and sculpture with recognizable subject matter derived from contemporary mass culture, which came to be known as Pop Art.

The imagery of Pop Art can be seen as the new American landscape. Landscape painting has always selected, idealized, and described man's environment. The subject of landscape has shifted from nature to urban life in the twentieth century, and Pop Art, in its development since 1960, has used the close-up technique of film on the artifacts and data of contemporary communication, making billboards, comic strips, packaging, picture magazines, and advertising the legitimate subjects of an art that is peculiarly American and of our decade.

No movement in the history of American art was named and received more quickly. A year after it hit the galleries and magazines, I had an air conditioner installed in my apartment. An Andy Warhol painting of six Marilyn Monroes was leaning against a wall. "What's that, Pop Art?" the air-conditioner man asked. Can you imagine someone in a similar situation in 1950, asking of a Jackson Pollock, "What's that, Abstract Expressionism?" For one thing, Pop Art was literally named before it began (Lawrence Alloway coined the phrase for certain English painters in the late 1950s), while the art of Pollock, Kline, and de Kooning was called Action Painting, New York School Painting, and still other names before it settled down as Abstract Expressionism.

Pop Art was radical and came as a surprise, yet somehow the American public was responsive to it. This, of course, became clear only after the fact. Nobody could have predicted it. There were critics in the fifties crying for a return to the figure, for a "new humanism." What they were hoping for was something comfortable and recognizable, a resuscitation of the art of the past veiled in the flaying brushstrokes of Abstract Expressionism. When they got their new figuration, it was not the tortured humanism of the postnuclear world

[7] Sam Hunter, "The United States," *Art Since 1945* (New York: Harry N. Abrams, 1958), p. 284.

for which they were longing but an art based on billboards, comic strips, and advertising. These critics cried "foul," and they cried it hard and long. Adolph Gottlieb has written, "Certain people always say we should go back to nature. I notice they never say we should go forward to nature. It seems to me they are more concerned that we should go back, than about nature." [8]

The situation in painting in New York in the late fifties offered the possibility of a return to representational art that would be both contemporary and meaningful. After two decades of tremendous energy and inventiveness in abstract painting, the reintroduction of recognizable content (objects, landscape, and figure) appeared at first *retardataire* and beside the point. The best and most mature artists at the time had created personal and distinct abstract manners and images. These men left little room for the younger artist dissatisfied with the choice between the manner of de Kooning and, let us say, Philip Guston.

Robert Rauschenberg pointed a way out of this dilemma by the mid-fifties by incorporating real objects in his work. Instead of representing a goat—that is, attempting to translate a goat into a two-dimensional painted image, Rauschenberg included the goat itself (stuffed, but only slightly less a goat for that). There was ample precedent for Rauschenberg's gesture, in kind if not in degree. His point of departure was collage, by then an eminently respectable Cubist technique, incorporating bits and pieces of reality such as newspaper and rope in works of art, a technique that Rauschenberg logically extended. Kurt Schwitters set the most specific precedent for Rauschenberg, as did Marcel Duchamp for Jasper Johns.

Younger than Rauschenberg, Jasper Johns, forms, with him, the bridge between Abstract Expressionism and Pop Art. Rauschenberg incorporated real objects and photographs in his work, imbedded in a matrix of brushed and spilled paint that was clearly Abstract Expressionist. Johns created images of objects that we know to be two-dimensional, flags, maps, numbers, and targets. The integrity of these objects in his work made it possible for the Pop artists to separate them from Johns's painterly style that was characteristic of the fifties. The Pop artists of the sixties (Warhol, Rosenquist, Oldenburg, Lichtenstein) seized upon the recognizable image and dropped the painterly style of the previous decade.

Just as Surrealism retreated from the almost frightening formal innovations and implications of Cubism (and its aftermath) to new subject matter (Freudianism and the interpretation of dreams), so Pop Art coming some fifteen years after another formal explosion, Abstract Expressionism, stepped back to legitimize another subject, the imagery of advertising and the mass media. Of course, there had been precursors in the history of art for both Surrealism and Pop Art. In the case of Pop, Duchamp, Schwitters, Gerald Murphy, Léger, and Stuart

[8] "The Ides of Art," *The Tiger's Eye*, Vol. 1, no. 2. (December, 1947), p. 43.

Davis may be cited. But the exclusive concern with comic strips, billboards, television commercials, and newspaper advertising in the fine arts of painting and sculpture was new in American art in 1959 and 1960. Both Surrealism and Pop Art were, to some extent, respites from problems of form; both returned to representation, distorted and dreamlike in the case of Surrealism, outsized and commercial in Pop Art.

Pop Art is seen by some to be radically different from the post-Abstract-Expressionist painting of the sixties by Noland, Stella, Kelly, and Frankenthaler. But art of any given period shares certain stylistic presuppositions no matter how varied it may seem in its time. The abstract painting of Olitski, Noland, and Frankenthaler and the Pop paintings of Lichtenstein, Warhol, and Rosenquist will come in time to look typical of the 1960s in New York. All have been concerned with the large canvas, the simple, flat, close-up image of the movie screen, all have used the new brilliant plastic colors. The aesthetic permission to project immense Pop images derives in part from these artists' awareness of the most advanced abstract art.

The tradition of American abstract painting and sculpture of the past three decades is still very much alive, both in the continuing work of the established masters and in the younger men who emerge every few years, making clear the ongoing vitality of abstract art. It seems today that Pop Art was an episode, an interesting one that has left its mark on the decade, and will continue to affect the future, but not a major modern movement which continues to spawn new artists. In fact, just about everything new and original in Pop Art was stated by a few artists in the first years of its existence. Since then no artists of first importance have been recruited and no second generation has come along. There is a strong possibility that the second generation of potential Pop artists has been fed directly into television and advertising, thus repaying art's debt to the media. Just as Surrealism continues to haunt Modernist art, cropping up as an influence in unexpected places, for example, New York painting of the 1940s, so Pop Art may well find its converts and adherents in unexpected future corners and pockets of major art.

Donald Judd, Robert Morris, and Dan Flavin are both the leading theoreticians of Minimal Sculpture and its most accomplished practitioners. Tony Smith, an architect whose involvement with the New American Painting dates from the late forties (he was among the first to realize the implications in the work of both Pollock and Newman), brings a richer and longer experience to his sculpture, making it more resonant and, conversely, less purely Minimal. This new sculpture of the sixties shares several of its presuppositions with the paintings of Burgoyne Diller, Ad Reinhardt, and Frank Stella; all chose to eliminate from their work the roughness of surface and eccentric evidences of

37

personality they associated with previous art. The Minimal sculptors strive for anonymity of craftsmanship, a clear projection of simple formal relationships, and a suppression of "signature."

The Minimal sculptors prefer to use common industrial material and processes, much as the Pop artists use common images and commercial techniques. Aluminum, fiberglas, and sheets of colored transparent plastic are their typical materials, materials which are familiar enough, but not in the context of sculpture. Dan Flavin uses light, first incandescent, now fluorescent, to create memorable icons with a minimum of construction and a minimum of compositional effects characteristic of the movement. Minimal Sculpture relies, for the most part, on three-dimensional geometric forms such as the cube; it avoids figurative references—it never stands on two legs—it hangs from the wall, leans in a corner, or sits foursquare on the floor. While the Pop artists still most often do their own work, these new sculptors are not sentimental about the artist's hand or touch. In fact, many of their pieces are fabricated industrially. Minimal Sculpture is the most recent movement in American art with a coherent body of work and a sizable critical literature.

This has been a brief recapitulation of what I consider to be the importance of the New York School as seen both in this book and in the exhibition it accompanies. We hope that by emphasizing aspects of the exhibiting history of the new American painting and sculpture in the past three decades we may call attention to New York's continuing responsibility to the arts that so enrich it. New York must provide an opportunity to see recent art in much the same way that Cubism and Surrealism are visible at The Museum of Modern Art. The achievement of the New York School merits such a permanent base. Rather than devoting an inordinate amount of time to an accelerated schedule of theme shows and retrospectives, museum directors and their staffs, when concentrating on modern art, might do better to expend their greatest efforts on providing gallery after gallery of important recent works by major artists so that our students, foreign and out-of-town visitors, New York's own passionate audience for art and, most importantly, practicing artists can always have before them a collection of challenging contemporary art of the highest quality and relevance. In this way we may hope to avoid the unfortunate situation of the past three decades in which the new art has not been consistently visible. This goal might be achieved through the cooperation of four museums, the Modern, Guggenheim, Whitney, and Metropolitan, or it might be the additive result of four separate but dovetailing programs. It is a goal eminently worth the best efforts of all concerned with New York art.

HENRY GELDZAHLER

Catalogue of the Exhibition

(Dimensions are given in feet and inches, height preceding width.)

JOSEF ALBERS

1. *Growing.* 1940. Oil on masonite. 15″ x 17¾″.
   The Collection of The San Francisco Museum of Art, San Francisco, California.
   Gift of Mrs. Charlotte Mack. (p. 113)

2. *Vice Versa C. ca.* 1943. Oil on masonite. 16¼″ x 31½″.
   Collection of the artist. (Not illustrated.)

3. *Indicating Solids.* 1949. Oil on masonite. 26″ x 25¾″.
   Collection of the artist. (p. 114)

4. *Transformations of a Scheme Series: No. 10.* 1950.
   Machine-engraved in laminated formica. 17″ x 22½″.
   Collection of the artist. (p. 114)

5. *Homage to the Square Series: New Gate.* 1951. Oil on masonite.
   24″ x 24″. Collection of the artist. (p. 115)

6. *Transformations of a Scheme Series: No. 26.* 1952.
   Machine-engraved in laminated formica. 17″ x 22½″.
   Collection of the artist. (p. 116)

7. *Homage to the Square Series: In Wide Light.* 1953. Oil on masonite.
   18″ x 18″. Collection of the artist. (p. 117)

8. *Homage to the Square Series: With Aura.* 1959. Oil on masonite.
   18″ x 18″. Collection of the artist. (Not illustrated.)

9. *Biconjugate Series: Red Orange Wall.* 1959. Oil on masonite.
   24″ x 34½″. Collection of the artist. (p. 117)

10. *Biconjugate Series: Chalk-Green Facade.* 1960. Oil on masonite.
    28″ x 40½″. Collection of the artist. (p. 118)

11. *Homage to the Square Series: Lone Light.* 1960. Oil on masonite.
    18″ x 18″. Collection of the artist. (Not illustrated.)

12. *Late Thought.* 1964. Oil on board. 48″ x 48″.
    The Woodward Foundation of Washington, D.C. (p. 65).

13. *Homage to the Square Series: Despite Mist* (diptych). 1967 and 1968.
    Oil on masonite. 40″ x 80″. Collection of the artist. (Not illustrated.)

MILTON AVERY

14. *Gaspé—Pink Sky.* 1940. Oil on canvas. 40″ x 50″.
    Collection of Mr. and Mrs. Maurice Geller, New York. (p. 119)

15. *Mother and Child.* 1944. Oil on canvas. 40″ x 30″.
    Tirca Karlis Gallery, Provincetown, Massachusetts. (p. 119)

16. *Sail.* 1958. Oil on canvas. 72″ x 50″.
    Grace Borgenicht Gallery, New York. (p. 120)

17. *Sunset Sea.* 1958. Oil on canvas. 49½″ x 73½″.
    The David Mirvish Gallery, Toronto, Canada. (p. 120)

18. *Speedboat's Wake.* 1959. Oil on canvas. 55″ x 73″.
    The David Mirvish Gallery, Toronto, Canada. (p. 66)

ALEXANDER CALDER

19. *Little Spider. ca.* 1940. Painted sheet metal and steel wire and rods. 55" x 50". Perls Galleries, New York. (p. 121)

20. *Mobile.* 1963. Sheet steel. 27'. The Connecticut Bank and Trust Company, Hartford, Connecticut. (p. 122)

21. *The Pregnant Whale.* 1963. Steel plate painted. 9'6" x 8'10" x 7'2". Collection of Mrs. Julius Epstein, Northfield, Illinois. (p. 67)

22. *Four Planes Écartés.* 1967. Painted sheet steel. *ca.* 10'6" (high). Perls Galleries, New York. (p. 123)

23. *Six Planes Écartés.* 1967. Painted sheet steel. *ca.* 10'6" (high). Perls Galleries, New York. (p. 123)

JOHN CHAMBERLAIN

24. *Fantail.* 1961. Painted steel. 70" x 75" x 60". Collection of Jasper Johns, New York. (p. 124)

25. *Velvet White.* 1962. Welded steel. 83" x 57" x 48". The Albert A. List Family Collection, New York. (p. 125)

26. *Dolores James.* 1962. Welded auto metal. 76" x 97" x 39". Leo Castelli Gallery, New York. (p. 68)

JOSEPH CORNELL

27. *Taglioni's Jewel Casket.* 1940. Wooden box containing glass ice cubes, jewelry, etc. 4¾" x 11⅞" x 8¼". The Museum of Modern Art, New York. Gift of James Thrall Soby, 1953. (Not illustrated.)

28. *L'Égypte de Mlle. Cléo de Mérode; cours élémentaire d'histoire naturelle.* 1940. Wood, glass, cork, and miscellaneous materials. 4¾" x 10¾" x 7¼". Collection of Mr. and Mrs. Richard L. Feigen, New York. (p. 126)

29. *Medici Slot Machine.* 1942. Construction. 15½" x 12" x 4⅜". Collection of Mr. and Mrs. Bernard J. Reis, New York. (p. 126)

30. *A Pantry Ballet (for Jacques Offenbach).* Summer, 1942. Wood, paper, plastic, metal, glass, etc. 10½" x 18" x 6". Collection of Mr. and Mrs. Richard L. Feigen, New York. (p. 127)

31. *Habitat Group for a Shooting Gallery.* 1943. Wood cabinet containing colored cut-out of parrots, printed cards, and papers, etc., behind shattered glass. 15½" x 11⅛" x 4¼". Collection of Irving Blum, Los Angeles, California. (p. 69)

32. *Pharmacy.* 1943. Wooden box with glass bottles. 15¼" x 12" x 3". Collection of Mrs. Marcel Duchamp, New York. (p. 127)

33. *Paolo and Francesca.* 1943–48. Box construction. 14¾" x 11⅜" x 3¹³⁄₁₆". Collection of Mr. and Mrs. Richard L. Feigen, New York. (Not illustrated.)

34. *American Rabbit.* 1945–46. Box construction. 11⅜" x 15½" x 3¹³⁄₁₆". Collection of Mr. and Mrs. Jacob Berman, Sherman Oaks, California. (Not illustrated.)

35. *Multiple Cubes.* 1946–48. Construction. 14" x 10⅜" x 2¼". Collection of Mr. and Mrs. E. A. Bergman, Chicago, Illinois. (Not illustrated.)

36. *Soap Bubble Set.* 1948. Black box construction. 15³⁄₁₆″ x 20⅜″ x 3¹³⁄₁₆″.
Collection of Mrs. Doris Starrels, Los Angeles, California.
(Not illustrated.)

37. *Cockatoo: "Keepsake Parakeet."* 1949–53. Construction in wood.
20¼″ x 12″ x 5″. Collection of Donald Windham, New York. (p. 128)

38. *Observatory.* 1950. Construction. 18″ x 11⅞″ x 5½″.
Collection of Mr. and Mrs. E. A. Bergman, Chicago, Illinois. (Not illustrated.)

39. *Grand Hotel Semiramis.* 1950. Construction of wood, glass, and diverse materials.
18″ x 12″ x 4″. Collection of Mr. and Mrs. Allan Frumkin, New York. (p. 128)

40. *Hotel (Night Sky). ca.* 1952. Wood box construction with glass face. 16½″ x 10″ x 6″.
Collection of Irving Blum, Los Angeles, California. (Not illustrated.)

41. *Medici Princess. ca.* 1952. Wood, glass, and diverse materials. 14½″ x 11″ x 5″.
Collection of Jean Frumkin, New York. (Not illustrated.)

42. *Hotel du Nord. ca.* 1953. Construction in wood, glass, and paper.
19″ x 13¼″. The Whitney Museum of American Art, New York. (p. 129)

43. *Grand Hotel de L'Observatoire.* 1954. Blue box construction.
18⁵⁄₁₆″ x 12⁵⁄₁₆″ x 3¹³⁄₁₆″. Collection of the artist. (Not illustrated.)

44. *Blériot.* 1956. Box containing painted wooden trapeze supported by
rusted steel spring. 18½″ x 11¼″ x 4¾″. Collection of Mr. and Mrs. E. A. Bergman,
Chicago, Illinois. (Not illustrated.)

45. *Hotel de L'Étoile. ca.* 1956–57. Painted wood construction.
18½″ x 14″ x 7½″. Collection of Mrs. Eleanor Ward, New York. (p. 129)

46. *Apollinaris.* (n.d.) Blue box construction. 19″ x 11¹⁄₁₆″ x 4⅝″.
Collection of the artist. (Not illustrated.)

47. *Grand Hotel de L'Univers.* (n.d.). Blue box construction. 19″ x 12⅝″ x 4¾″.
Anonymous loan courtesy of The Pasadena Art Museum, Pasadena, California.
(Not illustrated.)

48. *Hotel du Nord (Little Durer).* (n.d.). Box construction. 18″ x 12¼″ x 4″.
The Pasadena Art Museum, Funds donated by Mr. William Janss and the
Storrier-Stearns Fund. (Not illustrated.)

STUART DAVIS

49. *Hot Stillscape in Six Colors.* 1940. Oil on canvas. 36″ x 45″.
Courtesy of The Downtown Gallery, New York. (p. 70)

50. *New York Under Gaslight.* 1941. Oil on canvas. 32″ x 45″.
The Israel Museum, Jerusalem, gift of Mrs. Rebecca Shulman, New York.
(Not illustrated.)

51. *Owh! In San Paõ.* 1951. Oil on canvas. 52¼″ x 41¾″.
The Whitney Museum of American Art, New York. (p. 130)

52. *Colonial Cubism.* 1954. Oil on canvas. 45″ x 60″.
Collection of The Walker Art Center, Minneapolis, Minnesota. (p. 131)

53. *Pochade.* 1958. Oil on canvas. 60″ x 52″.
Courtesy of The Downtown Gallery, New York. (p. 131)

54. *Switchsky's Syntax.* 1961–64. Tempera on canvas. 42″ x 56″.
Courtesy of Mrs. Stuart Davis, New York. (p. 132)

WILLEM DE KOONING

55. *Seated Woman. ca.* 1940. Oil and charcoal on composition board.
54″ x 36″. Collection of Mrs. Albert M. Greenfield, Sr., Philadelphia,
Pennsylvania. (p. 133)

56. *Queen of Hearts.* 1943–46. Oil and charcoal on composition board.
46″ x 27½″. Joseph H. Hirshhorn Foundation. (p. 134)

57. *Pink Lady. ca.* 1944. Oil and charcoal on masonite composition board.
48¼″ x 35¼″. Collection of Mr. and Mrs. Stanley K. Sheinbaum,
Santa Barbara, California. (p. 135)

58. *The Marshes. ca.* 1945. Charcoal and oil on composition board.
32″ x 23⅞″. University Art Museum, Berkeley, California. Gift of Julian J. and
Joachim Jean Aberbach, New York. (p. 136)

59. *Light in August. ca.* 1946. Oil and enamel on paper, mounted on canvas.
55″ x 44½″. Collection of Elise C. Dixon, Scottsdale, Arizona. (p. 137)

60. *Bill-Lee's Delight. ca.* 1946. Oil on paper. 27½″ x 34¼″.
Collection of Mr. and Mrs. Lee V. Eastman, New York. (p. 71)

61. *Untitled.* 1948. Oil on paper, mounted on masonite. 24″ x 36″.
Collection of Mr. and Mrs. Stephen D. Paine, Boston, Massachusetts. (p. 138)

62. *Night Square.* 1950–51. Oil on masonite. 30″ x 40″.
Collection of Mrs. Martha K. Jackson, New York. (Not illustrated.)

63. *Police Gazette.* 1954–55. Oil on canvas. 43¼″ x 50¼″.
Collection of Mr. and Mrs. Robert C. Scull, New York. (p. 138)

64. *Easter Monday.* 1955–56. Oil and newspaper transfer on canvas. 96″ x 74″.
The Metropolitan Museum of Art, New York, Rogers Fund, 1956. (p. 139)

65. *Spike's Folly I.* 1959. Oil on canvas. 79″ x 68½″
Collection of Mr. and Mrs. Robert C. Scull, New York. (p. 140)

66. *Door to the River.* 1960. Oil on canvas. 80″ x 70″.
The Whitney Museum of American Art, New York. Gift of the Friends of The
Whitney Museum of American Art and purchase. (p. 141)

BURGOYNE DILLER

67. *First Theme.* 1962. Oil on canvas. 72″ x 72″.
The Art Institute of Chicago, Wilson L. Mead Fund Income. (p. 142)

68. *No. 33, First Theme.* 1962. Oil on canvas. 32″ x 32″.
Collection of Mr. and Mrs. Richard Hokin, New York. (p. 72)

69. *No. 5, Third Theme.* 1963. Oil on canvas. 42″ x 42″.
The Diller Estate, Courtesy of Noah Goldowsky and Richard Bellamy, New York.
(p. 143)

70. *No. 10, First Theme.* 1963–64. Oil on canvas. 72″ x 72″.
The Diller Estate, Courtesy of Noah Goldowsky and Richard Bellamy, New York.
(p. 144)

71. *No. 9, First Theme.* 1963–64. Oil on canvas. 72″ x 72″.
Albright-Knox Art Gallery, Buffalo, New York, Gift of Seymour H. Knox. (p. 144)

MARK DI SUVERO

72. *Hankchampion.* 1960. Wood and chain construction. 6′ x 10′.
Collection of Mr. and Mrs. Robert C. Scull, New York. (p. 145)

73. *Tom.* 1961. Wood and steel. 8′ x 10′ x 10′.
Lo Giudice Gallery, Chicago, Illinois, and Richard Bellamy, New York. (p. 146)

74. *Mohican.* 1967. Steel and wood, 15′ x 9′ x 30′.
Collection of Mr. Lewis Manilow, Chicago, Illinois. (p. 73)

DAN FLAVIN

75. *the nominal three (to William of Ockham).* 1963. Cool white fluorescent
light. 8′ (high). The National Gallery of Canada, Ottawa, Canada. (p. 74)

76. untitled. 1965. A set of seven cubes. White baked enamel on steel with
cool white fluorescent light. Size determined by length of fixture.
Dwan Gallery, New York. (Illustrated by drawing page 147.)

77. untitled. 1966. Cool white fluorescent light. 8′ (high).
Collection of Mr. and Mrs. Robert A. M. Stern, New York. (p. 147)

78. untitled. 1966. Cool white fluorescent light. *ca.* 8′ x 8′.
Collection of Irving Blum, Los Angeles, California. (p. 148)

HELEN FRANKENTHALER

79. *Abstract Landscape.* 1951. Oil on canvas. 69″ x 71⅞″.
Collection of the artist. (p. 149)

80. *Other Generations.* 1957. Oil on canvas. 70″ x 70″.
Collection of the artist. (p. 149)

81. *Europa.* 1957. Oil on canvas. 70½″ x 54″.
Collection of the artist. (p. 150)

82. *Yellow Caterpillar.* 1961. Oil on canvas. 90″ x 120″.
Private collection, New York. (p. 75)

83. *The Moors.* 1962. Acrylic on canvas. 107″ x 47″.
Collection of William S. Rubin, New York. (p. 151)

84. *Blue Atmosphere.* 1963. Acrylic on canvas. 117½″ x 70″.
Collection of the artist. (p. 152)

85. *Orange Shapes in Frame.* 1964. Acrylic on canvas. 93″ x 74″.
Collection of Mr. and Mrs. Robert B. Mayer, Winnetka, Illinois. (p. 153)

86. *One O'Clock.* 1966. Acrylic paint on canvas. 93¾″ x 75¾″.
Collection of Albert F. Weis, Savannah, Georgia. (p. 154)

87. *Gamut.* 1968. Acrylic on canvas. 11′2″ x 93″.
Collection of the artist. (p. 155)

ARSHILE GORKY

88. *Garden in Sochi.* 1940–41. Oil on canvas. 25″ x 29″
Private collection, courtesy of M. Knoedler & Company, Inc., New York. (p. 156)

89. *The Pirate I.* 1942. Oil on canvas. 29¼″ x 40⅛″.
Collection of Mr. and Mrs. Julien Levy, Bridgewater, Connecticut. (p. 158)

90. *The Pirate II.* 1943. Oil on canvas. 30" x 36".
Collection of Mr. and Mrs. Julien Levy, Bridgewater, Connecticut. (p. 158)

91. *Water of the Flowery Mill.* 1944. Oil on canvas. 42¼" x 48¾".
The Metropolitan Museum of Art, New York, George A. Hearn Fund, 1956. (p. 76)

92. *The Unattainable.* 1945. Oil on canvas. 41⅛" x 29¼".
The Baltimore Museum of Art, Baltimore, Maryland, Friends of Art Fund. (p. 159)

93. *The Plough and the Song.* 1947. Oil on burlap. 52⅛" x 64¼".
Collection of Mr. and Mrs. Milton A. Gordon, New York. (p. 160)

94. *The Plough and the Song.* 1947. Oil on canvas. 50¾" x 62¾".
Allen Memorial Art Museum, Oberlin College, Oberlin, Ohio. (p. 160)

95. *The Betrothal, II.* 1947. Oil on canvas. 50¾" x 38".
The Whitney Museum of American Art, New York. (p. 161)

96. *The Limit.* 1947. Oil on paper over burlap. 50¾" x 62½".
Private collection, courtesy of M. Knoedler & Company, Inc., New York. (p. 162)

97. *Dark Green Painting.* ca. 1948. Oil on canvas. 43¾" x 56".
Collection of Mrs. H. Gates Lloyd, Haverford, Pennsylvania. (p. 163)

ADOLPH GOTTLIEB

98. *Masquerade.* 1945. Oil and egg tempera on canvas. 36" x 24".
Collection of Mrs. Esther Gottlieb, New York. (p. 164)

99. *Recurrent Apparition.* 1946. Oil on canvas. 36" x 54".
Collection of Mrs. Esther Gottlieb, New York. (p. 165)

100. *Oracle.* 1947–48. Oil on canvas. 60" x 44".
The Albert A. List Family Collection, New York. (Not illustrated.)

101. *Dream.* 1948. Oil on canvas. 20" x 24".
Isaac Delgado Museum of Art, New Orleans, Louisiana,
Gift of William Edward Campbell, 1951. (p. 165)

102. *Thrust.* 1959. Oil on canvas. 108" x 90".
The Metropolitan Museum of Art, New York, George A. Hearn Fund, 1959. (p. 166)

103. *Aureole.* 1959. Oil on canvas. 108" x 90".
Collection of Mrs. Esther Gottlieb, New York. (p. 167)

104. *Una.* 1959. Oil on canvas. 108" x 90".
Collection of the artist. (p. 77)

105. *Sign.* 1962. Oil on canvas. 90" x 84".
Collection of the artist. (p. 168)

106. *Red, Blue, Yellow.* 1966. Oil on canvas. 84" x 90".
Collection of William S. Rubin, New York. (p. 169)

107. *Petaloid.* 1967. Cor-Ten steel. 96" x 96" x 48".
Collection of Mrs. Esther Gottlieb, New York. (p. 169)

108. *Wall.* 1969. Painted aluminum. 7½' x 4½' x 11'.
Collection of the artist. (Illustrated by model page 78.)

PHILIP GUSTON

109. *To B. W. T.* 1952. Oil on canvas. 48" x 51".
Collection of Mr. Leonard M. Brown, Springfield, Massachusetts. (p. 170)

110. *Painting*. 1952. Oil on canvas. 50¾″ x 48″.
Collection of Mrs. Albert H. Newman, Chicago, Illinois. (p. 79)

111. *Attar*. 1953. Oil on canvas. 48½″ x 46″.
Collection of Morton Feldman, New York. (Not illustrated.)

112. *Zone*. 1954. Oil on canvas. 46″ x 48⅛″.
Collection of Mr. and Mrs. Ben Heller, New York. (p. 171)

113. *Untitled*. 1954. Oil on canvas. 51″ x 48¾″.
Collection of Mr. and Mrs. C. B. Wright, Seattle, Washington. (p. 171)

114. *For M*. 1955. Oil on canvas. 76¼″ x 72″.
Private collection, Los Angeles, California. (p. 172)

115. *Cythera*. 1957. Oil on canvas. 72″ x 64″.
Collection of Mr. and Mrs. Donald Blinken, New York. (p. 173)

HANS HOFMANN

116. *In the Wake of the Hurricane*. 1960. Oil on canvas. 72¼″ x 60″.
University Art Museum, Berkeley, California, Gift of the artist. (p. 174)

117. *Summer Night's Bliss*. 1961. Oil on canvas. 84″ x 78″.
The Baltimore Museum of Art, Baltimore, Maryland, Gift of the artist. (p. 175)

118. *Agrigento*. 1961. Oil on canvas. 84¼″ x 72″.
University Art Museum, Berkeley, California, Gift of the artist. (p. 176)

119. *Memoria in Aeterne*. 1962. Oil on canvas. 84″ x 72⅛″.
The Museum of Modern Art, New York, Gift of the artist, 1963. (p. 177)

120. *Veluti in Speculum*. 1962. Oil on canvas. 85¼″ x 73½″.
The Metropolitan Museum of Art, Gift of Mr. and Mrs. Richard Rodgers and the
Francis Lathrop Fund, 1963. (p. 80)

121. *Gloriamundi*. 1963. Oil on canvas. 60⅛″ x 52″.
University Art Museum, Berkeley, California, Gift of the artist. (p. 178)

122. *Song of a Nightingale*. 1964. Oil on canvas. 7′ x 6′.
Collection of Mr. and Mrs. Eugene M. Schwartz, New York. (p. 179)

123. *In Sober Ecstasy*. 1965. Oil on canvas. 73½″ x 61½″.
Collection of Mr. and Mrs. David Mirvish, Toronto, Canada. (p. 180)

124. *Little Cherry* (Renata Series No. 1). 1965. Oil on canvas. 84″ x 78″.
Estate of Hans Hofmann. (p. 181)

125. *Lust and Delight* (Renata Series No. 2). 1965. Oil on canvas. 84″ x 60″.
Estate of Hans Hofmann. (p. 181)

EDWARD HOPPER

126. *Gas*. 1940. Oil on canvas. 26¼″ x 40¼″.
The Museum of Modern Art, New York, Mrs. Simon Guggenheim Fund, 1943.
(p. 182)

127. *First Row, Orchestra*. 1951. Oil on canvas. 31″ x 40″.
Joseph H. Hirshhorn Foundation. (p. 183)

128. *Office in a Small City*. 1953. Oil on canvas. 28″ x 40″.
The Metropolitan Museum of Art, New York, George A. Hearn Fund, 1953. (p. 184)

129. *Western Motel*. 1957. Oil on canvas. 30¼″ x 50⅛″.
Yale University Art Gallery, Bequest of Stephen Carlton Clark, B.A., 1903. (p. 82)

JASPER JOHNS

130. *Green Target.* 1955. Encaustic on newspaper on canvas. 60″ x 60″.
The Museum of Modern Art, New York, Richard S. Zeisler Fund, 1958. (p. 184)

131. *White Flag.* 1955. Encaustic and collage on canvas. 72″ x 144″.
Collection of the artist. (p. 185)

132. *Three Flags.* 1958. Encaustic on canvas. 30⅞″ x 45½″.
Collection of Mr. and Mrs. Burton Tremaine, Meriden, Connecticut. (p. 185)

133. *Device Circle.* 1959. Encaustic and collage on canvas. 40″ x 40″.
Collection of Mr. and Mrs. Burton Tremaine, Meriden, Connecticut. (p. 186)

134. *Jubilee.* 1959. Oil on canvas. 60″ x 44″.
Collection of Robert Rauschenberg, New York. (p. 187)

135. *False Start.* 1959. Oil on canvas. 67¼″ x 54″.
Collection of Mr. and Mrs. Robert C. Scull, New York. (p. 188)

136. *Painting with Two Balls.* 1960. Encaustic and collage on canvas with
objects. 65″ x 54″ (three panels). Collection of the artist. (p. 83)

137. *Studio.* 1964. Oil on canvas. 73½″ x 145½″.
The Whitney Museum of American Art, New York, Gift of the Friends of The
Whitney Museum of American Art and purchase. (p. 188)

138. *Double White Map.* 1965. Encaustic and collage on canvas. 90″ x 70″.
Collection of Mr. and Mrs. Robert C. Scull, New York. (p. 189)

139. *Screen Piece.* 1967. Oil on canvas. 72″ x 50″.
Collection of David Whitney, New York. (p. 190)

140. *Screen Piece 2.* 1968. Oil on canvas. 72″ x 50″.
Collection of Mr. and Mrs. Victor W. Ganz, New York. (p. 191)

141. *Flag (64 stars).* 1955. Pencil on paper. 7″ x 9″.
Collection of the artist. (Not illustrated.)

142. *Target with Four Faces.* 1955. Pencil on paper. 8½″ x 7¼″.
Collection of the artist. (Not illustrated.)

143. *Green Flag.* 1956. Pencil and crayon on canvas. 7″ x 9″.
Collection of Lois Long, New York. (Not illustrated.)

144. *Flag on Orange Field.* 1957. Day-Glo, watercolor, chalk, pencil on paper.
10½″ x 7¾″. Collection of the artist. (Not illustrated.)

145. *Alphabets.* 1957. Pencil and pasted index tabs. 13¾″ x 9¾″.
Collection of Robert Rosenblum, New York. (Not illustrated.)

146. *Light Bulb.* 1958. Pencil and graphite wash. 6½″ x 8¾″.
Collection of Andy Warhol, New York. (Not illustrated.)

147. *Flag.* 1958. Pencil and graphite wash on paper. 7½″ x 10⅜″.
Collection of Leo Castelli, New York. (p. 192)

148. *Tennyson.* 1958. Ink on paper. 14¾″ x 9¾″.
Collection of the artist. (Not illustrated.)

149. *Study for Painting with a Ball.* 1958. Conté on paper. 15″ x 14½″.
Collection of the artist. (p. 192)

150. *Three Flags.* 1959. Pencil on paper. 14½″ x 23½″.
Collection of the Victoria & Albert Museum, London, England. (Not illustrated.)

151. *Study for Painting with Two Balls.* 1960. Charcoal on paper. 19½″ x 15½″. Joseph H. Hirshhorn Collection. (p. 193)

152. *Numbers.* 1960. Pencil on paper. Ten drawings matted separately. 2¾″ x 2¼″ each. Collection of Edward Carey, New York. (p. 194)

153. *Device Circle.* 1960. Pencil on paper. 15″ x 14½″. Collection of Mr. and Mrs. Ben Heller, New York. (p. 194)

154. *Two Flags.* 1960. Graphite wash on paper. 26″ x 19″. Collection of the artist. (Not illustrated.)

155. *Out the Window.* 1960. Charcoal and pastel. 34½″ x 28½″. Collection of Dr. and Mrs. Bernard Brodsky, New York. (Not illustrated.)

156. *0 through 9.* 1960. Charcoal on paper. 29″ x 23″. Collection of the artist. (Not illustrated.)

157. *Gray Alphabets.* 1960. Graphite wash on paper. 32″ x 23½″. Collection of Mr. and Mrs. Leo Castelli, New York. (Not illustrated.)

158. *Numbers.* 1960. Charcoal on paper. 9½″ x 7½″. Collection of the artist. (Not illustrated.)

159. *Jubilee.* 1960. Graphite wash. 28″ x 21″. Collection of Mr. and Mrs. Lester Francis Avnet, New York. (Not illustrated.)

160. *Floral Design.* 1961. Watercolor on paper and collage. 20¼″ x 10½″. Collection of the artist. (Not illustrated.)

161. *0 through 9.* 1961. Charcoal and pastel on paper. 54″ x 45″. Collection of Mr. and Mrs. Robert C. Scull, New York. (p. 195)

162. *Study for Skin I.* 1962. Charcoal on paper. 22″ x 34″. Collection of the artist. (p. 196)

163. *Study for Skin II.* 1962. Charcoal on paper. 22″ x 34″. Collection of the artist. (p. 196)

164. *Study for Skin III.* 1962. Charcoal on paper. 22″ x 34″. Collection of the artist. (p. 196)

165. *Study for Skin IV.* 1962. Charcoal on paper. 22″ x 34″. Collection of the artist. (p. 196)

166. *Diver.* 1963. Charcoal, pastel, paper on canvas. 86½″ x 71″. Collection of Mr. and Mrs. Victor W. Ganz, New York. (p. 197)

167. *Map.* 1965. Graphite wash on paper. 13¼″ x 20½″. Collection of the artist. (Not illustrated.)

168. *Study for Flags.* 1965. Watercolor. 29″ x 21¼″. Collection of the artist. (Not illustrated.)

169. *Studies for 0–9 lithographs.* 1969. Watercolor. Ten watercolors, each 2¼″ x 2″. Collection of Jason Ferus Blum, Los Angeles, California. (Not illustrated.)

DONALD JUDD

170. Untitled. 1963. Painted wood and aluminum. 48″ x 83″ x 48″. Collection of Julie Judd, New York. (p. 84)

171. Untitled. 1965. Perforated steel. 8″ x 120″ x 66″. Leo Castelli Gallery, New York. (p. 198)

172. Untitled. 1969. Stainless steel and plexiglas.
Six units, each 34″ x 34″ x 34″. Leo Castelli Gallery, New York. (p. 198)

173. Untitled. 1969. Aluminum. 5′ x 7′ x 12′ approximately.
Leo Castelli Gallery. New York. (Not illustrated.)

ELLSWORTH KELLY

174. *White Relief with Blue.* 1950. Oil on wood. 45″ x 17½″.
Private collection, New York. (p. 199)

175. *Blue Red Green.* 1962–63. Oil on canvas. 91″ x 82″.
The Metropolitan Museum of Art, New York, Arthur H. Hearn Fund, 1963. (p. 200)

176. *3 Panels: Red, Yellow, Blue.* 1963. Acrylic on canvas. 90″ x 90″.
Fondation Maeght, Saint Paul, France. (p. 200)

177. *Orange White.* 1964. Oil on canvas. 122″ x 96″.
Courtesy of Sidney Janis Gallery, New York. (p. 201)

178. *Red Blue Green Yellow.* 1965. Oil on canvas. 86″ x 53½″.
Collection of Mr. and Mrs. Robert B. Mayer, Winnetka, Illinois. (p. 85)

179. *2 Panels: White Dark Blue.* 1968. Oil on canvas. 96″ x 144″.
Courtesy of Sidney Janis Gallery, New York. (p. 202)

180. *13 Panels: Spectrum V.* 1969. Oil on canvas. 84″ x 443″.
Courtesy of Sidney Janis Gallery, New York. (Not illustrated.)

181. *White Ring.* 1963. Epoxy on aluminum. 70″ x 72″ x 12″.
Private collection, New York. (p. 202)

182. *Blue White Angle.* 1966. Epoxy on aluminum. 72″ x 36″ x 72″.
Private collection, New York. (p. 86)

183. *Green.* 1968. Painted aluminum. 21″ x 105″ x 112″.
Collection of The Walker Art Center, Minneapolis, Minnesota. (p. 203)

184. Untitled. 1968. Painted aluminum. 100½″ x 146½″ x 38⅜″.
Collection of William S. Rubin, New York. (p. 204)

185. *Black White.* 1968. Painted aluminum. 100½″ x 146½″ x 38⅜″.
Courtesy of Sidney Janis Gallery, New York. (p. 205)

186. *Rubber Tree.* 1958. Pencil on paper. 29″ x 23″.
Private collection, New York. (Not illustrated.)

187. *Tulip.* 1958. Pencil on paper. 29″ x 23″.
Private collection, New York. (p. 206)

188. *Mango.* 1959. Pencil on paper. 28½″ x 22½″.
Private collection, New York. (Not illustrated.)

189. *Avocado.* 1960. Pencil on paper. 28½″ x 22½″.
Private collection, New York. (Not illustrated.)

190. *Sweet Pea.* 1960. Pencil on paper. 22½″ x 28½″.
Private collection, New York. (Not illustrated.)

191. *Lily.* 1960. Ink on paper. 28½″ x 22½″.
Private collection, New York. (Not illustrated.)

192. *Wild Grape.* 1960. Pencil on paper, 28½ ″x 45″.
Private collection, New York. (Not illustrated.)

193. *Brier.* 1960. Pencil on paper, 28½" x 22½".
Private collection, New York. (Not illustrated.)

194. *Brier.* 1960. Pencil on paper. 28½" x 22½".
Private collection, New York. (Not illustrated.)

195. *Grass.* 1961. Pencil on paper. 28½" x 22½".
Private collection, New York. (p. 206)

196. *Wild Grape.* 1961. Ink on paper. 22½" x 28½".
Private collection, New York. (Not illustrated.)

197. *Castor Bean.* 1961. Ink on paper, 22½ x 28½".
Private collection, New York. (p. 206)

198. *Philodendron.* 1963. Ink on paper, 28½" x 22½".
Private collection, New York. (Not illustrated.)

199. *Oak.* 1964. Pencil on paper. 28½" x 22½".
Private collection, New York. (p. 207)

200. *Lemon Branch.* 1964. Pencil on paper. 28½" x 22½".
Private collection, New York. (Not illustrated.)

201. *Catalpa.* 1964. Pencil on paper. 28½" x 45".
Private collection, New York. (Not illustrated.)

202. *Chrysanthemum.* 1965. Pencil on paper. 28½" x 22½".
Private collection, New York. (Not illustrated.)

203. *Leaves.* 1965. Pencil on paper. 29" x 23".
Private collection, New York. (Not illustrated.)

204. *Oranges.* 1966. Pencil on paper. 22½" x 28½".
Private collection, New York. (Not illustrated.)

205. *Magnolia.* 1966. Pencil on paper. 29" x 23".
Private collection, New York. (p. 207)

206. *Woodland Plant.* 1967. Pencil on paper. 29" x 23".
Private collection, New York. (Not illustrated.)

207. *Avocado.* 1967. Pencil on paper. 29" x 23".
Private collection, New York. (Not illustrated.)

208. *Oak.* 1967. Pencil on paper. 22" x 30".
Private collection, New York. (Not illustrated.)

209. *Avocado.* 1967. Pencil on paper. 29" x 23".
Private collection, New York. (p. 207)

210. *Woodland Plant.* 1967. Pencil on paper. 30" x 22".
Private collection, New York. (Not illustrated.)

211. *Ghinko.* 1967. Pencil on paper. 29" x 23".
Private collection, New York. (Not illustrated.)

212. *Avocado.* 1967. Pencil on paper. 30" x 22".
Private collection, New York. (Not illustrated.)

213. *Cyclamen.* 1967. Pencil on paper, 29" x 23".
Private collection, New York. (Not illustrated.)

214. *Chrysanthemum.* 1967. Pencil on paper. 30" x 22".
Private collection, New York. (p. 208)

215. *Water Lily.* 1968. Pencil on paper. 29" x 23".
Private collection, New York. (p. 208)

FRANZ KLINE

216. *Nijinsky.* 1949. Oil on canvas. 33″ x 28″.
Collection of Mr. and Mrs. David I. Orr, New York. (p. 209)

217. *Wotan.* 1950. Oil on canvas. 55⅛″ x 79¼″.
Collection of Mr. and Mrs. Robert C. Scull, New York. (p. 210)

218. *Horizontals Two.* 1952. Oil on canvas. 77″ x 100″.
Estate of Franz Kline. Courtesy of Marlborough-Gerson Gallery, New York. (p. 210)

219. *Figure Eight.* 1952. Oil on canvas. 80½″ x 63½″.
Collection of William S. Rubin, New York. (p. 211)

220. Untitled. 1953–54. Oil on canvas. 57¼″ x 82″.
Collection of Robert H. Halff and Carl W. Johnson, Beverly Hills, California. (p. 212)

221. Untitled. 1954. Oil on canvas. 43″ x 36″.
Collection of Mr. and Mrs. David I. Orr, New York. (p. 212)

222. *White Forms.* 1955. Oil on canvas. 74″ x 50″.
Collection of Philip Johnson, New Canaan, Connecticut. (p. 213)

223. *Blue Center.* 1958. Oil on canvas. 36″ x 40″.
Collection of Mr. and Mrs. Robert C. Scull, New York. (p. 87)

224. *Orange and Black Wall.* 1959. Oil on canvas. 66½″ x 144″.
Collection of Mr. and Mrs. Robert C. Scull, New York. (p. 214)

225. *Riverbed.* 1961. Oil on canvas. 78⅞″ x 109¼″.
Collection of William M. White, Jr., New York. (p. 214)

GABE KOHN

226. *Acrotère.* 1960. Laminated wood. 35¼″ x 31″ x 22¼″.
The Museum of Modern Art, New York, Given anonymously, 1963. (p. 88)

227. *Long Beach Contract.* 1965. Laminated redwood. 10′ x 7′.
California State College, Long Beach, California. (p. 215)

ROY LICHTENSTEIN

228. *I Can See the Whole Room. . . .* 1961. Oil on canvas. 48″ x 48″.
Collection of Mr. and Mrs. Burton Tremaine, Meriden, Connecticut. (p. 216)

229. *The Engagement Ring.* 1961. Oil on canvas. 67¾″ x 79½″.
Collection of Mr. and Mrs. Robert A. Rowan, Pasadena, California. (p. 89)

230. *Live Ammo.* 1962. Oil on canvas. 68″ x 92″ (two panels).
Collection of Mr. and Mrs. Morton Neumann, Chicago, Illinois. (p. 217)

231. *Sussex.* 1964. Oil and magna on canvas. 36″ x 68″.
Collection of Robert Rosenblum, New York. (p. 217)

232. *Big Painting #6.* 1965. Oil and magna on canvas. 92½″ x 129″.
Collection of Mr. and Mrs. Robert C. Scull, New York. (p. 218)

233. *Haystacks.* 1968. Oil and magna on canvas. 18″ x 24″.
Private collection, New York. (p. 219)

234. *Haystacks.* 1969. Oil and magna on canvas. 16″ x 24″.
Private collection, New York. (Not illustrated.)

235. *Haystacks*. 1969. Oil and magna on canvas. 16″ x 24″.
Private collection, New York. (p. 219)

236. *Rouen Cathedral (seen at five different times of day) III*. 1969.
Oil and magna on canvas. 63″ x 42″. (#1 of five paintings in set.)
Private collection, New York. (p. 220)

237. *Rouen Cathedral (seen at five different times of day) III*. 1969.
Oil and magna on canvas. 63″ x 42″. (#2 of five paintings in set.)
Private collection, New York. (Not illustrated.)

238. *Rouen Cathedral (seen at five different times of day) III*. 1969.
Oil and magna on canvas. 63″ x 42″. (#3 of five paintings in set.)
Private collection, New York. (p. 221)

MORRIS LOUIS

239. *Iris*. 1954. Acrylic on canvas. 80″ x 106″.
Collection of Mr. and Mrs. Eugene M. Schwartz, New York. (p. 90)

240. *Saraband*. 1959. Acrylic on canvas. 100½″ x 149″.
The Solomon R. Guggenheim Museum, New York. (p. 222)

241. *Terranean*. 1959. Acrylic resin paint on canvas. 90½″ x 146″.
Collection of Mr. and Mrs. Kenneth Noland, New York. (p. 223)

242. *While*. 1959. Acrylic on canvas. 96½″ x 136⅜″.
Harry N. Abrams Family Collection, New York. (p. 224)

243. *Aleph*. 1960. Magna acrylic on canvas. 105″ x 92¾″.
Collection of Jaime C. del Amo, Madrid, Spain. (p. 225)

244. *Alpha-Pi*. 1961. Acrylic on canvas. 102½″ x 177″.
The Metropolitan Museum of Art, New York, Arthur H. Hearn Fund, 1967. (p. 91)

245. *Alpha-Delta*. 1961. Acrylic on canvas. 8′8″ x 20′.
Everson Museum of Art, Syracuse, New York. (p. 225)

246. *Moving In*. 1961. Magna acrylic on canvas. 87½″ x 41½″.
Private collection. New York. (p. 226)

247. *Hot Half*. 1962. Acrylic resin on canvas. 63″ x 63″.
Collection of Mrs. Abner Brenner, Washington, D.C. (p. 227)

ROBERT MORRIS

248. Untitled. 1964. Painted plywood. 6′6″ x 9 .
Collection of Dott. Giuseppe Panza di Buomo, Milan, Italy.
Courtesy of Leo Castelli Gallery, New York. (p. 228)

249. Untitled. 1965. Aluminum construction. 6′ x 11′7″ x 3″.
Collection of Mr. and Mrs. Robert C. Scull, New York. (p. 92)

250. Untitled. 1966. Steel mesh. 31″ x 106″ x 106″.
Lent by The Kleiner Foundation, Beverly Hills, California.
Courtesy of Los Angeles County Museum of Art, Los Angeles, California. (p. 228)

251. Untitled. 1967–68. Felt. 180″ x 72″ x 1″.
The Detroit Institute of Arts, Gift of the Friends of Modern Art. (p. 229)

252. Untitled. 1968. Translucent fiberglas. Nine units, each 48″ x 24″ x 24″.
Collection of Philip Johnson, New Canaan, Connecticut. (p. 230)

ROBERT MOTHERWELL

253. *The Little Spanish Prison.* 1941–44. Oil on canvas. 27⅛″ x 17″.
Collection of the artist. (p. 231)

254. *Mallarmé's Swan.* 1944. Collage using gouache, crayon, and paper on cardboard.
43½″ x 35½″. Contemporary Collection of The Cleveland Museum of Art, Cleveland, Ohio. (p. 93)

255. *Homely Protestant.* 1948. Oil on composition board. 96″ x 48″.
Collection of Helen Frankenthaler, New York. (p. 232)

256. *Elegy to the Spanish Republic, 70.* 1961. Oil on canvas. 69″ x 114″.
The Metropolitan Museum of Art, New York, Anonymous gift, 1965. (p. 233)

257. *Africa.* 1965. Acrylic on canvas. 80″ x 225″.
The Baltimore Museum of Art, Baltimore, Maryland, Gift of the artist. (p. 233)

258. *Beige Figuration No. 3.* 1967. Collage (paper). 30″ x 22″.
Collection of the artist. (p. 234)

259. *"Open" No. 14: In Ochre with Charcoal Line.* 1968.
Polymer paint and charcoal on canvas. 114″ x 69″.
Collection of the artist. (p. 235)

260. *"Open" No. 17: In Ultramarine with Charcoal Line.* 1968.
Polymer paint and charcoal on canvas. 100″ x 197″.
Collection of the artist. (p. 236)

261. *"Open" No. 31B: In Raw Sienna.* 1968. Charcoal on blotting paper.
17″ x 37½″. Collection of the artist. (p. 236)

BARNETT NEWMAN

262. *Pagan Void.* 1946. Oil on canvas. 33″ x 38″.
Collection of Mrs. Annalee Newman, New York. (p. 237)

263. *The Euclidian Abyss.* 1946–47. Oil and crayon on fabric. 28″ x 22″.
Collection of Mr. and Mrs. Burton Tremaine, Meriden, Connecticut. (p. 237)

264. *Concord.* 1949. Oil on canvas. 89¾″ x 53⅝″.
The Metropolitan Museum of Art, New York, George A. Hearn Fund, 1968. (p. 94)

265. *Onement III.* 1949. Oil on canvas. 72″ x 34″.
Collection of Mr. and Mrs. Joseph Slifka, New York. (p. 238)

266. *Covenant.* 1949. Oil on canvas. 48″ x 60″.
Joseph H. Hirshhorn Collection. (p. 239)

267. *Prometheus Bound.* 1952. Oil on canvas. 131¾″ x 50″.
Collection of William S. Rubin, New York. (p. 240)

268. *Shining Forth (for George).* 1961. Oil on canvas. 9½′ x 14½′.
Collection of Mrs. Annalee Newman, New York. (p. 241)

269. *Who's Afraid of Red, Yellow, Blue I.* 1966. Oil on canvas. 60″ x 50″.
Collection of S. I. Newhouse, Jr., New York. (p. 242)

270. *Anna's Light.* 1968. Acrylic on canvas. 9′ x 20′.
M. Knoedler & Company, Inc., New York. (p. 243)

271. *Jericho.* 1968–69. Acrylic on canvas. 9′6″ x 9′6″.
M. Knoedler & Company, Inc., New York. (p. 243)

272. *Here I (to Marcia)*. 1950. Bronze. 8′ x 26″ x 27″.
Collection of Mrs. Annalee Newman, New York. (p. 244)

273. *Here III*. 1966. Stainless steel and Cor-Ten steel.
10′5″ x 23½″ x 18½″. M. Knoedler & Company, Inc., New York. (p. 244)

274. *Broken Obelisk*. 1967. Cor-Ten steel. 26′ x 10½′ x 10½′.
M. Knoedler & Company, Inc., New York. (p. 245)

ISAMU NOGUCHI

275. *The Cry*. 1959. Balsa wood with steel base. 84″ x 30″ x 18″.
The Solomon R. Guggenheim Museum, New York. (p. 246)

276. *Life of a Cube*. 1962. Black granite. 21″ x 21″ x 21″.
Cordier & Ekstrom, Inc., New York. (p. 247)

277. *Sky Frame*. 1966. Rose Aurora Portuguese marble. 22″ x 28″ x 8¼″.
Cordier & Ekstrom, Inc., New York. (p. 247)

278. *White Sun*. 1966. White Italian Saravezza marble. 28½″ (diameter).
Cordier & Ekstrom, Inc., New York. (p. 95)

279. *Euripides*. 1966. White Italian Altissimo marble. Two pieces, 45″ and
90″ (high). Cordier & Ekstrom, Inc., New York. (p. 248)

KENNETH NOLAND

280. *Teton Noir*. 1961. Acrylic on canvas. 81″ x 81″.
Collection of Carter Burden, New York. (p. 249)

281. *Mach II*. 1964. Acrylic resin on canvas. 9′ x 17′. Collection of
Kimiko and John Powers, Aspen, Colorado. (p. 250)

282. *17th Stage*. 1964. Acrylic on canvas. 8′ x 7′.
Collection of Mr. and Mrs. Eugene M. Schwartz, New York. (p. 251)

283. *Bend Sinister*. 1964. Acrylic on canvas. 98″ x 161¾″.
Joseph H. Hirshhorn Collection. (p. 252)

284. *Embrown*. 1964. Acrylic on canvas. 96″ x 145″.
Collection of Mr. and Mrs. David Mirvish, Toronto, Canada. (p. 252)

285. *Trans-Median*. 1968. Acrylic on canvas. 7½′ x 7½′.
Collection of Mr. and Mrs. David Mirvish, Toronto, Canada. (p. 253)

286. *Trans-Median II*. 1968. Acrylic emulsion on canvas. 90½″ x 160″.
Collection of Lawrence Rubin, New York. (p. 96)

287. *Dawn-Dusk*. 1968. Water-miscible acrylic on cotton duck. 30½″ x
141½″. Collection of Mr. and Mrs. Clement Greenberg, New York. (p. 254)

288. *Via Lime*. 1968–69. Acrylic emulsion on canvas. 90½″ x 240″.
Collection of Ondine Vaughn and Steve Schapiro, New York. (p. 254)

CLAES OLDENBURG

289. *7-up*. 1961. Enamel on plaster. 50⅛″ x 37⅜″ x 6¼″.
Collection of Mr. and Mrs. Burton Tremaine, Meriden, Connecticut. (p. 255)

290. *Strong Arm*. 1961. Enamel on plaster. 43⅜″ x 32⅜″ x 5½″.
Collection of Mr. and Mrs. Burton Tremaine, Meriden, Connecticut. (p. 256)

291. *Soft Typewriter*. 1963. Vinyl, kapok, cloth, and plexiglas.
9″ x 27½″ x 26″. Collection of Alan Power, London, England. (p. 257)

292. *Ironing Board with Shirt and Iron*. 1964. Wood, cloth, vinyl, nylon, and hydrostone.
80″ x 67½″ x 24″. Collection of Mr. and Mrs. Sonnabend, Paris, France. (p. 257)

293. *Tub (hard model)*. 1966. Corrugated paper, wood, enamel.
80″ x 32½″ x 28″. Collection of Mrs. Claes Oldenburg, New York. (p. 258)

294. *Giant Pool Balls*. 1967. Sixteen plexiglas balls, 24″ each, wood rack,
120″ x 120″ x 108″. Courtesy of Sidney Janis Gallery, New York. (p. 97)

JULES OLITSKI

295. *Ten O'Clock*. 1959. Paint, spackle, polymer emulsion on panel.
36″ x 36″. Collection of the artist. (p. 259)

296. *Bathsheba*. 1959. Oil on canvas. 78″ x 70″.
Collection of J. Patrick Lannan, Palm Beach, Florida. (p. 260)

297. *Ritual of L*. 1959. Paint, spackle, polymer emulsion on canvas.
6′ x 7′. Collection of the artist. (p. 261)

298. *Commissar Demikovsky*. 1965. Acrylic on canvas. 8′ x 7′.
Collection of Mr. and Mrs. Eugene M. Schwartz, New York. (p. 262)

299. *Thigh Smoke*. 1966. Acrylic on canvas. 167″ x 92½″.
Seattle–First National Bank Collection, Seattle, Washington. (p. 263)

300. *Disarmed*. 1968. Acrylic on canvas. 9′10″ x 16′.
Collection of Mr. and Mrs. Eugene M. Schwartz, New York. (p. 98)

301. *Green Volya*. 1969. Acrylic emulsion on canvas. 9′9″ x 17′5″.
Collection of Lawrence Rubin, New York. (p. 264)

302. *Warehouse Light*. 1969. Acrylic on canvas. 118″ x 174″.
Collection of Lawrence Rubin, New York. (p. 265)

303. *Twelve Nights*. 1968. Aluminum and acrylic, air drying lacquer.
9′ x 16½′ x 12′. Collection of the artist. (p. 265)

JACKSON POLLOCK

304. *Male and Female*. 1942. Oil on canvas. 73¼″ x 49″.
Collection of Mrs. H. Gates Lloyd, Haverford, Pennsylvania. (p. 266)

305. *Moon Woman Cuts the Circle*. 1943. Oil on canvas. 43″ x 41″.
Courtesy of Marlborough-Gerson Gallery, New York. (p. 267)

306. *Night Ceremony*. 1944. Oil and enamel on canvas. 72″ x 43⅛″.
Collection of Mrs. Barbara Reis Poe, New York. (p. 268)

307. *Cathedral*. 1947. Duco and aluminum paint on canvas. 71½″ x 35¹⁄₁₆″.
Dallas Museum of Fine Arts, Gift of Mr. and Mrs. Bernard J. Reis. (p. 269)

308. *Lucifer*. 1947. Oil, enamel, and aluminum paint on canvas.
41″ x 8′9½″. Collection of Joseph H. Hazen, New York. (p. 270)

309. *Mural*. 1950. Oil, enamel, and aluminum paint on canvas, mounted on
wood. 6′ x 8′. Collection of William S. Rubin, New York. (p. 99)

310. *Autumn Rhythm*. 1950. Oil on canvas. 105″ x 207″.
The Metropolitan Museum of Art, New York, Estate of Jackson Pollock,
George A. Hearn Fund, 1957. (p. 270)

311. *Portrait and a Dream.* 1953. Enamel on canvas. 58⅛″ x 134¼″.
Dallas Museum of Fine Arts, Gift of Mr. and Mrs. Algur H. Meadows and
the Meadows Foundation, Inc. (p. 271)

312. *The Deep.* 1953. Oil and duco on canvas. 86¾″ x 51⅛″.
Collection of Samuel Wagstaff, Jr., Detroit, Michigan. (p. 272)

LARRY POONS

313. *Double Speed.* 1962–63. Acrylic and fabric dye on canvas. 72″ x 144″.
Collection of Frank Stella, New York. (p. 273)

314. *Enforcer.* 1963. Liquitex and fabric spray on canvas. 80″ x 80″.
Collection of Mr. and Mrs. Robert C. Scull, New York. (p. 273)

315. *Mary Queen of Scots.* 1965. Acrylic on canvas. 12′ x 90″.
Collection of Mr. and Mrs. Robert C. Scull, New York. (p. 274)

316. *Rosewood.* 1966. Acrylic on canvas. 120″ x 160″.
Collection of William S. Rubin, New York. (p. 275)

317. *Brown Sound.* 1968. Acrylic on canvas. 96″ x 125″.
The Woodward Foundation of Washington, D.C. (p. 100)

318. *Night Journey.* 1968. Acrylic on canvas. 108″ x 124″.
Collection of Carter Burden, New York. (p. 276)

319. *Doge's Palace.* 1969. Acrylic on canvas. 112″ x 17′10″.
Collection of Lawrence Rubin, New York. (p. 277)

ROBERT RAUSCHENBERG

320. *Bed.* 1955. Combine painting. 74″ x 31″.
Collection of Mr. and Mrs. Leo Castelli, New York. (p. 101)

321. *Rebus.* 1955. Combine painting. 96″ x 144″.
Collection of Mr. and Mrs. Victor W. Ganz, New York. (p. 278)

322. *Odalisk.* 1955–58. Construction. 81″ x 25″ x 25″.
Collection of Mr. and Mrs. Victor W. Ganz, New York. (p. 279)

323. *Factum I.* 1957. Combine painting. 62″ x 35½″.
Collection of Dott. Giuseppe Panza di Buomo, Milan, Italy. (p. 280)

324. *Factum II.* 1957. Oil and collage on canvas. 61½″ x 35½″.
Collection of Mr. and Mrs. Morton Neumann, Chicago, Illinois. (p. 281)

325. *Third Time Painting.* 1961. Oil on canvas with clock. 84″ x 60″.
Harry N. Abrams Family Collection, New York. (p. 282)

326. *Tracer.* 1964. Oil on canvas with silkscreen. 84″ x 60″.
Collection of Mr. and Mrs. Frank M. Titelman, Altoona, Pennsylvania. (p. 283)

AD REINHARDT

327. *Yellow Painting.* 1949. Oil on canvas. 40″ x 60″.
Collection of Anna Reinhardt, New York. (p. 284)

328. *Abstract Painting Grey.* 1950. Oil on canvas. 30″ x 40″.
Collection of Rita Reinhardt, New York. (p. 284)

329. *White.* 1950. Oil on canvas. 80″ x 36″.
Collection of Rita Reinhardt, New York. (p. 285)

330. *Red Painting.* 1952. Oil on canvas. 60″ x 82″.
Courtesy of Marlborough-Gerson Gallery, New York. (p. 102)

331. *Red Painting.* 1952. Oil on canvas. 6½′ x 12′.
The Metropolitan Museum of Art, New York, Arthur H. Hearn Fund, 1968. (p. 286)

332. *Abstract Painting.* 1956–60. Oil on canvas. 108″ x 40″.
Courtesy of Marlborough-Gerson Gallery, New York. (p. 287)

333. *Abstract Painting.* 1959. Oil on canvas. 108″ x 40″.
Courtesy of Marlborough-Gerson Gallery, New York. (p. 288)

334. *Abstract Painting.* 1964. Oil on canvas. 60″ x 60″.
Courtesy of Marlborough-Gerson Gallery, New York. (p. 103)

335. *Black Quadruptych.* 1966. Oil on canvas. 120″ x 120″.
Courtesy of Marlborough-Gerson Gallery, New York. (Not illustrated.)

JAMES ROSENQUIST

336. *The Lines Were Deeply Etched on the Map of Her Face.* 1961–62.
Oil on canvas. 66″ x 78″. Collection of Mr. and Mrs. Robert C. Scull,
New York. (p. 104)

337. *Four Young Revolutionaries.* 1962. Glass, wood, and oil paint. 24″ x 32″.
Collection of Mr. and Mrs. Lewis V. Winter, New York. (p. 289)

338. Untitled. 1962. Oil on canvas. 84″ x 72″.
Collection of Mr. and Mrs. Robert A. Rowan, Pasadena, California. (p. 290)

339. *Silver Skies.* 1962. Oil on canvas. 78″ x 16½″.
Collection of Mr. and Mrs. Robert C. Scull, New York. (p. 291)

340. *Early in the Morning.* 1963. Oil on canvas. 95″ x 56″.
Collection of Mr. and Mrs. Robert C. Scull, New York. (p. 292)

341. *Nomad.* 1963. Oil on canvas, plastic paint, wood. 84″ x 210″.
Albright-Knox Art Gallery, Buffalo, New York, Gift of Seymour H. Knox. (p. 293)

342. *Growth Plan.* 1966. Oil on canvas. 70″ x 140″ (2 panels).
Museum of Contemporary Art, Nagaoka, Japan. (p. 293)

343. *Tumbleweed.* 1963–66. Chromed barbed wire and neon. 54″ x 60″ x 60″ approximately. Leo Castelli Gallery, New York. (p. 294)

MARK ROTHKO

344. Untitled. 1946. Watercolor. 38¾″ x 25½″.
Collection of Mr. and Mrs. Donald Blinken, New York. (p. 295)

345. *Vessels of Magic.* 1946–47. Watercolor. 38¾″ x 25¾″.
The Brooklyn Museum, New York. (p. 296)

346. *Fantasy.* 1947. Watercolor. 25½″ x 39½″.
Collection of Mr. and Mrs. Donald Blinken, New York. (p. 297)

347. *No. 26.* 1947. Oil on canvas. 34″ x 45¼″.
Collection of Mrs. Betty Parsons, New York. (p. 297)

348. *Black, Pink and Yellow over Orange.* 1951–52. Oil on canvas.
116″ x 92¼″. Collection of William S. Rubin, New York. (p. 298)

349. *No. 10.* 1952. Oil on canvas. 81½″ x 42½″.
Collection of Mr. and Mrs. C. B. Wright, Seattle, Washington. (p. 299)

350. *No. 8.* 1952. Oil on canvas. 80½″ x 68″.
Collection of Mr. and Mrs. Burton Tremaine, Meriden, Connecticut. (p. 300)

351. *Brown, Black and Blue.* 1958. Oil on canvas. 5′9″ x 5′.
Collection of Dr. and Mrs. Edward Massie, St. Louis, Missouri. (p. 301)

352. *Reds, No. 16.* 1960. Oil on canvas. 102″ x 119½″.
Collection of Mr. and Mrs. Robert C. Scull, New York. (p. 105)

353. *Number 207 (Red Over Dark Blue on Dark Gray).* 1961. Oil on canvas.
92¾″ x 81⅛″. University Art Museum, Berkeley, California. Acquired from the
artist. (p. 302)

GEORGE SEGAL

354. *The Gas Station.* 1963. Plaster and mixed media. 8′6″ x 24′ x 4′.
The National Gallery of Canada, Ottawa, Canada. (p. 106)

DAVID SMITH

355. *False Peace Specter.* 1945. Bronze and steel painted blue.
21½″ x 27¼″ x 10¾″. Private collection. (Not illustrated.)

356. *Billiard Player II.* 1945. Steel. 16¾″ x 17⅞″ x 6⅝″.
Collection of Mr. and Mrs. Louis D. Cohen, Great Neck, New York.
(Not illustrated.)

357. *Deserted Garden Landscape.* 1946. Steel, bronze. 11¾″ x 10⅛″ x 4¾″.
Collection of Mr. and Mrs. Harry W. Anderson, Atherton, California. (p. 303)

358. *Puritan Landscape.* 1946. Steel, bronze, cast iron, nickel.
28¼″ x 15″ x 10″. Collection of Peter Brant, New York. (p. 304)

359. *Australia.* 1951. Painted steel. 97½″ x 107⅞″ x 16⅛″ (including base).
Collection of William S. Rubin, New York. (p. 305)

360. *Forging No. 4.* 1955. Steel. 90⅝″ x 8½″ x 8¼″. Estate of David Smith.
Courtesy of Marlborough-Gerson Gallery, New York. (Not illustrated.)

361. *Forging No. 10.* 1955. Steel. 70½″ x 11″ x 12″.
Estate of David Smith. Courtesy of Marlborough-Gerson Gallery,
New York. (Not illustrated.)

362. *Forging No. 11.* 1955. Steel. 8⅝″ x 8½″ x 7⅞″.
Estate of David Smith. Courtesy of Marlborough-Gerson Gallery,
New York. (Not illustrated.)

363. *Albany III.* 1959. Painted steel. 26½″ x 19¼″ x 13⅛″.
Estate of David Smith. Courtesy of Marlborough-Gerson Gallery,
New York. (Not illustrated.)

364. *Albany XII.* 1961. Welded steel painted black. 30″ x 14½″ x 21½″.
Collection of Mr. and Mrs. Stephen D. Paine, Boston, Massachusetts. (p. 305)

365. *2 Circles IV.* 1962. Painted steel. 124″ x 60″ x 28½″.
Estate of David Smith. Courtesy of Marlborough-Gerson Gallery, New York. (p. 306)

366. *Primo Piano III.* 1962. Painted steel. 124″ x 145″ x 18″.
Courtesy of Marlborough-Gerson Gallery, New York. (p. 307)

367. *Voltri VI.* 1962. Steel. 103″ x 102¾″ x 25½″.
Private collection, New York. (p. 307)

368. *Voltri XIII.* 1962. Steel. 64⅛″ x 103¾″ x 26″.
University Art Museum, Berkeley, California, Gift of Mr. and Mrs. Eugene E.
Trefethen, Jr., Piedmont, California. (p. 308)

369. *Voltri XIX.* 1962. Welded and shaped iron and found objects. 55″ x 45″ x 50″.
Collection of Mr. and Mrs. Stephen D. Paine, Boston, Massachusetts. (p. 308)

370. Untitled. 1962–63. Stainless steel. 96¼″ x 63″ x 26″.
Art Gallery of Ontario, Purchase with assistance from the Women's
Committee Fund, 1968. (p. 309)

371. *Voltron XII.* 1963. Steel. 95³⁄₁₆″ x 18″.
Collection of Anne and Robert Simon, Jr., New York. (Not illustrated.)

372. *Wagon II.* 1964. Forged iron. 84″ x 112″ x 45″.
Estate of David Smith. Courtesy of Marlborough-Gerson Gallery, New York. (p. 310)

373. *Cubi XXIV.* 1964. Stainless steel. 114¼″ x 83½″.
Museum of Art, Carnegie Institute, Pittsburgh, Pennsylvania,
Howard Heinz Endowment Purchase Fund. (p. 311)

374. Untitled. 1965. Stainless steel. 102½″ x 120″ x 31¼″.
Estate of David Smith. Courtesy of Marlborough-Gerson Gallery, New York. (p. 312)

375. *Cubi XXV.* 1965. Stainless steel. 119¼″ x 120¾″ x 31¼″.
Estate of David Smith. Courtesy of Marlborough-Gerson Gallery, New York. (p. 313)

376. *Becca.* 1965. Stainless steel. 116″ x 120¼″ x 31½″.
Estate of David Smith. Courtesy of Marlborough-Gerson Gallery, New York. (p. 107)

TONY SMITH

377. *Die.* 1962. Steel. 6′ x 6′ x 6′.
Collection of Samuel Wagstaff, Jr., Detroit, Michigan. (p. 108)

378. *Black Box.* 1962. Steel. 22½″ x 33″ x 25″.
Collection of Mr. and Mrs. Norman Ives, Woodbridge, Connecticut. (p. 314)

379. *Free Ride.* 1962. Steel. (#2 of an edition of three.) 6′8″ x 6′8″ x 6′8″.
Courtesy of Fischbach Gallery, New York. (p. 314)

FRANK STELLA

380. *Zambesi.* 1959. Enamel on canvas. 90″ x 78″.
Collection of Lawrence Rubin, New York. (p. 315)

381. *Nunca Pasa Nada.* 1964. Metallic powder in acrylic emulsion on canvas.
9′ x 18′ approximately. The Lannan Foundation. (p. 316)

382. *Valparaiso (flesh and green).* 1964. Metallic paint on canvas.
84″ x 144″. Collection of the artist. (p. 316)

383. *Ossippee I.* 1966. Fluorescent alkyd and epoxy paint on canvas.
95″ x 138″. Collection of Dr. and Mrs. Ernest Kafka, New York. (p. 317)

384. *Union IV.* 1966. Fluorescent alkyd and epoxy paint on canvas.
103″ x 174″. Collection of Richard Meier, New York. (p. 318)

385. *Sangre de Cristo.* 1967. Metallic powder in polymer emulsion.
10′ x 42′. Collection of Dr. and Mrs. Charles Hendrickson,
Newport Beach, California. (p. 319)

386. *Hagmatana II.* 1967. Acrylic on canvas. 10′ x 15′.
Collection of Mr. and Mrs. Eugene M. Schwartz, New York. (p. 320)

387. *Sinjerli Variation IV.* 1968. Fluorescent acrylic on canvas. 120″ (diameter).
Collection of Mr. and Mrs. David Mirvish, Toronto, Canada. (p. 109)

388. *Ctesiphon III.* 1968. Fluorescent acrylic on canvas. 10′ x 20′.
Wallraf-Richartz Museum, Köln, Germany, Sammlung Ludwig. (p. 320)

CLYFFORD STILL

389. *Painting 1948-D.* 1948. Oil on canvas. 93⅛″ x 79⅝″.
Collection of William S. Rubin, New York. (p. 321)

390. *No. 5.* 1951. Oil on canvas. 55″ x 46″.
Wadsworth Atheneum, Hartford, Connecticut, (p. 322)

391. *Painting.* 1951. Oil on canvas. 93¼″ x 75¾″.
The Detroit Institute of Arts, W. Hawkins Ferry Fund. (p. 323)

392. *1957-D No. 1.* 1957. Oil on canvas. 113″ x 159″.
Albright-Knox Art Gallery, Buffalo, New York, Gift of Seymour H. Knox. (p. 110)

393. *Painting.* 1958. Oil on canvas. 113¾″ x 159½″.
Collection of J. Patrick Lannan, Palm Beach, Florida. (p. 324)

BRADLEY WALKER TOMLIN

394. *All Souls' Night.* 1948. Oil on canvas. 42½″ x 64″.
Betty Parsons Gallery, New York. (p. 325)

395. *Tension by Moonlight.* 1948. Oil on canvas. 32″ x 44″.
Betty Parsons Gallery, New York. (p. 326)

396. *Number 3.* 1948. Oil on canvas. 40″ x 50⅛″.
The Museum of Modern Art, New York, Fractional gift of John E.
Hutchins in memory of Frances E. Marder Hutchins, 1960. (p. 327)

397. *Number 4.* 1949. Oil on canvas. 43″ x 61″. Collection of
Mr. and Mrs. Edward L. Diehl, Cambridge, Massachusetts. (Not illustrated.)

398. *Number 10-A.* 1949. Oil on canvas. 46″ x 31″.
Collection of Dustin Rice, New York. (p. 111)

399. *Number 11.* 1949. Oil on canvas. 44⅛″ x 29″.
Munson-Williams-Proctor Institute, Utica, New York, Edward W. Root Bequest.
(p. 328)

400. *Number 9: In Memory of Gertrude Stein.* 1950. Oil on canvas.
49″ x 8′6¼″. The Museum of Modern Art, New York,
Gift of Mrs. John D. Rockefeller, III, 1955. (p. 329)

401. *Number 5.* 1952. Oil on canvas. 79″ x 45″.
Collection of Mrs. Betty Parsons, New York. (p. 330)

ANDY WARHOL

402. *Dick Tracy.* 1960. Casein on canvas. 70⅛″ x 52¼″.
Gordon Locksley Gallery, Minneapolis, Minnesota. (p. 331)

403. *Campbell's Soup Cans.* 1961–62. Oil on canvas. 32 panels, each 20″ x 16″
Collection of Irving Blum, Los Angeles, California. (pp. 332–33)

404. *Do It Yourself.* 1962. Liquitex on canvas. 72″ x 54″.
    Collection of Kimiko and John Powers, Aspen, Colorado. (p. 334)

405. *Marilyn Monroe Diptych.* 1962. Oil on canvas. 82″ x 114″.
    Collection of Mr. and Mrs. Burton Tremaine, Meriden, Connecticut. (p. 335)

406. *Ethel Scull 36 times.* 1963. Silkscreen media on canvas. 12′ x 8′4″.
    Collection of Mr. and Mrs. Robert C. Scull, New York. (p. 112)

407. *Orange Disaster.* 1963. Oil on canvas. 106″ x 82″.
    Harry N. Abrams Family Collection, New York. (p. 336)

408. *Brillo Box.* 1964. Silkscreen ink on wood. 17″ x 17″ x 17″.
    Leo Castelli Gallery, New York. (p. 337)

Josef Albers:
Late Thought. 1964. Oil on board. 48″ x 48″.
The Woodward Foundation of Washington, D.C.

Milton Avery:
Speedboat's Wake. 1959. Oil on canvas. 55″ x 73″.
The David Mirvish Gallery, Toronto, Canada.

Alexander Calder:
The Pregnant Whale. 1963. Steel plate painted. 9′6″ x 8′10″ x 7′2″.
Collection of Mrs. Julius Epstein, Northfield, Illinois.

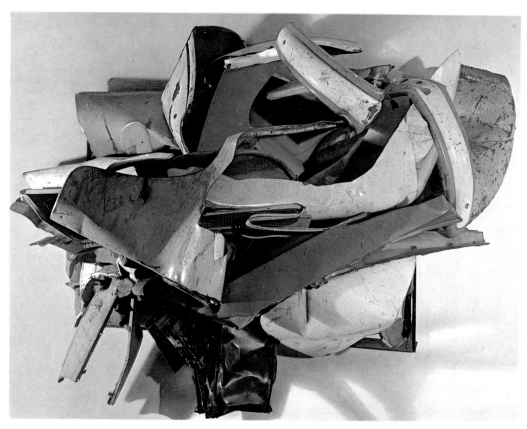

John Chamberlain:
Dolores James. 1962. Welded auto metal. 76″ x 97″ x 39″.
Leo Castelli Gallery, New York.

Joseph Cornell:
Habitat Group for a Shooting Gallery. 1943.
Wood cabinet containing colored cutouts of parrots,
printed cards, and papers, etc. behind shattered glass.
15½″ x 11⅛″ x 4¼″.
Collection of Irving Blum, Los Angeles, California.

Stuart Davis:
Hot Stillscape in Six Colors. 1940. Oil on canvas. 36″ x 45″.
Courtesy of The Downtown Gallery, New York.

Willem de Kooning:
Bill-Lee's Delight. ca. 1946. Oil on paper. 27½″ x 34¼″.
Collection of Mr. and Mrs. Lee V. Eastman, New York.

Burgoyne Diller:
No. 33, First Theme. 1962. Oil on canvas. 32″ x 32″.
Collection of Mr. and Mrs. Richard Hokin, New York.

Mark di Suvero:
Mohican. 1967. Steel and wood. 15′ x 9′ x 30′.
Collection of Mr. Lewis Manilow, Chicago, Illinois.

Dan Flavin:
the nominal three (to William of Ockham). 1963.
Cool white fluorescent light. 8′ (high).
The National Gallery of Canada, Ottawa, Canada.

Helen Frankenthaler:
Yellow Caterpillar. 1961. Oil on canvas. 90″ x 120″.
Private collection, New York.

Arshile Gorky:
Water of the Flowery Mill. 1944. Oil on canvas. 42¼″ x 48¾″.
The Metropolitan Museum of Art, New York, George A. Hearn Fund, 1956.

Adolph Gottlieb:
Una. 1959. Oil on canvas. 108″ x 90″.
Collection of the artist.

Adolph Gottlieb:
Wall (maquette). 1968. Painted steel.
27½″ x 40½″ x 24½″ (one-third size of projected sculpture).
Collection of the artist.

Philip Guston:
Painting. 1952. Oil on canvas. 50¾″ x 48″.
Collection of Mrs. Albert H. Newman, Chicago, Illinois.

Hans Hofmann: *Veluti in Speculum.* 1962.
Oil on canvas. 85¼″ x 73½″.
The Metropolitan Museum of Art, New York,
Gift of Mr. and Mrs. Richard Rodgers
and the Francis Lathrop Fund, 1963.

Hans Hofmann:
Lust and Delight (Renata Series No. 2).
1965. Oil on canvas. 84″ x 60″.
Estate of Hans Hofmann.

Edward Hopper:
Western Motel. 1957. Oil on canvas. 30¼″ x 50⅛″.
Yale University Art Gallery, Bequest of Stephen Carlton Clark, B.A., 1903.

Jasper Johns:
Painting with Two Balls. 1960. Encaustic and collage on canvas with objects. 65″ x 54″
(three panels). Collection of the artist.

83

Donald Judd:
Untitled. 1963. Painted wood and aluminum. 48″ x 83″ x 48″.
Collection of Julie Judd, New York.

Franz Kline:
Blue Center. 1958. Oil on canvas. 36″ x 40″.
Collection of Mr. and Mrs. Robert C. Scull, New York.

Ellsworth Kelly:
Blue White Angle. 1966. Epoxy on aluminum. 72″ x 36″ x 72″.
Private collection, New York.

Gabe Kohn:
Acrotere. 1960. Laminated wood. 35¼″ x 31″ x 22¼″.
The Museum of Modern Art, New York, Given anonymously, 1963.

Roy Lichtenstein:
The Engagement Ring. 1961. Oil on canvas. 67¾″ x 79½″.
Collection of Mr. and Mrs. Robert A. Rowan, Pasadena, California.

Morris Louis:
Iris. 1954. Acrylic on canvas. 80″ x 106″.
Collection of Mr. and Mrs. Eugene M. Schwartz, New York.

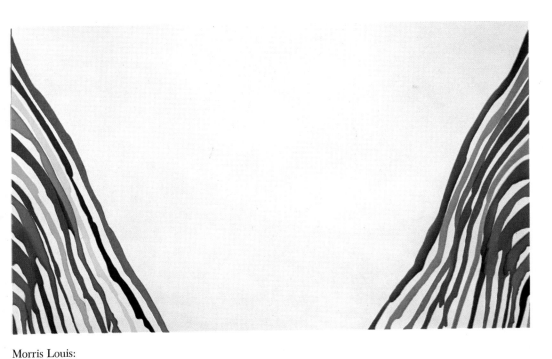

Morris Louis:
Alpha-Pi. 1961. Acrylic on canvas. 102½" x 177".
The Metropolitan Museum of Art, New York, Arthur H. Hearn Fund, 1967.

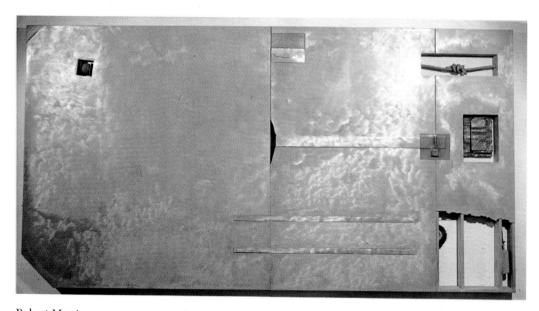

Robert Morris:
Untitled. 1965. Aluminum construction. 6′ x 11′7″ x 3″.
Collection of Mr. and Mrs. Robert C. Scull, New York.

Robert Motherwell:
Mallarmé's Swan. 1944. Collage using gouache, crayon, and paper on
cardboard. 43½″ x 35½″.
Contemporary Collection of The Cleveland Museum of Art, Cleveland, Ohio.

Isamu Noguchi:
White Sun. 1966. White Italian Saravezza marble. 28½″ (diameter).
Cordier & Ekstrom, Inc., New York.

Barnett Newman:
Concord. 1949. Oil on canvas. 89¾″ x 53⅝″.
The Metropolitan Museum of Art, New York, George A. Hearn Fund, 1968.

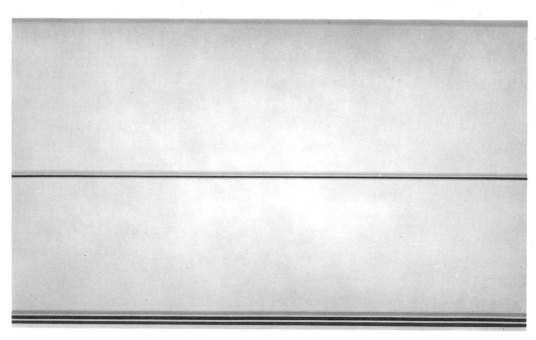

Kenneth Noland:
Trans-Median II. 1968. Acrylic emulsion on canvas. 90½″ x 160″.
Collection of Lawrence Rubin, New York.

Claes Oldenburg:
Giant Pool Balls. 1967. Sixteen plexiglas balls 24″ each, wood rack.
120″ x 120″ x 108″.
Courtesy of Sidney Janis Gallery, New York.

Jules Olitski:
Disarmed. 1968. Acrylic on canvas. 9′10″ x 16′.
Collection of Mr. and Mrs. Eugene M. Schwartz, New York.

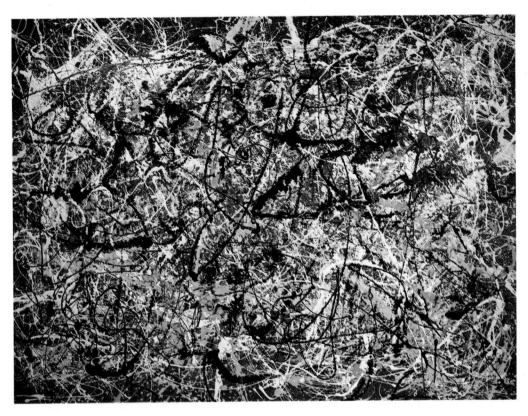

Jackson Pollock:
Mural. 1950. Oil, enamel, and aluminum paint on canvas, mounted on wood.
6′ x 8′. Collection of William S. Rubin, New York.

Larry Poons:
Brown Sound. 1968. Acrylic on canvas. 96″ x 125″.
The Woodward Foundation of Washington, D.C.

Robert Rauschenberg:
Bed. 1955. Combine painting. 74″ x 31″.
Collection of Mr. and Mrs. Leo Castelli,
New York.

Ad Reinhardt:
Red Painting. 1952. Oil on canvas. 60″ x 82″.
Courtesy of Marlborough-Gerson Gallery, New York.

Ad Reinhardt:
Abstract Painting. 1964. Oil on canvas. 60″ x 60″.
Courtesy of Marlborough-Gerson Gallery, New York.

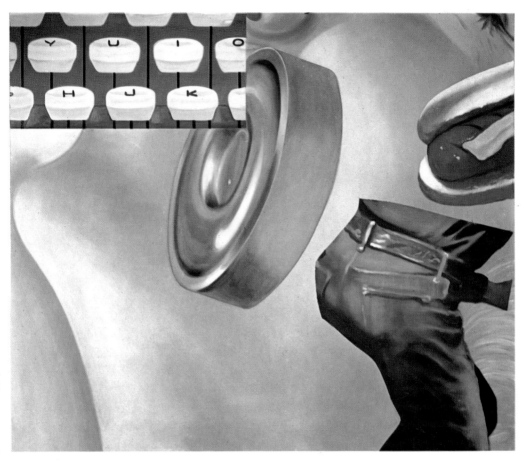

James Rosenquist:
The Lines Were Deeply Etched on the Map of Her Face. 1961–62.
Oil on canvas. 66″ x 78″.
Collection of Mr. and Mrs. Robert C. Scull, New York.

Mark Rothko:
Reds, No. 16. 1960. Oil on canvas. 102″ x 119½″.
Collection of Mr. and Mrs. Robert C. Scull, New York.

George Segal:
The Gas Station. 1964. Plaster and mixed media. 8'6" x 24' x 4'.
The National Gallery of Canada, Ottawa, Canada.

David Smith:
Becca. 1965. Stainless steel. 116" x 120¼" x 31½".
Estate of David Smith. Courtesy of Marlborough-Gerson Gallery, New York.

Frank Stella:
Sinjerli Variation IV. 1968. Fluorescent acrylic on canvas. 120″ (diameter).
Collection of Mr. and Mrs. David Mirvish, Toronto, Canada.

Tony Smith:
Die. 1962. Steel. 6′ x 6′ x 6′.
Collection of Samuel Wagstaff, Jr., Detroit, Michigan.

Clyfford Still:
1957-D no. 1. 1957. Oil on canvas. 113″ x 159″.
Albright-Knox Art Gallery, Buffalo, New York, Gift of Seymour H. Knox.

Bradley Walker Tomlin:
Number 10-A. 1949. Oil on canvas. 46″ x 31″.
Collection of Dustin Rice, New York.

Andy Warhol:
Ethel Scull 36 Times. 1963. Silkscreen media on canvas. 12′ x 8′4″.
Collection of Mr. and Mrs. Robert C. Scull, New York.

Josef Albers:
Growing. 1940. Oil on masonite. 15″ x 17¾″.
The Collection of The San Francisco Museum of Art, San Francisco, California,
Gift of Mrs. Charlotte Mack.

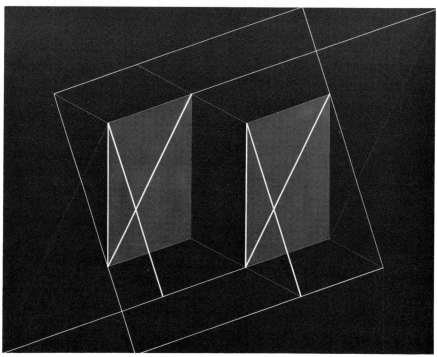

LEFT, ABOVE. Josef Albers:
Indicating Solids. 1949. Oil on masonite. 26″ x 25¾″.
Collection of the artist.

LEFT, BELOW. Josef Albers:
Transformations of a Scheme Series: No. 10. 1950.
Machine-engraved in laminated formica. 17″ x 22½″.
Collection of the artist.

ABOVE. Josef Albers:
Homage to the Square Series: New Gate. 1951.
Oil on masonite. 24″ x 24″. Collection of the artist.

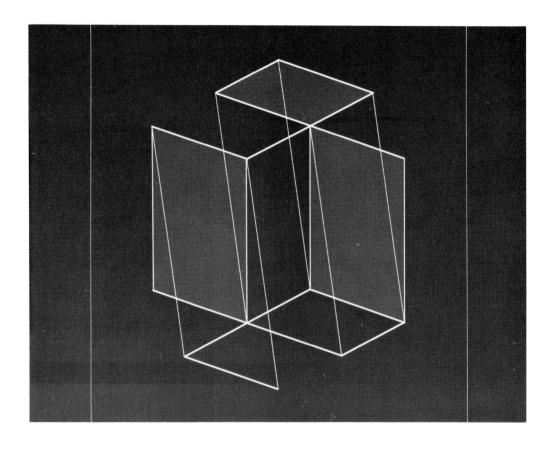

ABOVE. Josef Albers:
Transformations of a Scheme Series: No. 26. 1952.
Machine-engraved in laminated formica. 17″ x 22½″.
Collection of the artist.

RIGHT, ABOVE. Josef Albers:
Homage to the Square Series: In Wide Light. 1953.
Oil on masonite. 18″ x 18″. Collection of the artist.

RIGHT, BELOW. Josef Albers:
Biconjugate Series: Red Orange Wall. 1959.
Oil on masonite. 24″ x 34½″. Collection of the artist.

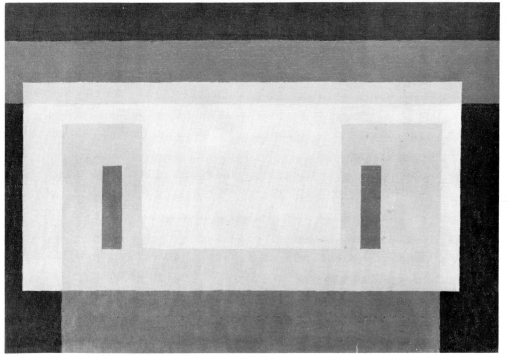

ABOVE. Josef Albers:
Biconjugate Series: Chalk-Green Facade. 1960.
Oil on masonite. 28″ x 40½″. Collection of the artist.

RIGHT, ABOVE. Milton Avery:
Gaspé—Pink Sky. 1940. Oil on canvas. 40″ x 50″.
Collection of Mr. and Mrs. Maurice Geller, New York.

RIGHT, BELOW. Milton Avery:
Mother and Child. 1944. Oil on canvas. 40″ x 30″.
Tirca Karlis Gallery, Provincetown, Massachusetts.

119

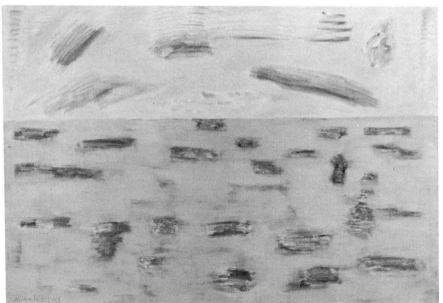

LEFT, ABOVE. Milton Avery:
Sail. 1958. Oil on canvas. 72″ x 50″.
Grace Borgenicht Gallery, New York.

LEFT, BELOW. Milton Avery:
Sunset Sea. 1958. Oil on canvas. 49½″ x 73½″.
The David Mirvish Gallery, Toronto, Canada.

ABOVE. Alexander Calder:
Little Spider. ca. 1940. Painted sheet metal and steel wire and rods.
55″ x 50″. Perls Galleries, New York.

ABOVE. Alexander Calder:
Mobile. 1963. Sheet steel. 27'.
The Connecticut Bank and Trust Company, Hartford, Connecticut.

RIGHT, ABOVE. Alexander Calder:
Four Planes Écartés. 1967. Painted sheet steel. *ca.* 10'6" (high).
Perls Galleries, New York.

RIGHT, BELOW. Alexander Calder:
Six Planes Écartés. 1967. Painted sheet steel. *ca.* 10'6" (high).
Perls Galleries, New York.

John Chamberlain:
Fantail. 1961. Painted steel. 70″ x 75″ x 60″.
Collection of Jasper Johns, New York.

John Chamberlain:
Velvet White. 1962. Welded steel. 83″ x 57″ x 48″.
The Albert A. List Family Collection, New York.

Joseph Cornell:
L'Egypte de Mlle. Cléo de Mérode; cours élémentaire d'histoire naturelle.
1940. Wood, glass, cork, and miscellaneous materials. 4¾" x 10¾" x 7¼".
Collection of Mr. and Mrs. Richard L. Feigen, New York.

Joseph Cornell:
Medici Slot Machine. 1942. Construction. 15½" x 12" x 4⅜".
Collection of Mr. and Mrs. Bernard J. Reis, New York.

Joseph Cornell:
A Pantry Ballet (for Jacques Offenbach).
Summer, 1942.
Wood, paper, plastic, metal, glass, etc.
10½″ x 18″ x 6″.
Collection of Mr. and Mrs. Richard L.
Feigen, New York.

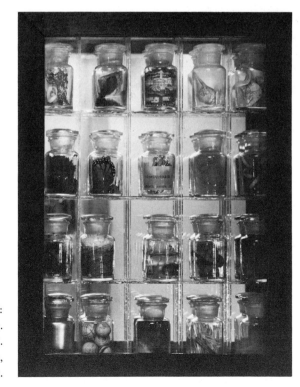

Joseph Cornell:
Pharmacy. 1943.
Wooden box with glass bottles. 15¼″ x 12″ x 3″.
Collection of Mrs. Marcel Duchamp,
New York.

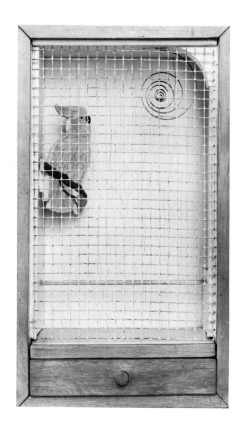 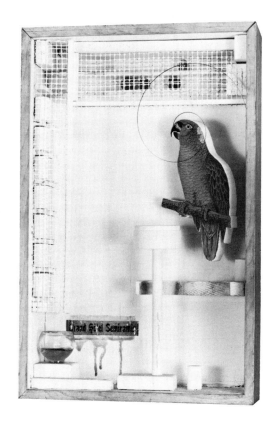

LEFT. Joseph Cornell:
Cockatoo: "Keepsake Parakeet." 1949–53. Construction in wood.
20¼″ x 12″ x 5″. Collection of Donald Windham, New York.

RIGHT. Joseph Cornell:
Grand Hotel Semiramis. 1950. Construction of wood, glass, and diverse
materials. 18″ x 12″ x 4″. Collection of Mr. and Mrs. Allan Frumkin, New York.

LEFT. Joseph Cornell:
Hotel du Nord. ca. 1953. Construction in wood, glass, and paper.
19″ x 13¼″. The Whitney Museum of American Art, New York.

RIGHT. Joseph Cornell:
Hotel de L'Étoile. ca. 1956–57. Painted wood construction.
18½″ x 14″ x 7½″. Collection of Mrs. Eleanor Ward, New York.

ABOVE. Stuart Davis:
Owh! In San Paõ. 1951. Oil on canvas. 52¼″ x 41¾″.
The Whitney Museum of American Art, New York.

RIGHT, ABOVE. Stuart Davis:
Colonial Cubism. 1954. Oil on canvas. 45″ x 60″.
Collection of The Walker Art Center, Minneapolis, Minnesota.

RIGHT, BELOW. Stuart Davis:
Pochade. 1958. Oil on canvas. 60″ x 52″.
Courtesy of The Downtown Gallery, New York.

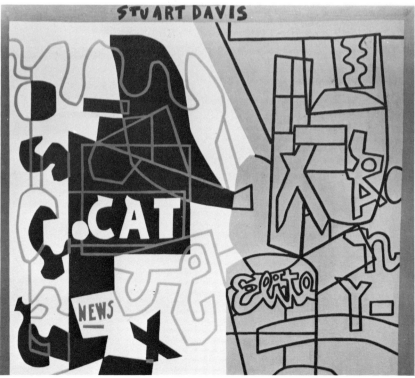

Stuart Davis:
Switchsky's Syntax. 1961–64. Tempera on canvas. 42″ x 56″.
Courtesy of Mrs. Stuart Davis, New York.

Willem de Kooning:
Seated Woman. ca. 1940. Oil and charcoal on composition board.
54″ x 36″. Collection of Mrs. Albert M. Greenfield, Sr., Philadelphia, Pennsylvania.

Willem de Kooning:
Queen of Hearts. 1943–46. Oil and charcoal on composition board.
46″ x 27½″. Joseph H. Hirshhorn Foundation.

Willem de Kooning:
Pink Lady. ca. 1944. Oil and charcoal on masonite composition board.
48¼″ x 35¼″.
Collection of Mr. and Mrs. Stanley K. Sheinbaum, Santa Barbara, California.

Willem de Kooning:
The Marshes. ca. 1945. Charcoal and oil on composition board.
32″ x 23⅞″. University Art Museum, Berkeley, California,
Gift of Julian J. and Joachim Jean Aberbach, New York.

Willem de Kooning:
Light in August. ca. 1946. Oil and enamel on paper, mounted on canvas.
55″ x 44½″. Collection of Elise C. Dixon, Scottsdale, Arizona.

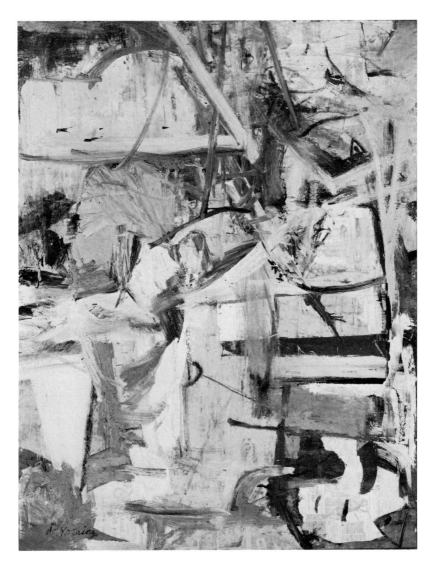

LEFT, ABOVE. Willem de Kooning:
Untitled. 1948. Oil on paper, mounted on masonite. 24″ x 36″.
Collection of Mr. and Mrs. Stephen D. Paine, Boston, Massachusetts.

LEFT, BELOW. Willem de Kooning:
Police Gazette. 1954–55. Oil on canvas. 43¼″ x 50¼″.
Collection of Mr. and Mrs. Robert C. Scull, New York.

ABOVE. Willem de Kooning:
Easter Monday. 1955–56. Oil and newspaper transfer on canvas.
96″ x 74″. The Metropolitan Museum of Art, New York, Rogers Fund, 1956.

Willem de Kooning:
Spike's Folly I. 1959. Oil on canvas. 79″ x 68½″.
Collection of Mr. and Mrs. Robert C. Scull, New York.

Willem de Kooning:
Door to the River. 1960. Oil on canvas. 80″ x 70″.
The Whitney Museum of American Art, New York, Gift of the Friends of The
Whitney Museum of American Art and purchase.

Burgoyne Diller:
First Theme. 1962. Oil on canvas. 72″ x 72″.
The Art Institute of Chicago, Wilson L. Mead Fund Income.

Burgoyne Diller:
No. 5, Third Theme. 1963. Oil on canvas. 42″ x 42″.
The Diller Estate, Courtesy of Noah Goldowsky and Richard Bellamy, New York.

LEFT, ABOVE. Burgoyne Diller:
No. 10, First Theme. 1963–64. Oil on canvas. 72″ x 72″.
The Diller Estate, Courtesy of Noah Goldowsky and Richard Bellamy, New York.

LEFT, BELOW. Burgoyne Diller:
No. 9, First Theme. 1963–64. Oil on canvas. 72″ x 72″.
Albright–Knox Art Gallery, Buffalo, New York, Gift of Seymour H. Knox.

ABOVE. Mark di Suvero:
Hankchampion. 1960. Wood and chain construction. 6′ x 10′.
Collection of Mr. and Mrs. Robert C. Scull, New York.

ABOVE. Mark di Suvero:
Tom. 1961. Wood and steel. 8′ x 10′ x 10′.
Lo Giudice Gallery, Chicago, Illinois, and Richard Bellamy, New York.

RIGHT, ABOVE. Dan Flavin:
untitled. 1965. (Drawing for.)
A set of seven cubes. White baked enamel on steel with cool white
fluorescent light. Size determined by length of fixture. Dwan Gallery, New York.

RIGHT, BELOW. Dan Flavin:
untitled. 1966. Cool white fluorescent light. 8′ (high).
Collection of Mr. and Mrs. Robert A. M. Stern, New York.

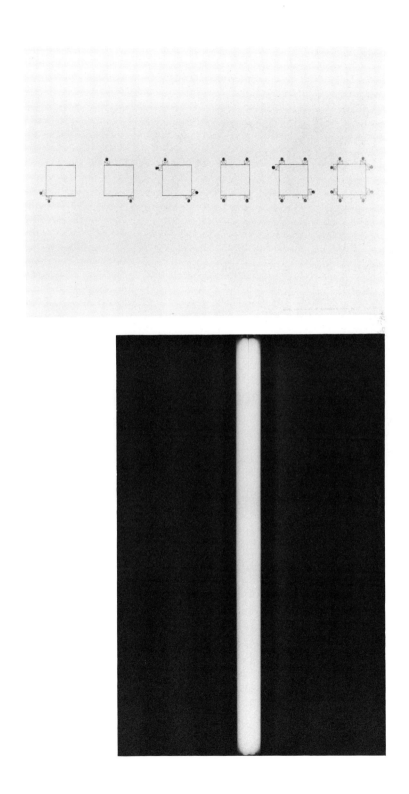

ABOVE. Dan Flavin:
untitled. 1966. Cool white fluorescent light. *ca.* 8' x 8'.
Collection of Irving Blum, Los Angeles, California.

RIGHT, ABOVE. Helen Frankenthaler:
Abstract Landscape. 1951. Oil on canvas. 69" x 71⅞".
Collection of the artist.

RIGHT, BELOW. Helen Frankenthaler:
Other Generations. 1957. Oil on canvas. 70" x 70".
Collection of the artist.

ABOVE. Helen Frankenthaler:
Europa. 1957. Oil on canvas. 70½″ x 54″.
Collection of the artist.

RIGHT. Helen Frankenthaler:
The Moors. 1962. Acrylic on canvas. 107″ x 47″.
Collection of William S. Rubin, New York.

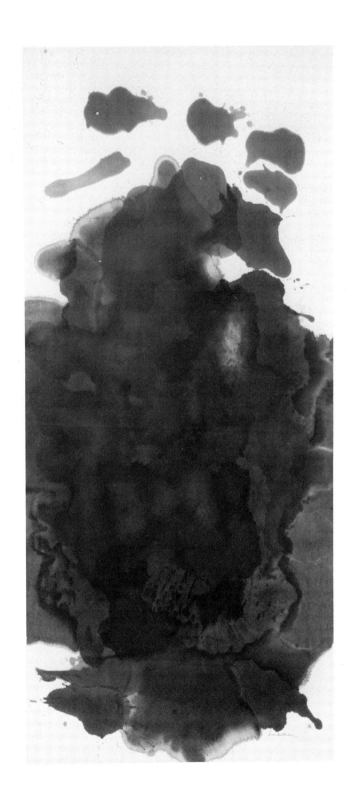

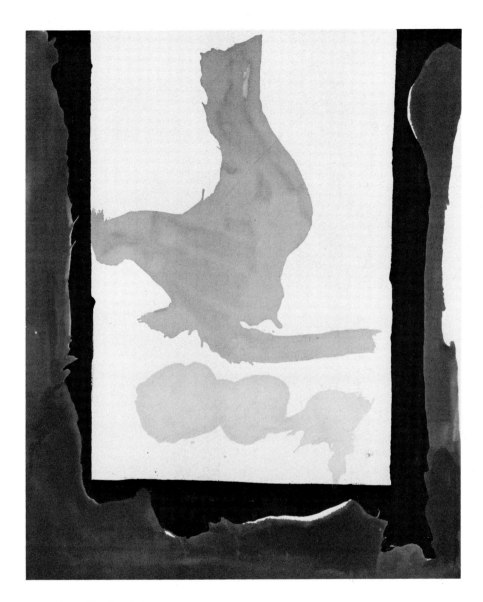

LEFT. Helen Frankenthaler:
Blue Atmosphere. 1963. Acrylic on canvas. 117½″ x 70″.
Collection of the artist.

ABOVE. Helen Frankenthaler:
Orange Shapes in Frame. 1964. Acrylic on canvas. 93″ x 74″.
Collection of Mr. and Mrs. Robert B. Mayer, Winnetka, Illinois.

Helen Frankenthaler:
One O'Clock. 1966. Acrylic paint on canvas. 93¾″ x 75¾″.
Collection of Albert F. Weis, Savannah, Georgia.

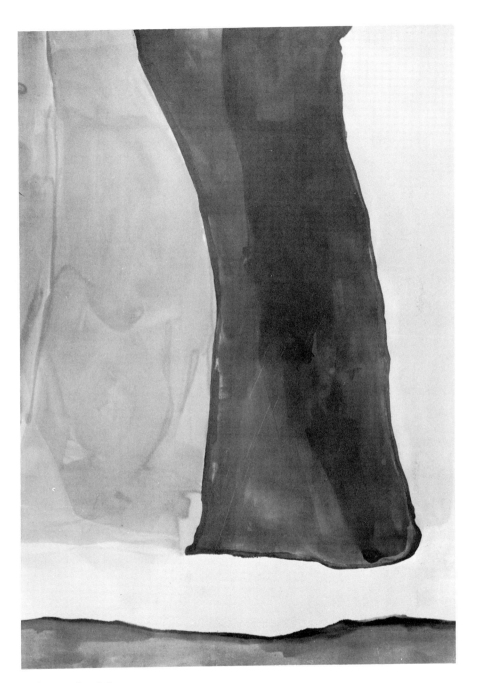

Helen Frankenthaler:
Gamut. 1968. Acrylic on canvas. 11′2″ x 93″.
Collection of the artist.

Arshile Gorky:
Garden in Sochi. 1940–41. Oil on canvas. 25″ x 29″.
Private collection, Courtesy of M. Knoedler & Company, Inc., New York.

Arshile Gorky:
Garden in Sochi. ca. 1943. Oil on canvas. 31″ x 39″.
The Museum of Modern Art, New York, Purchase, 1969. (Not in exhibition.)

LEFT, ABOVE. Arshile Gorky:
The Pirate I. 1942. Oil on canvas. 29¼″ x 40⅛″.
Collection of Mr. and Mrs. Julien Levy, Bridgewater, Connecticut.

LEFT, BELOW. Arshile Gorky:
The Pirate II. 1943. Oil on canvas. 30″ x 36″.
Collection of Mr. and Mrs. Julien Levy, Bridgewater, Connecticut.

ABOVE. Arshile Gorky:
The Unattainable. 1945. Oil on canvas. 41⅛″ x 29¼″.
The Baltimore Museum of Art, Baltimore, Maryland, Friends of Art Fund.

LEFT, ABOVE. Arshile Gorky:
The Plough and the Song. 1947. Oil on burlap. 52⅛″ x 64¼″.
Collection of Mr. and Mrs. Milton A. Gordon, New York.

LEFT, BELOW. Arshile Gorky:
The Plough and the Song. 1947. Oil on canvas. 50¾″ x 62¾″.
Allen Memorial Art Museum, Oberlin College, Oberlin, Ohio.

ABOVE. Arshile Gorky:
The Betrothal II. 1947. Oil on canvas. 50¾″ x 38″.
The Whitney Museum of American Art, New York.

Arshile Gorky:
The Limit. 1947. Oil on paper over burlap. 50¾″ x 62½″.
Private collection, Courtesy of M. Knoedler & Company, Inc., New York.

Arshile Gorky:
Dark Green Painting. ca. 1948. Oil on canvas. 43¾″ x 56″.
Collection of Mrs. H. Gates Lloyd, Haverford, Pennsylvania.

ABOVE. Adolph Gottlieb:
Masquerade. 1945. Oil and egg tempera on canvas. 36″ x 24″.
Collection of Mrs. Esther Gottlieb, New York.

RIGHT, ABOVE. Adolph Gottlieb:
Recurrent Apparition. 1946. Oil on canvas. 36″ x 54″.
Collection of Mrs. Esther Gottlieb, New York.

RIGHT, BELOW. Adolph Gottlieb:
Dream. 1948. Oil on canvas. 20″ x 24″.
Isaac Delgado Museum of Art, New Orleans, Louisiana,
Gift of William Edward Campbell, 1951.

Adolph Gottlieb:
Thrust. 1959. Oil on canvas. 108″ x 90″.
The Metropolitan Museum of Art, New York, George A. Hearn Fund, 1959.

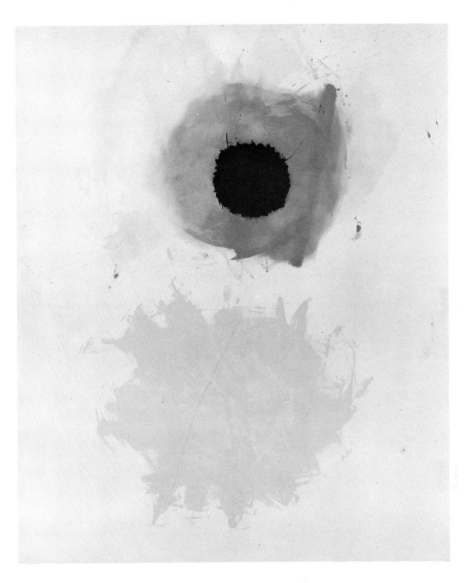

Adolph Gottlieb:
Aureole. 1959. Oil on canvas. 108″ x 90″.
Collection of Mrs. Esther Gottlieb, New York.

ABOVE. Adolph Gottlieb:
Sign. 1962. Oil on canvas. 90″ x 84″.
Collection of the artist.

RIGHT, ABOVE. Adolph Gottlieb:
Red, Blue, Yellow. 1966. Oil on canvas. 84″ x 90″.
Collection of William S. Rubin, New York.

RIGHT, BELOW. Adolph Gottlieb:
Petaloid. 1967. Cor-Ten steel. 96″ x 96″ x 48″.
Collection of Mrs. Esther Gottlieb, New York.

169

ABOVE. Philip Guston:
To B. W. T. 1952. Oil on canvas. 48″ x 51″.
Collection of Leonard M. Brown, Springfield, Massachusetts.

RIGHT, ABOVE. Philip Guston:
Zone. 1954. Oil on canvas. 46″ x 48⅛″.
Collection of Mr. and Mrs. Ben Heller, New York.

RIGHT, BELOW. Philip Guston:
Untitled. 1954. Oil on canvas. 51″ x 48¾″.
Collection of Mr. and Mrs. C. B. Wright, Seattle, Washington.

Philip Guston:
For M. 1955. Oil on canvas. 76¼″ x 72″.
Private collection, Los Angeles, California.

Philip Guston:
Cythera. 1957. Oil on canvas. 72" x 64".
Collection of Mr. and Mrs. Donald Blinken, New York.

Hans Hofmann:
In the Wake of the Hurricane. 1960. Oil on canvas. 72¼" x 60".
University Art Museum, Berkeley, California,
Gift of the artist.

Hans Hofmann:
Summer Night's Bliss. 1961. Oil on canvas. 84″ x 78″.
The Baltimore Museum of Art, Baltimore, Maryland, Gift of the artist.

Hans Hofmann:
Agrigento. 1961. Oil on canvas. 84¼″ x 72″.
University Art Museum, Berkeley, California,
Gift of the artist.

Hans Hofmann:
Memoria in Aeterne. 1962. Oil on canvas. 84″ x 72⅛″.
The Museum of Modern Art, New York, Gift of the artist, 1963.

Hans Hofmann:
Gloriamundi. 1963. Oil on canvas. 60⅛″ x 52″.
University Art Museum, Berkeley, California,
Gift of the artist.

Hans Hofmann:
Song of a Nightingale. 1964. Oil on canvas. 7′ x 6′.
Collection of Mr. and Mrs. Eugene M. Schwartz, New York.

Hans Hofmann:
In Sober Ecstasy. 1965. Oil on canvas. 73½″ x 61½″.
Collection of Mr. and Mrs. David Mirvish, Toronto, Canada.

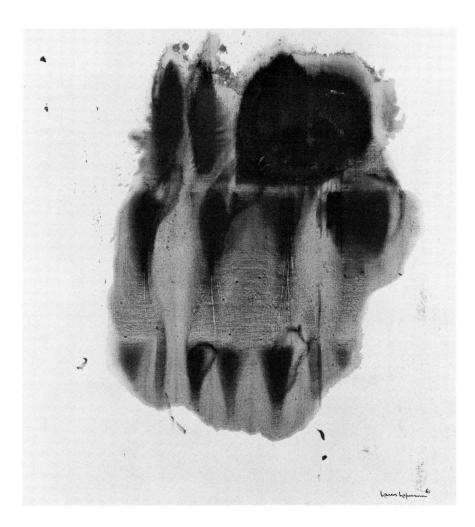

Hans Hofmann:
Little Cherry (Renata Series No. 1). 1965. Oil on canvas.
84″ x 78″. Estate of Hans Hofmann.

ABOVE. Edward Hopper:
Gas. 1940. Oil on canvas. 26¼″ x 40¼″.
The Museum of Modern Art, New York, Mrs. Simon Guggenheim Fund, 1943.

RIGHT, ABOVE. Edward Hopper:
First Row Orchestra. 1951. Oil on canvas. 31″ x 40″.
Joseph H. Hirshhorn Foundation.

RIGHT, BELOW. Edward Hopper:
Office in a Small City. 1953. Oil on canvas. 28″ x 40″.
The Metropolitan Museum of Art, New York, George A. Hearn Fund, 1953.

ABOVE. Jasper Johns:
Green Target. 1955. Encaustic on newspaper on canvas. 60″ x 60″.
The Museum of Modern Art, New York, Richard S. Zeisler Fund, 1958.

RIGHT, ABOVE. Jasper Johns:
White Flag. 1955. Encaustic and collage on canvas. 72″ x 144″.
Collection of the artist.

RIGHT, BELOW. Jasper Johns:
Three Flags. 1958. Encaustic on canvas. 30⅞″ x 45½″.
Collection of Mr. and Mrs. Burton Tremaine, Meriden, Connecticut.

Jasper Johns:
Device Circle. 1959. Encaustic and collage on canvas. 40″ x 40″.
Collection of Mr. and Mrs. Burton Tremaine, Meriden, Connecticut.

Jasper Johns:
Jubilee. 1959. Oil on canvas. 60″ x 44″.
Collection of Robert Rauschenberg, New York.

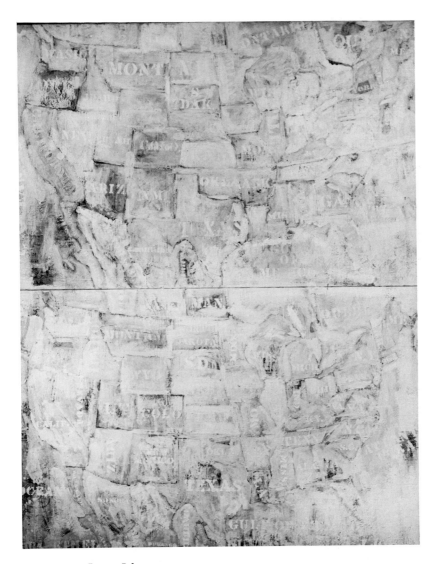

LEFT, ABOVE. Jasper Johns:
False Start. 1959. Oil on canvas. 67¼″ x 54″.
Collection of Mr. and Mrs. Robert C. Scull, New York.

LEFT, BELOW. Jasper Johns:
Studio. 1964. Oil on canvas. 73½″ x 145½″.
The Whitney Museum of American Art, New York, Gift of the Friends
of The Whitney Museum of American Art and purchase.

ABOVE. Jasper Johns:
Double White Map. 1965. Encaustic and collage on canvas. 90″ x 70″.
Collection of Mr. and Mrs. Robert C. Scull, New York.

Jasper Johns:
Screen Piece. 1967. Oil on canvas. 72″ x 50″.
Collection of David Whitney, New York.

Jasper Johns:
Screen Piece 2. 1968. Oil on canvas. 72″ x 50″.
Collection of Mr. and Mrs. Victor W. Ganz, New York.

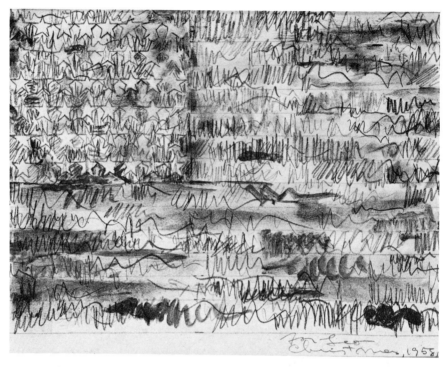

LEFT, ABOVE. Jasper Johns:
Flag. 1958. Pencil and graphite wash on paper. 7½″ x 10⅜″.
Collection of Leo Castelli, New York.

LEFT, BELOW. Jasper Johns:
Study for Painting with a Ball. 1958. Conté on paper. 15″ x 14½″.
Collection of the artist.

ABOVE. Jasper Johns:
Study for Painting with Two Balls. 1960. Charcoal on paper.
19½″ x 15½″. Joseph H. Hirshhorn Collection.

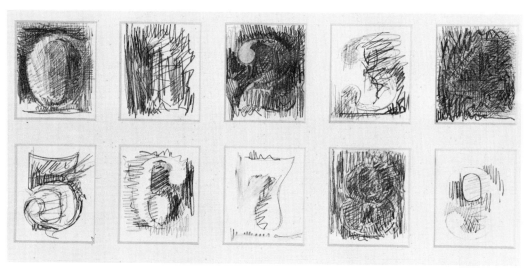

ABOVE. Jasper Johns:
Numbers. 1960. Pencil on paper; ten drawings each matted
separately. 2¾″ x 2¼″ each. Collection of Edward Carey, New York.

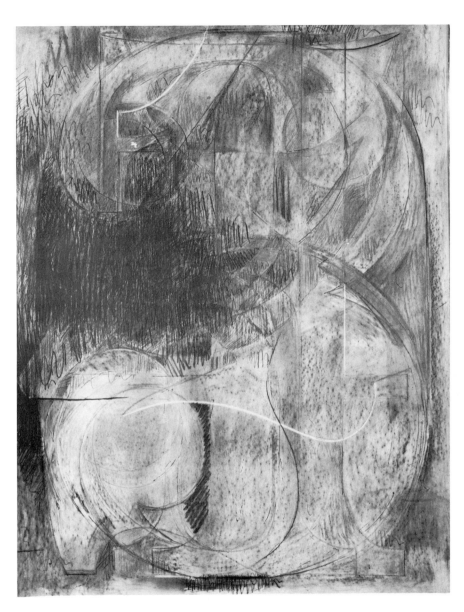

LEFT. Jasper Johns:
Device Circle. 1960. Pencil on paper. 15″ x 14½″.
Collection of Mr. and Mrs. Ben Heller, New York.

ABOVE. Jasper Johns:
0 through 9. 1961. Charcoal and pastel on paper. 54″ x 45″.
Collection of Mr. and Mrs. Robert C. Scull, New York.

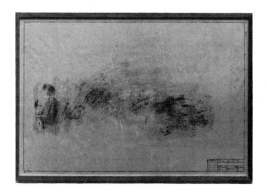 

Jasper Johns:
Study for Skin I. 1962. Charcoal on paper. 22″ x 34″.
Study for Skin II. 1962. Charcoal on paper. 22″ x 34″.
Study for Skin III. 1962. Charcoal on paper. 22″ x 34″.
Study for Skin IV. 1962. Charcoal on paper. 22″ x 34″.
Collection of the artist.

Jasper Johns:
Diver. 1963. Charcoal, pastel, paper on canvas. 86½″ x 71″.
Collection of Mr. and Mrs. Victor W. Ganz, New York.

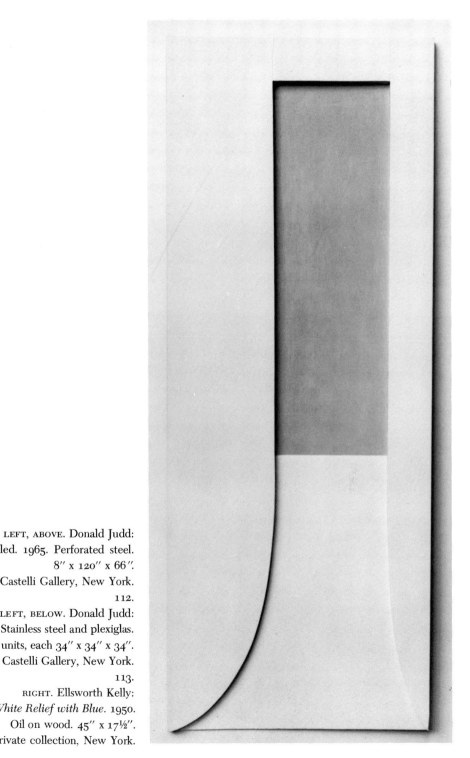

LEFT, ABOVE. Donald Judd:
Untitled. 1965. Perforated steel.
8″ x 120″ x 66″.
Leo Castelli Gallery, New York.
112.
LEFT, BELOW. Donald Judd:
Untitled. 1969. Stainless steel and plexiglas.
Six units, each 34″ x 34″ x 34″.
Leo Castelli Gallery, New York.
113.
RIGHT. Ellsworth Kelly:
White Relief with Blue. 1950.
Oil on wood. 45″ x 17½″.
Private collection, New York.

LEFT, ABOVE. Ellsworth Kelly:
Blue Red Green. 1962–63. Oil on canvas. 91″ x 82″.
The Metropolitan Museum of Art, Arthur H. Hearn Fund, 1963.

LEFT, BELOW. Ellsworth Kelly:
3 Panels: Red, Yellow, Blue. 1963. Acrylic on canvas. 90″ x 90″.
Fondation Maeght, Saint Paul, France.

ABOVE. Ellsworth Kelly:
Orange White. 1964. Oil on canvas. 122″ x 96″.
Courtesy of Sidney Janis Gallery, New York.

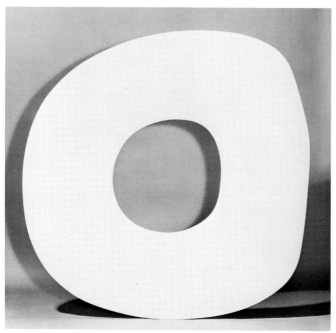

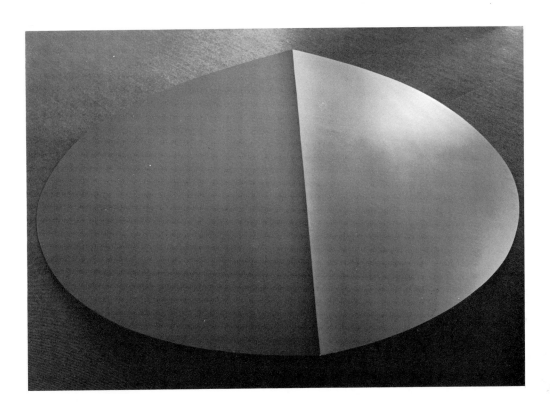

LEFT, ABOVE. Ellsworth Kelly:
2 Panels: White Dark Blue. 1968. Oil on canvas. 96″ x 144″.
Courtesy of Sidney Janis Gallery, New York.

LEFT, BELOW. Ellsworth Kelly:
White Ring. 1963. Epoxy on aluminum. 70″ x 72″ x 12″.
Private collection, New York.

ABOVE. Ellsworth Kelly:
Green. 1968. Painted aluminum. 21″ x 105″ x 112″.
Collection of The Walker Art Center, Minneapolis, Minnesota.

Ellsworth Kelly:
Untitled. 1968. Painted aluminum. 100½″ x 146½″ x 38⅜″.
Collection of William S. Rubin, New York.

Ellsworth Kelly:
Black White. 1968. Painted aluminum. 100½″ x 146½″ x 38⅜″.
Courtesy of Sidney Janis Gallery, New York.

Ellsworth Kelly:
Tulip. 1958. Pencil on paper.
29″ x 23″.
Private collection, New York.

Ellsworth Kelly:
Grass. 1961. Pencil on paper.
28½″ x 22½″.
Private collection, New York.

Ellsworth Kelly:
Castor Bean. 1961. Ink on paper.
22½″ x 28½″.
Private collection, New York.

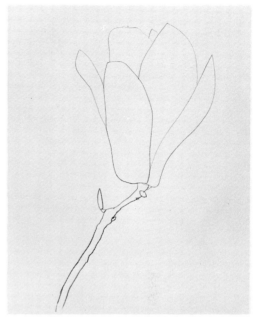

Ellsworth Kelly:
Oak. 1964. Pencil on paper.
28½″ x 22½″.
Private collection, New York.

Ellsworth Kelly:
Magnolia. 1966. Pencil on paper.
29″ x 23″.
Private collection, New York.

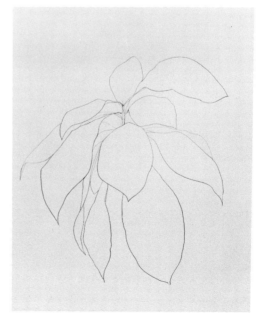

Ellsworth Kelly:
Avocado. 1967. Pencil on paper.
29″ x 23″.
Private collection, New York.

Ellsworth Kelly:
Chrysanthemum. 1967. Pencil on paper.
30″ x 22″.
Private collection, New York.

Ellsworth Kelly:
Water Lily. 1968. Pencil on paper.
29″ x 23″.
Private collection, New York.

Franz Kline:
Nijinsky. 1949. Oil on canvas. 33″ x 28″.
Collection of Mr. and Mrs. David I. Orr, New York.

LEFT, ABOVE. Franz Kline:
Wotan. 1950. Oil on canvas. 55⅛″ x 79¼″.
Collection of Mr. and Mrs. Robert C. Scull, New York.

LEFT, BELOW. Franz Kline:
Horizontals Two. 1952. Oil on canvas. 77″ x 100″.
Estate of Franz Kline, Courtesy of Marlborough-Gerson Gallery, New York.

ABOVE. Franz Kline:
Figure Eight. 1952. Oil on canvas. 80½″ x 63½″.
Collection of William S. Rubin, New York.

LEFT, ABOVE. Franz Kline:
Untitled. 1953–54. Oil on canvas. 57¼″ x 82″.
Collection of Robert H. Halff and Carl W. Johnson, Beverly Hills, California.

LEFT, BELOW. Franz Kline:
Untitled. 1954. Oil on canvas. 43″ x 36″.
Collection of Mr. and Mrs. David I. Orr, New York.

ABOVE. Franz Kline:
White Forms. 1955. Oil on canvas. 74″ x 50″.
Collection of Philip Johnson, New Canaan, Connecticut.

LEFT, ABOVE. Franz Kline:
Orange and Black Wall. 1959. Oil on canvas. 66½″ x 144″.
Collection of Mr. and Mrs. Robert C. Scull, New York.

LEFT, BELOW. Franz Kline:
Riverbed. 1961. Oil on canvas. 78⅞″ x 109¼″.
Collection of William M. White, Jr., New York.

ABOVE. Gabe Kohn:
Long Beach Contract. 1965. Laminated redwood. 10′ x 7′.
California State College, Long Beach, California.

ABOVE. Roy Lichtenstein:
I Can See the Whole Room. . . . 1961. Oil on canvas. 48″ x 48″.
Collection of Mr. and Mrs. Burton Tremaine, Meriden, Connecticut.

RIGHT, ABOVE. Roy Lichtenstein:
Live Ammo. 1962. Oil on canvas. 68″ x 92″ (two panels).
Collection of Mr. and Mrs. Morton Neumann, Chicago, Illinois.

RIGHT, BELOW. Roy Lichtenstein:
Sussex. 1964. Oil and magna on canvas. 36″ x 68″.
Collection of Robert Rosenblum, New York.

TAKE COVER!

Live Ammo

RIGHT NOW -- IF THEY'RE WATCHIN' ME -- THEY'VE GOT TO MAKE UP THEIR MINDS WHETHER I DON'T KNOW THEY'RE HERE -- AND WILL PASS BY -- LETTIN' THE OUTFIT BE SUCKED INTO A TRAP-- OR WHETHER I KNOW THEY'RE HERE -- AND AM ABOUT TO FIRE AT THEM! BUT WHERE DID THEY COME FROM? NOT THE SEA--WE'VE HAD OUR EYES GLUED TO IT! AND WE KNOW THERE AIN'T AN AIR FIELD ON THIS ISLAND! WHERE'D THEY COME FROM? WHERE'D THEY COME FROM!

ABOVE. Roy Lichtenstein:
Big Painting #6. 1965. Oil and magna on canvas. 92½″ x 129″.
Collection of Mr. and Mrs. Robert C. Scull, New York.

RIGHT, ABOVE. Roy Lichtenstein:
Haystacks. 1968. Oil and magna on canvas. 18″ x 24″.
Private collection, New York.

RIGHT, BELOW. Roy Lichtenstein:
Haystacks. 1969. Oil and magna on canvas. 16″ x 24″.
Private collection, New York.

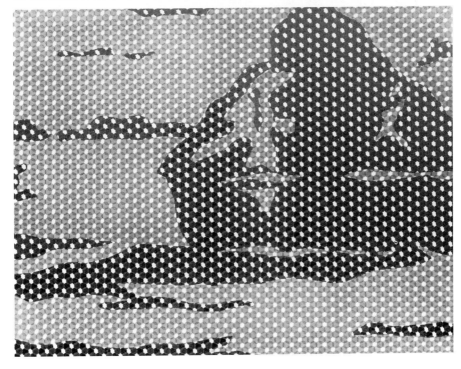

Roy Lichtenstein:
Rouen Cathedral (seen at five different times of day), III. 1969.
Oil and magna on canvas. 63″ x 42″. (#1 of five paintings in set.)
Private collection, New York.

Roy Lichtenstein:
Rouen Cathedral (seen at five different times of day), III. 1969.
Oil and magna on canvas. 63″ x 42″. (#3 of five paintings in set.)
Private collection, New York.

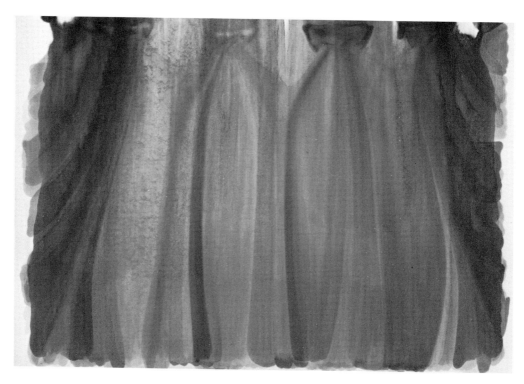

Morris Louis:
Saraband. 1959. Acrylic on canvas. 100½″ x 149″.
The Solomon R. Guggenheim Museum, New York.

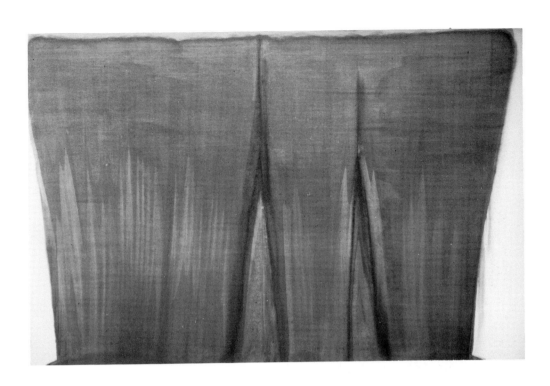

Morris Louis:
Terranean. 1959. Acrylic resin paint on canvas. 90½″ x 146″.
Collection of Mr. and Mrs. Kenneth Noland, New York.

ABOVE. Morris Louis:
While. 1959. Acrylic on canvas. 96½" x 136⅜".
Harry N. Abrams Family Collection, New York.

RIGHT, ABOVE. Morris Louis:
Aleph. 1960. Magna acrylic on canvas. 105" x 92¾".
Collection of Jaime C. del Amo, Madrid, Spain.

RIGHT, BELOW. Morris Louis:
Alpha-Delta. 1961. Acrylic on canvas. 8'8" x 20'.
Everson Museum of Art, Syracuse, New York.

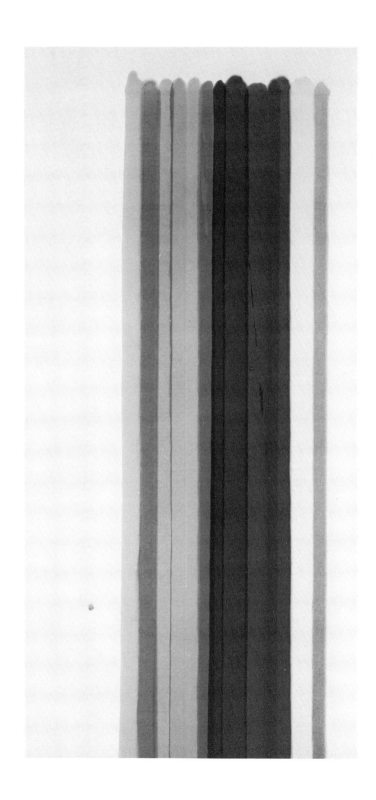

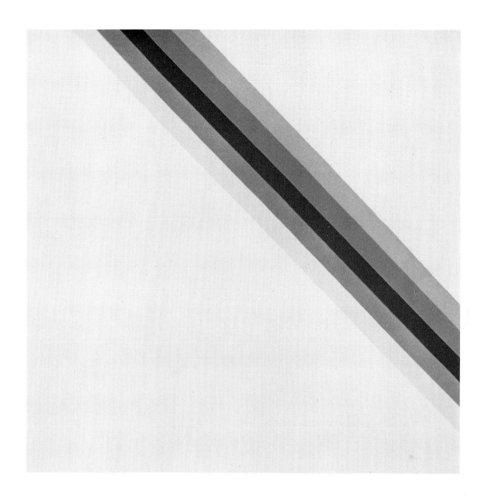

LEFT. Morris Louis:
Moving In. 1961. Magna acrylic on canvas. 87½″ x 41½″.
Private collection, New York.

ABOVE. Morris Louis:
Hot Half. 1962. Acrylic resin on canvas. 63″ x 63″.
Collection of Mrs. Abner Brenner, Washington, D.C.

LEFT, ABOVE. Robert Morris:
Untitled. 1964. Painted plywood. 6'6" x 9'.
Collection Dott. Giuseppe Panza di Buomo, Milan, Italy,
Courtesy of Leo Castelli Gallery, New York.

LEFT, BELOW. Robert Morris:
Untitled. 1966. Steel mesh. 31" x 106" x 106".
Lent by The Kleiner Foundation, Beverly Hills, Courtesy of
Los Angeles County Museum of Art, Los Angeles, California.

ABOVE. Robert Morris:
Untitled. 1967–68. Felt. 180" x 72" x 1".
The Detroit Institute of Arts, Gift of The Friends of Modern Art.

Robert Morris:
Untitled. 1968. Translucent fiberglas. Nine units, each 48″ x 24″ x 24″.
Collection of Philip Johnson, New Canaan, Connecticut.

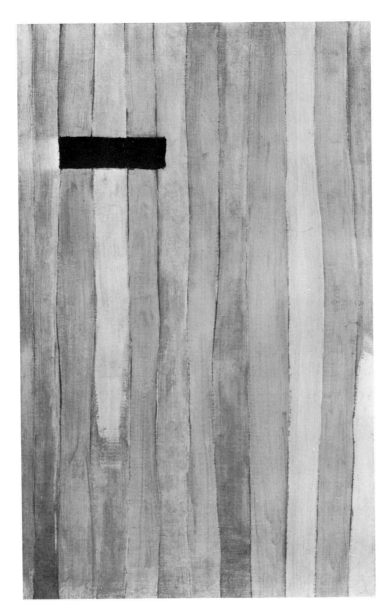

Robert Motherwell:
The Little Spanish Prison. 1941–44. Oil on canvas. 27⅛″ x 17″.
Collection of the artist.

LEFT. Robert Motherwell:
Homely Protestant. 1948. Oil on composition board. 96″ x 48″.
Collection of Helen Frankenthaler, New York.

ABOVE. Robert Motherwell:
Elegy to the Spanish Republic, 70. 1961. Oil on canvas. 69″ x 114″.
The Metropolitan Museum of Art, Anonymous gift, 1965.

BELOW. Robert Motherwell:
Africa. 1965. Acrylic on canvas. 80″ x 225″.
The Baltimore Museum of Art, Baltimore, Maryland, Gift of the artist.

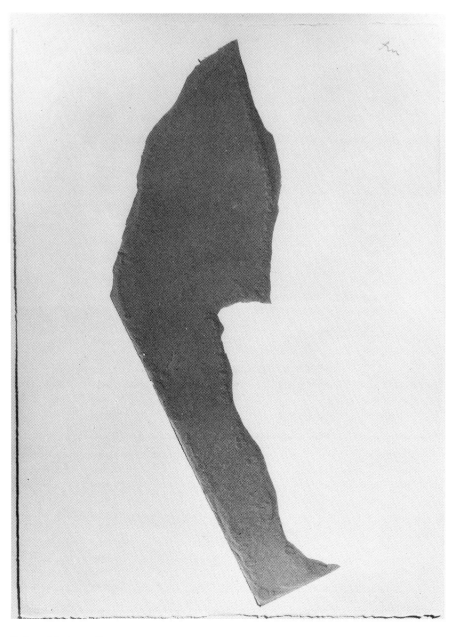

Robert Motherwell:
Beige Figuration No. 3. 1967. Collage (paper). 30″ x 22″.
Collection of the artist.

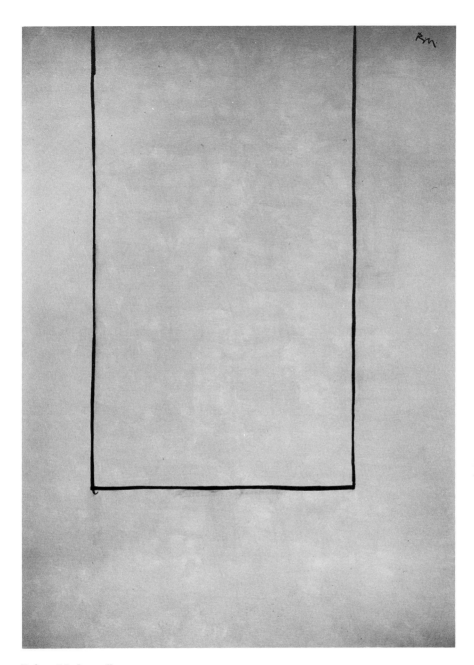

Robert Motherwell:
"Open" No. 14: In Ochre with Charcoal Line. 1968.
Polymer paint and charcoal on canvas. 114″ x 69″.
Collection of the artist.

Robert Motherwell:
"Open" No. 17: In Ultramarine with Charcoal Line. 1968.
Polymer paint and charcoal on canvas. 100″ x 197″.
Collection of the artist.

Robert Motherwell:
"Open" No. 31B: In Raw Sienna. 1968. Charcoal on blotting paper.
17″ x 37½″. Collection of the artist.

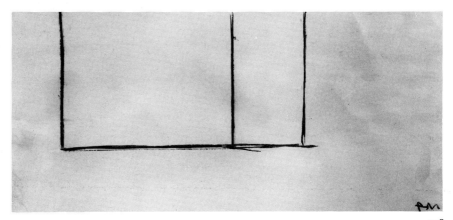

Barnett Newman:
Pagan Void. 1946. Oil on canvas.
33″ x 38″.
Collection of Mrs. Annalee Newman,
New York.

Barnett Newman:
The Euclidian Abyss. 1946–47.
Oil and crayon on fabric. 28″ x 22″.
Collection of Mr. and Mrs. Burton
Tremaine, Meriden, Connecticut.

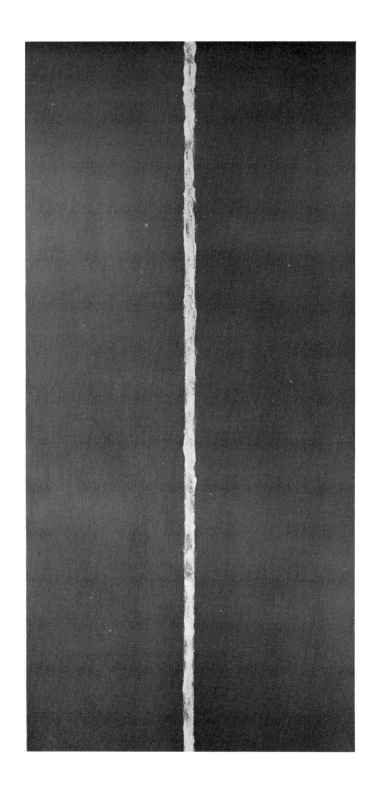

LEFT. Barnett Newman:
Onement III. 1949. Oil on canvas. 72″ x 34″.
Collection of Mr. and Mrs. Joseph Slifka, New York.

ABOVE. Barnett Newman:
Covenant. 1949. Oil on canvas. 48″ x 60″. Joseph H. Hirshhorn Collection.

Barnett Newman:
Prometheus Bound. 1952.
Oil on canvas. 131¾″ x 50″.
Collection of William S. Rubin,
New York.

Barnett Newman:
Shining Forth (for George). 1961. Oil on canvas. 9½' x 14½'.
Collection of Mrs. Annalee Newman, New York.

ABOVE. Barnett Newman:
Who's Afraid of Red, Yellow, Blue I. 1966. Oil on canvas. 60″ x 50″.
Collection of S. I. Newhouse, Jr., New York.

RIGHT, ABOVE. Barnett Newman:
Anna's Light. 1968. Acrylic on canvas. 9′ x 20′.
M. Knoedler & Company, Inc., New York.

RIGHT, BELOW. Barnett Newman:
Jericho. 1968–69. Acrylic on canvas. 9′ 6″ x 9′ 6″.
M. Knoedler & Company, Inc., New York.

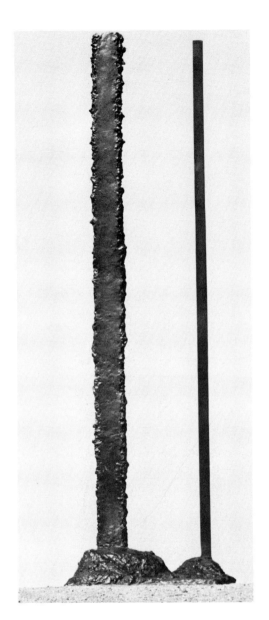

LEFT. Barnett Newman:
Here I (to Marcia). 1950. Bronze. 8′ x 26″ x 27″.
Collection of Mrs. Annalee Newman, New York.

RIGHT. Barnett Newman:
Here III. 1966. Stainless steel and Cor-Ten steel. 10′ 5″ x 23½″ x 18½″.
M. Knoedler & Company, Inc., New York.

Barnett Newman:
Broken Obelisk. 1967. Cor-Ten steel. 26′ x 10½′ x 10½′.
M. Knoedler & Company, Inc., New York.

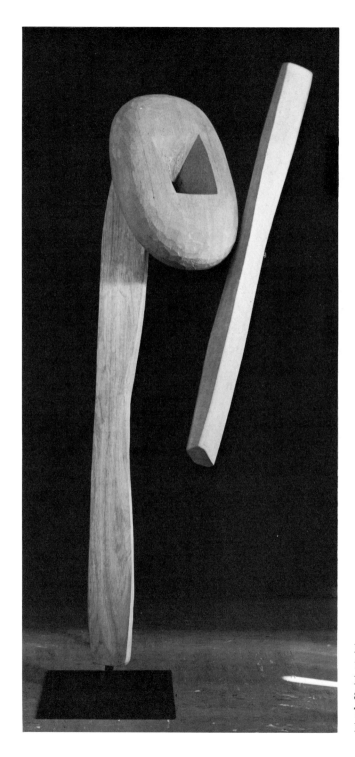

Isamu Noguchi:
The Cry. 1959.
Balsa wood with steel base.
84″ x 30″ x 18″.
The Solomon R. Guggenheim Museum,
New York.

Isamu Noguchi:
Life of a Cube. 1962.
Black granite.
21″ x 21″ x 21″.
Cordier & Ekstrom, Inc.,
New York.

Isamu Noguchi:
Sky Frame. 1966.
Rose Aurora Portuguese Marble.
22″ x 28″ x 8¼″.
Cordier & Ekstrom,
Inc., New York.

Isamu Noguchi:
Euripides. 1966. White Italian Altissimo marble.
Two pieces, 45″ and 90″ (high).
Cordier & Ekstrom, Inc., New York.

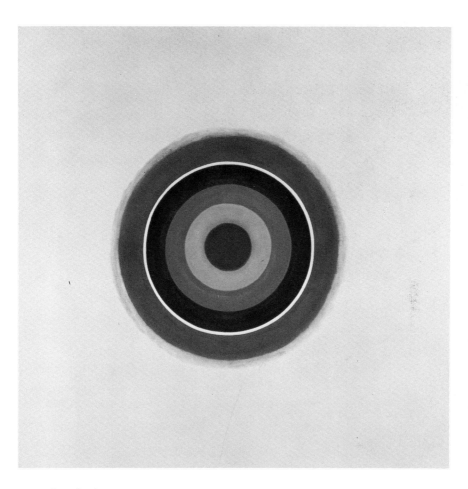

Kenneth Noland:
Teton Noir. 1961. Acrylic on canvas. 81″ x 81″.
Collection of Carter Burden, New York.

Kenneth Noland:
Mach II. 1964. Acrylic resin on canvas. 9′ x 17′.
Collection of Kimiko and John Powers, Aspen, Colorado.

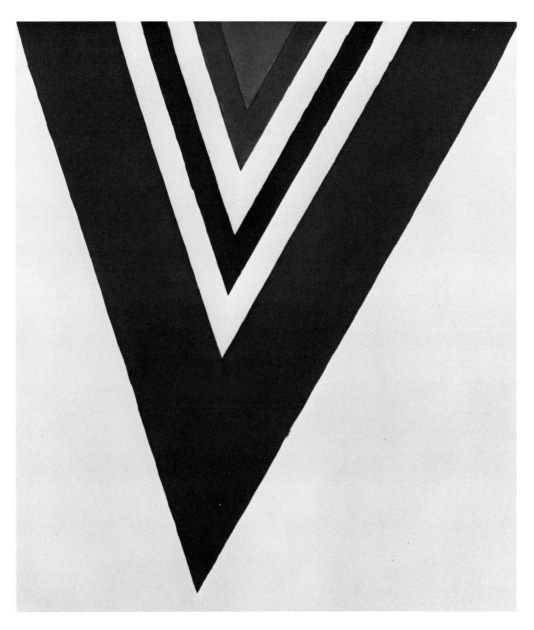

Kenneth Noland:
17th Stage. 1964. Acrylic on canvas. 8′ x 7′.
Collection of Mr. and Mrs. Eugene M. Schwartz, New York.

LEFT, ABOVE. Kenneth Noland:
Bend Sinister. 1964. Acrylic on canvas. 98″ x 161¾″.
Joseph H. Hirshhorn Collection.

LEFT, BELOW. Kenneth Noland:
Embrown. 1964. Acrylic on canvas. 96″ x 145″.
Collection of Mr. and Mrs. David Mirvish, Toronto, Canada.

ABOVE. Kenneth Noland:
Trans-Median. 1968. Acrylic on canvas. 7½′ x 7½′.
Collection of Mr. and Mrs. David Mirvish, Toronto, Canada.

Kenneth Noland:
Dawn-Dusk. 1968. Water-miscible acrylic on cotton duck. 30½″ x 141½″.
Collection of Mr. and Mrs. Clement Greenberg, New York.

Kenneth Noland:
Via Lime. 1968–69. Acrylic emulsion on canvas. 90½″ x 240″.
Collection of Ondine Vaughn and Steve Schapiro, New York.

Claes Oldenburg:
7-up. 1961. Enamel on plaster. 50⅛″ x 37⅜″ x 6¼″
Collection of Mr. and Mrs. Burton Tremaine, Meriden, Connecticut.

ABOVE. Claes Oldenburg:
Strong Arm. 1961. Enamel on plaster. 43⅜″ x 32⅜″ x 5½″.
Collection of Mr. and Mrs. Burton Tremaine, Meriden, Connecticut.

RIGHT, ABOVE. Claes Oldenburg:
Soft Typewriter. 1963. Vinyl, kapok, cloth, and plexiglas. 9″ x 27½″ x 26″.
Collection of Alan Power, London, England.

RIGHT, BELOW. Claes Oldenburg:
Ironing Board with Shirt and Iron. 1964. Wood, cloth, vinyl, nylon, and hydrostone.
80″ x 67½″ x 24″. Collection of Mr. and Mrs. Sonnabend, Paris, France.

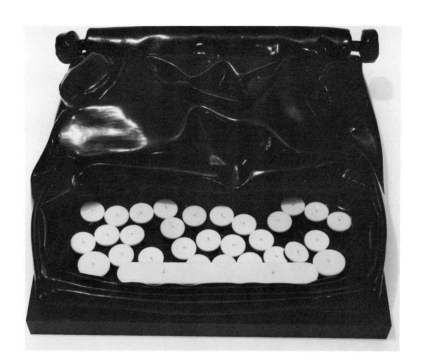

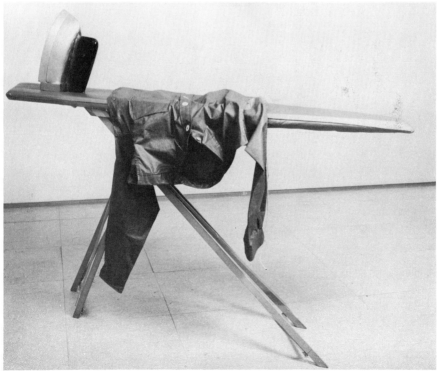

LEFT. Claes Oldenburg:
Tub (hard model). 1966. Corrugated paper, wood, enamel.
80″ x 32½″ x 28″. Collection of Mrs. Claes Oldenburg, New York.

ABOVE. Jules Olitski:
Ten O'Clock. 1959. Paint, spackle, polymer emulsion on panel.
36″ x 36″. Collection of the artist.

Jules Olitski:
Bathsheba. 1959. Oil on canvas. 78″ x 70″.
Collection of J. Patrick Lannan, Palm Beach, Florida.
198.

Jules Olitski:
Ritual of L. 1959. Paint, spackle, polymer emulsion on canvas.
6′ x 7′. Collection of the artist.

ABOVE. Jules Olitski:
Commissar Demikovsky. 1965. Acrylic on canvas: 8′ x 7′.
Collection of Mr. and Mrs. Eugene M. Schwartz, New York.

RIGHT. Jules Olitski:
Thigh Smoke. 1966. Acrylic on canvas. 167″ x 92½″.
Seattle–First National Bank Collection, Seattle, Washington.

ABOVE. Jules Olitski:
Green Volya. 1969. Acrylic emulsion on canvas. 9′ 9″ x 17′ 5″.
Collection of Lawrence Rubin, New York.

RIGHT, ABOVE. Jules Olitski:
Warehouse Light. 1969. Acrylic on canvas. 118″ x 174″.
Collection of Lawrence Rubin, New York.

RIGHT, BELOW. Jules Olitski:
Twelve Nights. 1968. Aluminum and acrylic, air drying lacquer. 9′ x 16½′ x 12′.
Collection of the artist.

LEFT. Jackson Pollock:
Male and Female. 1942. Oil on canvas. 73¼″ x 49″.
Collection of Mrs. H. Gates Lloyd, Haverford, Pennsylvania.

ABOVE. Jackson Pollock:
Moon Woman Cuts the Circle. 1943. Oil on canvas. 43″ x 41″.
Courtesy of Marlborough-Gerson Gallery, New York.

LEFT. Jackson Pollock:
Night Ceremony. 1944.
Oil and enamel on canvas.
72″ x 43⅛″.
Collection of Mrs. Barbara
Reis Poe, New York.

RIGHT. Jackson Pollock:
Cathedral. 1947.
Duco and aluminum paint on canvas.
71½″ x 35⅟₁₆″.
Dallas Museum of Fine Arts,
Gift of Mr. and Mrs.
Bernard J. Reis.

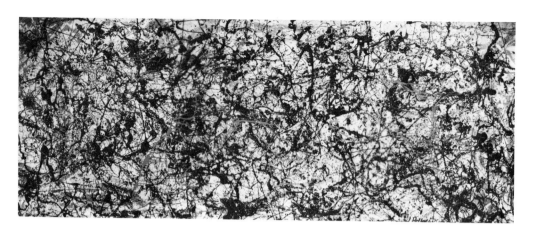

Jackson Pollock:
Lucifer. 1947. Oil, enamel, and aluminum paint on canvas.
41″ x 8′ x 9½″. Collection of Joseph H. Hazen, New York.

Jackson Pollock:
Autumn Rhythm. 1950. Oil on canvas. 105″ x 207″.
The Metropolitan Museum of Art, New York,
Estate of Jackson Pollock, George A. Hearn Fund, 1957.

Jackson Pollock:
Portrait and a Dream. 1953. Enamel on canvas. 58⅛″ x 134¼″.
Dallas Museum of Fine Arts, Gift of Mr. and Mrs. Algur H. Meadows
and the Meadows Foundation, Inc.

ABOVE. Jackson Pollock:
The Deep. 1953. Oil and duco on canvas. 86¾″ x 51⅛″.
Collection of Samuel Wagstaff, Jr., Detroit, Michigan.

RIGHT, ABOVE. Larry Poons:
Double Speed. 1962–63. Acrylic and fabric dye on canvas.
72″ x 144″. Collection of Frank Stella, New York.

RIGHT, BELOW. Larry Poons:
Enforcer. 1963. Liquitex and fabric spray on canvas. 80″ x 80″.
Collection of Mr. and Mrs. Robert C. Scull, New York.

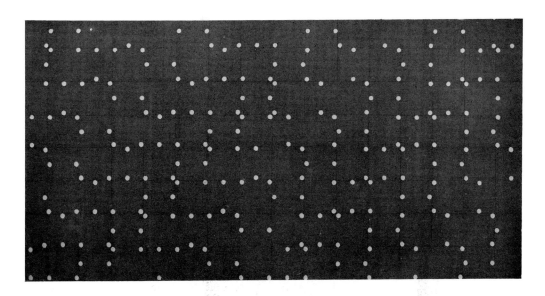

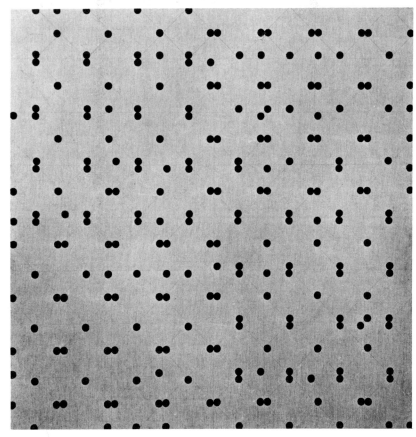

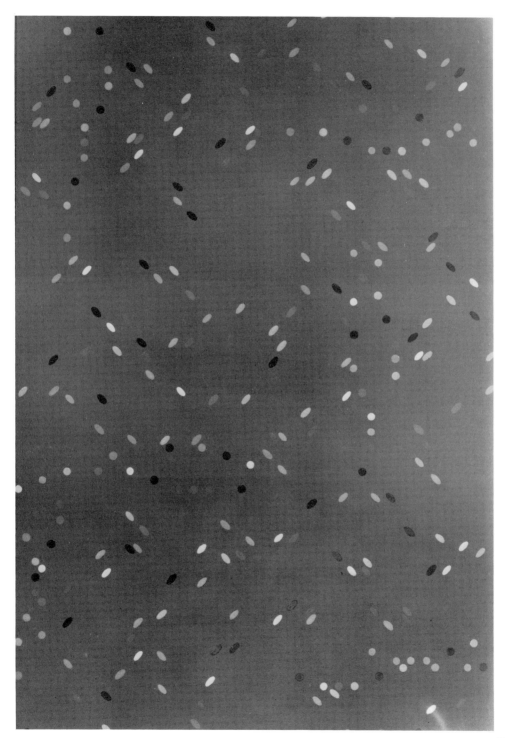

274

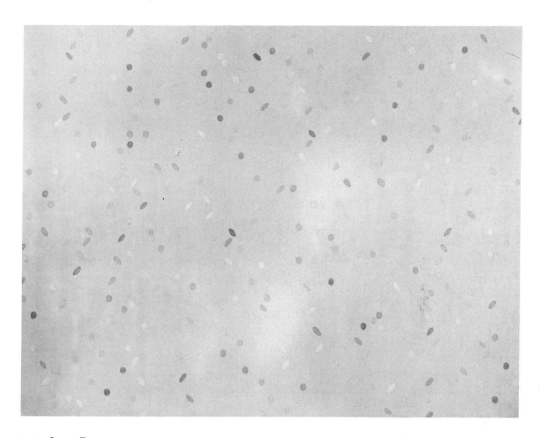

LEFT. Larry Poons:
Mary Queen of Scots. 1965. Acrylic on canvas. 12′ x 90″.
Collection of Mr. and Mrs. Robert C. Scull, New York.

ABOVE. Larry Poons:
Rosewood. 1966. Acrylic on canvas. 120″ x 160″.
Collection of William S. Rubin, New York.

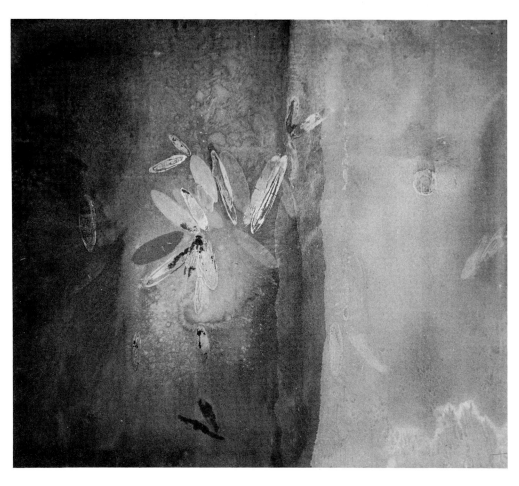

Larry Poons:
Night Journey. 1968. Acrylic on canvas. 108″ x 124″.
Collection of Carter Burden, New York.

Larry Poons:
Doge's Palace. 1969. Acrylic on canvas. 112″ x 17′ 10″.
Collection of Lawrence Rubin, New York.

Robert Rauschenberg:
Rebus. 1955. Combine painting. 96″ x 144″.
Collection of Mr. and Mrs. Victor W. Ganz, New York.

Robert Rauschenberg:
Odalisk. 1955–58. Construction.
81″ x 25″ x 25″.
Collection of Mr. and Mrs.
Victor W. Ganz, New York.

Robert Rauschenberg:
Factum I. 1957. Combine painting. 62″ x 35½″.
Collection of Dott. Giuseppe Panza di Buomo, Milan, Italy.

Robert Rauschenberg:
Factum II. 1957. Oil and collage on canvas. 61½" x 35½".
Collection of Mr. and Mrs. Morton Neumann, Chicago, Illinois.

Robert Rauschenberg:
Third Time Painting. 1961. Oil on canvas with clock. 84″ x 60″.
Harry N. Abrams Family Collection, New York.

Robert Rauschenberg:
Tracer. 1964. Oil on canvas with silkscreen. 84″ x 60″.
Collection of Mr. and Mrs. Frank M. Titelman, Altoona, Pennsylvania.

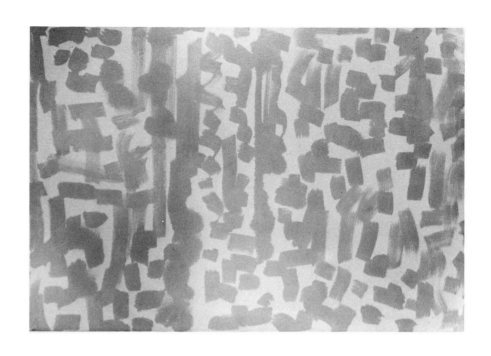

LEFT, ABOVE. Ad Reinhardt: *Yellow Painting.* 1949. Oil on canvas. 40″ x 60″. Collection of Anna Reinhardt, New York.

LEFT, BELOW. Ad Reinhardt: *Abstract Painting Grey.* 1950. Oil on canvas. 30″ x 40″. Collection of Rita Reinhardt, New York.

RIGHT. Ad Reinhardt: *White.* 1950. Oil on canvas. 80″ x 36″. Collection of Rita Reinhardt, New York.

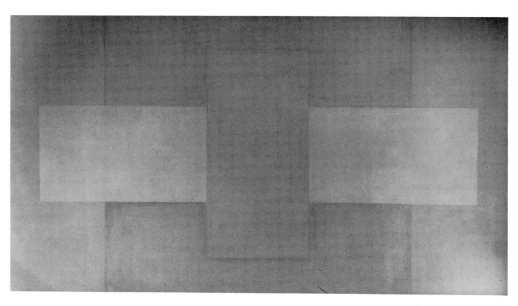

Ad Reinhardt:
Red Painting. 1952. Oil on canvas. 6½′ x 12′.
The Metropolitan Museum of Art, New York, Arthur H. Hearn Fund, 1968.

Ad Reinhardt:
Abstract Painting. 1956–60.
Oil on canvas. 108″ x 40″.
Courtesy of Marlborough-Gerson
Gallery, New York.

287

Ad Reinhardt:
Abstract Painting. 1959.
Oil on canvas. 108″ x 40″.
Courtesy of Marlborough-Gerson
Gallery, New York.

James Rosenquist:
Four Young Revolutionaries. 1962. Glass, wood, and oil paint.
24″ x 32″. Collection of Mr. and Mrs. Lewis V. Winter, New York.

James Rosenquist:
Untitled. 1962. Oil on canvas. 84″ x 72″.
Collection of Mr. and Mrs. Robert A. Rowan, Pasadena, California.

James Rosenquist:
Silver Skies. 1962. Oil on canvas. 78″ x 16½″.
Collection of Mr. and Mrs. Robert C. Scull, New York.

James Rosenquist:
Early in the Morning. 1963. Oil on canvas. 95″ x 56″.
Collection of Mr. and Mrs. Robert C. Scull, New York.

James Rosenquist:
Nomad. 1963. Oil on canvas, plastic paint, wood. 84″ x 210″.
Albright-Knox Art Gallery, Buffalo, New York, Gift of Seymour H. Knox.

James Rosenquist:
Growth Plan. 1966. Oil on canvas. 70″ x 140″ (2 panels).
Museum of Contemporary Art, Nagaoka, Japan.

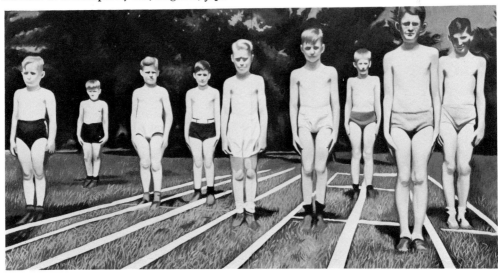

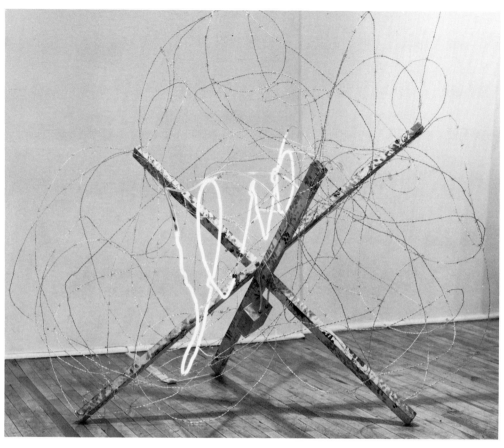

James Rosenquist:
Tumbleweed. 1963–66. Chromed barbed wire and neon.
54″ x 60″ x 60″ approximately. Leo Castelli Gallery, New York.

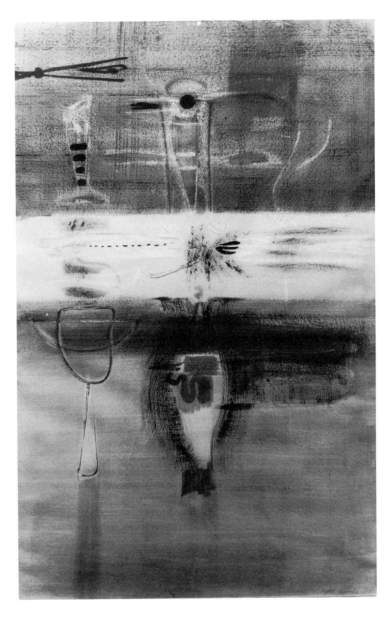

Mark Rothko:
Untitled. 1946. Watercolor. 38¾" x 25½".
Collection of Mr. and Mrs. Donald Blinken, New York.

ABOVE. Mark Rothko:
Vessels of Magic. 1946–47. Watercolor. 38¾″ x 25¾″.
The Brooklyn Museum, New York.

RIGHT, ABOVE. Mark Rothko:
Fantasy. 1947. Watercolor. 25½″ x 39½″.
Collection of Mr. and Mrs. Donald Blinken, New York.

RIGHT, BELOW. Mark Rothko:
No. 26. 1947. Oil on canvas. 34″ x 45¼″.
Collection of Mrs. Betty Parsons, New York.

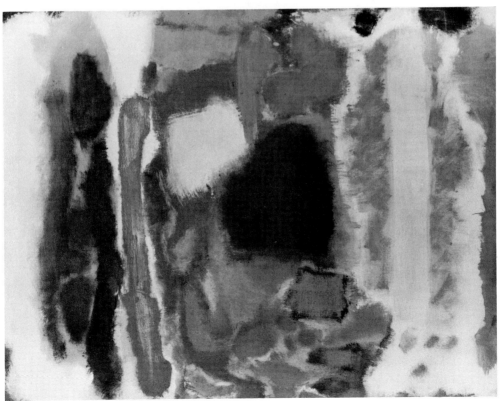

Mark Rothko:
Black, Pink, and Yellow over Orange. 1951–52. Oil on canvas.
116″ x 92¼″. Collection of William S. Rubin, New York.

Mark Rothko:
No. 10. 1952. Oil on canvas. 81½″ x 42½″.
Collection of Mr. and Mrs. C. B. Wright, Seattle, Washington.

Mark Rothko:
No. 8. 1952. Oil on canvas. 80½″ x 68″.
Collection of Mr. and Mrs. Burton Tremaine, Meriden, Connecticut.

Mark Rothko:
Brown, Black, and Blue. 1958. Oil on canvas. 5′9″ x 5′.
Collection of Dr. and Mrs. Edward Massie, St. Louis, Missouri.

Mark Rothko:
Number 207 (Red Over Dark Blue on Dark Gray). 1961.
Oil on canvas. 92¾″ x 81⅛″.
University Art Museum, Berkeley, California,
Acquired from the artist.

David Smith:
Deserted Garden Landscape. 1946. Steel, bronze. 11¾″ x 10⅛″ x 4¾″
Collection of Mr. and Mrs. Harry W. Anderson, Atherton, California.

David Smith:
Puritan Landscape. 1946. Steel, bronze, cast iron, nickel.
28¼″ x 15″ x 10″
Collection of Peter Brant, New York.

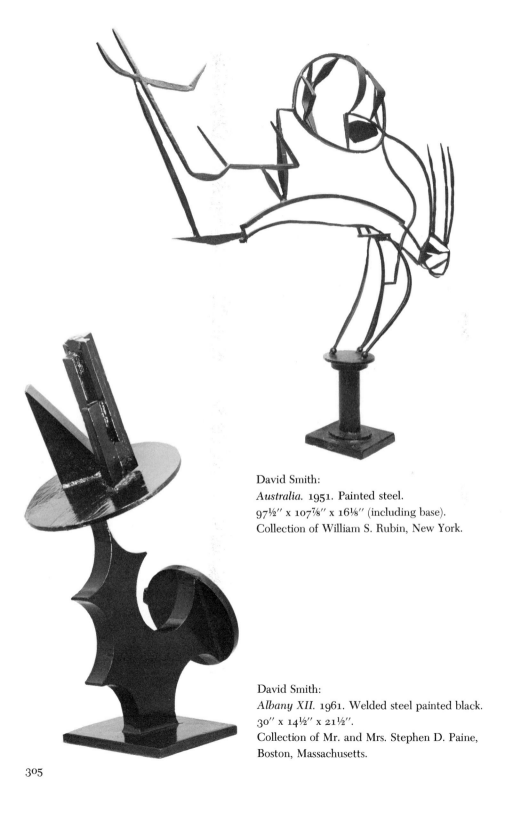

David Smith:
Australia. 1951. Painted steel.
97½″ x 107⅞″ x 16⅛″ (including base).
Collection of William S. Rubin, New York.

David Smith:
Albany XII. 1961. Welded steel painted black.
30″ x 14½″ x 21½″.
Collection of Mr. and Mrs. Stephen D. Paine,
Boston, Massachusetts.

ABOVE. David Smith:
2 Circles IV. 1962. Painted steel. 124″ x 60″ x 28½″.
Estate of David Smith, Courtesy of Marlborough-Gerson Gallery, New York.

RIGHT, ABOVE. David Smith:
Primo Piano III. 1962. Painted steel. 124″ x 145″ x 18″.
Courtesy of Marlborough-Gerson Gallery, New York.

RIGHT, BELOW. David Smith:
Voltri VI. 1962. Steel. 103″ x 102¾″ x 25½″.
Private collection, New York.

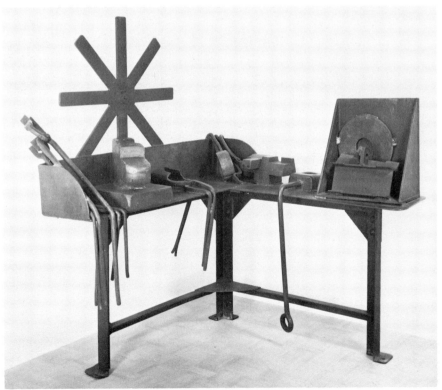

LEFT, ABOVE. David Smith:
Voltri XIII. 1962. Steel. 64⅛″ x 103¾″ x 26″.
University Art Museum, Berkeley, California.
Gift of Mr. and Mrs. Eugene E. Trefethen, Jr., Piedmont, California.

LEFT, BELOW. David Smith:
Voltri XIX. 1962. Welded and shaped iron and found objects. 55″ x 45″ x 50″.
Collection of Mr. and Mrs. Stephen D. Paine, Boston, Massachusetts.

ABOVE. David Smith:
Untitled. 1962–63. Stainless steel. 96¼″ x 63″ x 26″.
Art Gallery of Ontario, Purchase with assistance from the Women's Committee Fund, 1968.

David Smith:
Wagon II. 1964. Forged iron. 84″ x 112″ x 45″. Estate of David Smith, Courtesy of Marlborough-Gerson Gallery, New York.

David Smith:
Cubi XXIV. 1964. Stainless steel. 114¼″ x 83½″.
Museum of Art, Carnegie Institute, Pittsburgh, Pennsylvania,
Howard Heinz Endowment Purchase Fund.

David Smith:
Untitled. 1965. Stainless steel, 102½″ x 120″ x 31¼″.
Estate of David Smith, Courtesy of Marlborough-Gerson Gallery, New York.

David Smith:
Cubi XXV. 1965. Stainless steel. 119¼″ x 120¾″ x 31¼″.
Estate of David Smith, Courtesy of Marlborough-Gerson Gallery, New York.

Tony Smith:
Black Box. 1962. Steel.
22½″ x 33″ x 25″.
Collection of Mr. and Mrs. Norman Ives,
Woodbridge, Connecticut.

Tony Smith:
Free Ride. 1962. Steel.
(#2 of an edition of three.)
6′ 8″ x 6′ 8″ x 6′ 8″.
Courtesy of Fischbach Gallery, New York.

Frank Stella:
Zambesi. 1959. Enamel on canvas. 90″ x 78″.
Collection of Lawrence Rubin, New York.

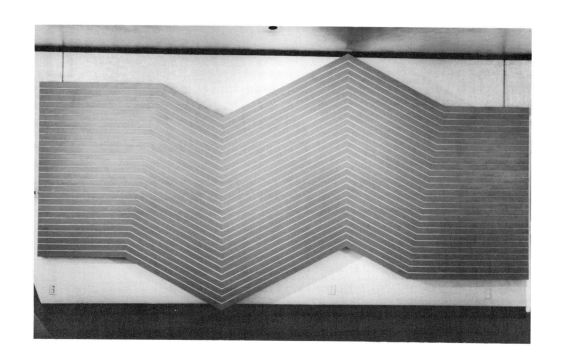

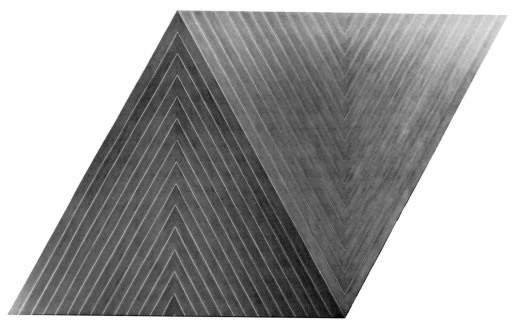

LEFT, ABOVE. Frank Stella:
Nunca Pasa Nada. 1964. Metallic powder in acrylic emulsion on canvas.
9′ x 18′ approximately. The Lannan Foundation.

LEFT, BELOW. Frank Stella:
Valparaiso (flesh and green). 1964. Metallic paint on canvas.
84″ x 144″. Collection of the artist.

ABOVE. Frank Stella:
Ossippee I. 1966. Fluorescent alkyd and epoxy paint on canvas.
95″ x 138″. Collection of Dr. and Mrs. Ernest Kafka, New York.

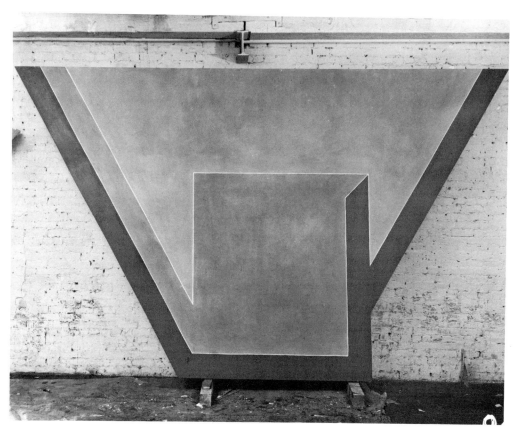

Frank Stella:
Union IV. 1966. Fluorescent alkyd and epoxy paint on canvas.
103″ x 174″. Collection of Richard Meier, New York.

Frank Stella:
Sangre de Cristo. 1967. Metallic powder in polymer emulsion.
10′ x 42′. Collection of Dr. and Mrs. Charles Hendrickson, Newport Beach, California.

LEFT, ABOVE. Frank Stella:
Hagmatana II. 1967. Acrylic on canvas. 10′ x 15′.
Collection of Mr. and Mrs. Eugene M. Schwartz, New York.

LEFT, BELOW. Frank Stella:
Ctesiphon III. 1968. Fluorescent acrylic on canvas. 10′ x 20′.
Wallraf-Richartz Museum, Köln, Germany, Sammlung Ludwig.

ABOVE. Clyfford Still:
Painting 1948-D. 1948. Oil on canvas. 93⅛″ x 79⅝″.
Collection of William S. Rubin, New York.

Clyfford Still:
No. 5. 1951. Oil on canvas. 55″ x 46″.
Wadsworth Atheneum, Hartford, Connecticut.

Clyfford Still:
Painting. 1951. Oil on canvas. 93¼″ x 75¾″.
The Detroit Institute of Arts, W. Hawkins Ferry Fund.

Clyfford Still:
Painting. 1958. Oil on canvas. 113¾″ x 159½″.
Collection of J. Patrick Lannan, Palm Beach, Florida.

Bradley Walker Tomlin:
All Souls' Night. 1948. Oil on canvas. 42½″ x 64″.
Betty Parsons Gallery, New York.

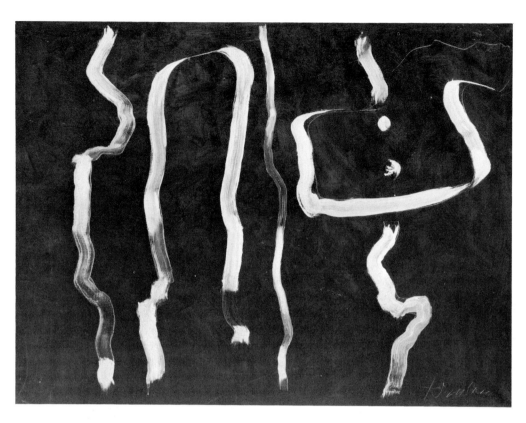

Bradley Walker Tomlin:
Tension by Moonlight. 1948. Oil on canvas. 32″ x 44″.
Betty Parsons Gallery, New York.

Bradley Walker Tomlin:
Number 3. 1948. Oil on canvas. 40″ x 50⅛″.
The Museum of Modern Art, New York, Fractional gift of
John E. Hutchins in memory of Frances E. Marder Hutchins, 1960.

Bradley Walker Tomlin:
Number 11. 1949. Oil on canvas. 44⅛″ x 29″.
Munson-Williams-Proctor Institute, Utica, New York.
Edward W. Root Bequest.

Bradley Walker Tomlin:
Number 9: In Memory of Gertrude Stein. 1950. Oil on canvas. 49″ x 8′ 6¼″.
The Museum of Modern Art, New York, Gift of Mrs. John D. Rockefeller, III, 1955.

LEFT. Bradley Walker Tomlin:
Number 5. 1952. Oil on canvas. 79″ x 45″.
Collection of Mrs. Betty Parsons, New York.

ABOVE. Andy Warhol:
Dick Tracy. 1960. Casein on canvas. 70⅛″ x 52¼″.
Gordon Locksley Gallery, Minneapolis, Minnesota.

Andy Warhol:
Campbell's Soup Cans. 1961–62. Oil on canvas.
Thirty-two panels, each 20″ x 16″.
Collection of Irving Blum, Los Angeles, California.

Andy Warhol:
Do It Yourself. 1962. Liquitex on canvas. 72″ x 54″.
Collection of Kimiko and John Powers, Aspen, Colorado.

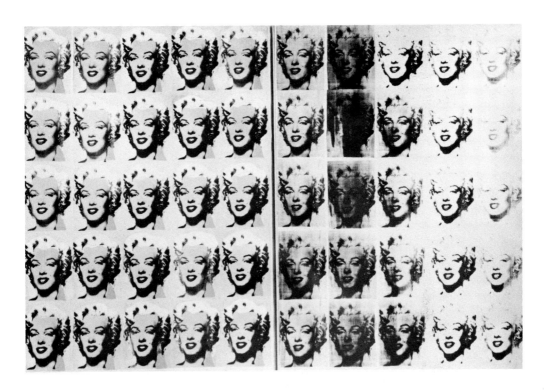

Andy Warhol:
Marilyn Monroe Diptych. 1962. Oil on canvas. 82″ x 114″.
Collection of Mr. and Mrs. Burton Tremaine, Meriden, Connecticut.

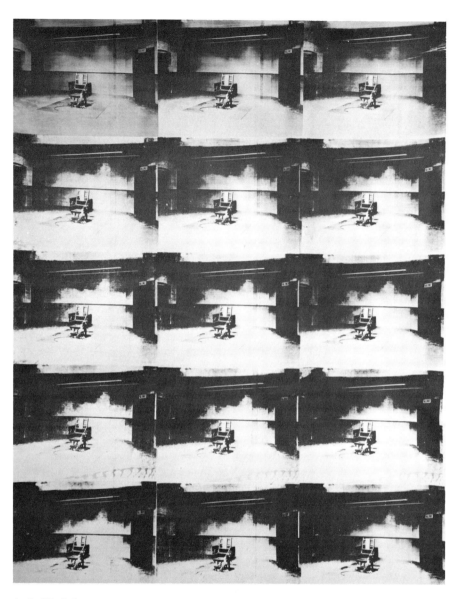

Andy Warhol:
Orange Disaster. 1963. Oil on canvas. 106″ x 82″.
Harry N. Abrams Family Collection, New York.

Andy Warhol:
Brillo Box. 1964. Silkscreen ink on wood. 17″ x 17″ x 17″.
Leo Castelli Gallery, New York.

Contemporary Criticism

The American Action Painters[*]

By Harold Rosenberg

"J'ai fait des gestes blanc parmi les solitudes."
— APOLLINAIRE

"The American will is easily satisfied
in its efforts to realize itself in knowing itself."
— WALLACE STEVENS

What makes any definition of a movement in art dubious is that it never fits the deepest artists in the movement—certainly not as well as, if successful, it does the others. Yet without the definition something essential in those best is bound to be missed. The attempt to define is like a game in which you cannot possibly reach the goal from the starting point but can only close in on it by picking up each time from where the last play landed.

Modern Art? Or an Art of the Modern?

Since the War every twentieth-century style in painting is being brought to profusion in the United States: thousands of "abstract" painters—crowded teaching courses in Modern Art—a scattering of new heroes—ambitions stimulated by new galleries, mass exhibitions, reproductions in popular magazines, festivals, appropriations.

Is this the usual catching up of America with European art forms? Or is something new being created? . . . For the question of novelty, a definition would seem indispensable.

Some people deny that there is anything original in the recent American painting. Whatever is being done here now, they claim, was done thirty years ago in Paris. You can trace this painter's boxes of symbols to Kandinsky, that one's moony shapes to Miró or even back to Cézanne.

Quantitatively, it is true that most of the symphonies in blue and red rectangles, the wandering pelvises and birdbills, the line constructions and plane suspensions, the virginal dissections of flat areas that crowd the art shows are accretions to the "School of Paris" brought into being by the fact that the mode of production of modern masterpieces has now been all too clearly rationalized. There are styles in the present displays that the painter could have acquired by putting a square inch of a Soutine or a Bonnard under a microscope. . . . All this is training based on a new conception of what art is, rather than original work demonstrating what art is about to become.

[*] Reprinted from *Art News*, Vol. 51, No. 5 (September, 1952).

At the center of this wide practicing of the immediate past, however, the work of some painters has separated itself from the rest by a consciousness of a function for painting different from that of the earlier "abstractionists," both the Europeans themselves and the Americans who joined them in the years of the Great Vanguard.

This new painting does not constitute a School. To form a School in modern times not only is a new painting consciousness needed but a consciousness of that consciousness—and even an insistence on certain formulas. A School is the result of the linkage of practice with terminology—different paintings are affected by the same words. In the American vanguard the words, as we shall see, belong not to the art but to the individual artists. What they think in common is represented only by what they do separately.

Getting Inside the Canvas

At a certain moment the canvas began to appear to one American painter after another as an arena in which to act—rather than as a space in which to reproduce, re-design, analyze, or "express" an object, actual or imagined. What was to go on the canvas was not a picture but an event.

The painter no longer approached his easel with an image in his mind; he went up to it with material in his hand to do something to that other piece of material in front of him. The image would be the result of this encounter.

It is pointless to argue that Rembrandt or Michelangelo worked in the same way. You don't get Lucrece with a dagger out of staining a piece of cloth or spontaneously putting forms into motion upon it. She had to exist someplace else before she got on the canvas, and the paint was Rembrandt's means for bringing her here. Now, everything must have been in the tubes, in the painter's muscles, and in the cream-colored sea into which he dives. If Lucrece should come out she will be among us for the first time—a surprise. To the painter, she *must* be a surprise. In this mood there is no point in an act if you already know what it contains.

"B. is not modern," one of the leaders of this mode said to me the other day. "He works from sketches. That makes him Renaissance."

Here the principle, and the difference from the old painting, is made into a formula. A sketch is the preliminary form of an image the *mind* is trying to grasp. To work from sketches arouses the suspicion that the artist still regards the canvas as a place where the mind records its contents—rather than itself the "mind" through which the painter thinks by changing a surface with paint.

If a painting is an action, the sketch is one action, the painting that follows it another. The second cannot be "better" or more complete than the first. There is just as much significance in their difference as in their similarity.

Of course, the painter who spoke had no right to assume that the other had the old mental conception of a sketch. There is no reason why an act cannot be prolonged from a piece of paper to a canvas. Or repeated on another scale and with more control. A sketch can have the function of a skirmish.

Call this painting "abstract" or "Expressionist" or "Abstract-Expressionist," what counts is its special motive for extinguishing the object, which is not the same as in other abstract or Expressionist phases of modern art.

The New American Painting is not "pure art," since the extrusion of the object was not for the sake of the aesthetic. The apples weren't brushed off the table in order to make room for perfect relations of space and color. They had to go so that nothing would get in the way of the act of painting. In this gesturing with materials the aesthetic, too, has been subordinated. Form, color, composition, drawing, are auxiliaries, any one of which—or practically all, as has been attempted, logically, with unpainted canvases—can be dispensed with. What matters always is the revelation contained in the act. It is to be taken for granted that in the final effect, the image, whatever be or be not in it, will be a *tension*.

Dramas of as if

A painting that is an act is inseparable from the biography of the artist. The painting itself is a "moment" in the adulterated mixture of his life—whether "moment" means, in one case, the actual minutes taken up with spotting the canvas or, in another, the entire duration of a lucid drama conducted in sign language. The act-painting is of the same metaphysical substance as the artist's existence. The new painting has broken down every distinction between art and life.

It follows that anything is relevant to it. Anything that has to do with action—psychology, philosophy, history, mythology, hero worship. Anything but art criticism. The painter gets away from Art through his act of painting; the critic can't get away from it. The critic who goes on judging in terms of schools, styles, form, as if the painter were still concerned with producing a certain kind of object (the work of art), instead of living on the canvas, is bound to seem a stranger.

Some painters take advantage of this stranger. Having insisted that their painting is an act, they then claim admiration for the act as art. This turns the act back toward the aesthetic in a petty circle. If the picture is an act, it cannot be justified *as an act of genius* in a field whose whole measuring apparatus has been sent to the devil. Its value must be found apart from art. Otherwise the "act" gets to be "making a painting" at sufficient speed to meet an exhibition date.

Art—relation of the painting to the works of the past, rightness of color, texture, balance, etc.—comes back into painting by way of psychology. As Stevens says of poetry, "it is a process of the personality of the poet." But the psychology is the psychology of creation. Not that of the so-called psychological criticism that wants to "read" a painting for clues to the artist's sexual preferences or debilities. The work, the act, translates the psychologically given into the intentional, into a "world"—and thus transcends it.

With traditional aesthetic references discarded as irrelevant, what gives the canvas its meaning is not psychological data but *role*, the way the artist organizes his emotional and intellectual energy as if he were in a living situation. The interest lies on the kind of act taking place in the four-sided arena, a dramatic interest.

Criticism must begin by recognizing in the painting the assumptions inherent in its mode of creation. Since the painter has become an actor, the spectator has to think in a vocabulary of action: its inception, duration, direction—psychic state, concentration and relaxation of the will, passivity, alert waiting. He must become a connoisseur of the gradations among the automatic, the spontaneous, the evoked.

"It's Not That, It's Not That, It's Not That"

With a few important exceptions, most of the artists of this vanguard found their way to their present work by being cut in two. Their type is not a young painter but a reborn one. The man may be over forty, the painter around seven. The diagonal of a grand crisis separates him from his personal and artistic past.

Many of the painters were "Marxists" (W.P.A. unions, artists' congresses)—they had been trying to paint Society. Others had been trying to paint Art (Cubism, Post-Impressionism)—it amounts to the same thing.

The big moment came when it was decided to paint. . . . Just *To Paint*. The gesture on the canvas was a gesture of liberation, from Value—political, aesthetic, moral.

If the war and the decline of radicalism in America had anything to do with this sudden impatience, there is no evidence of it. About the effects of large issues upon their emotions, Americans tend to be either reticent or unconscious. The French artist thinks of himself as a battleground of history; here one hears only of private Dark Nights. Yet it is strange how many segregated individuals came to a dead stop within the past ten years and abandoned, even physically destroyed, the work they had been doing. A far-off watcher, unable to realize that these events were taking place in silence, might have assumed they were being directed by a single voice.

At its center the movement was away from rather than toward. The Great Works of the Past and the Good Life of the Future became equally nil.

The refusal of Value did not take the form of condemnation or defiance of

344

society, as it did after World War I. It was diffident. The lone artist did not want the world to be different, he wanted his canvas to be a world. Liberation from the object meant liberation from the "nature," society, and art already there. It was a movement to leave behind the self that wished to choose its future and to nullify its promissory notes to the past.

With the American, heir of the pioneer and the immigrant, the foundering of Art and Society was not experienced as a loss. On the contrary, the end of Art marked the beginning of an optimism regarding himself as an artist.

The American vanguard painter took to the white expanse of the canvas as Melville's Ishmael took to the sea.

On the one hand, a desperate recognition of moral and intellectual exhaustion; on the other, the exhilaration of an adventure over depths in which he might find reflected the true image of his identity.

Painting could now be reduced to that equipment which the artist needed for an activity that would be an alternative to both utility and idleness. Guided by visual and somatic memories of paintings he had seen or made—memories which he did his best to keep from intruding into his consciousness—he gesticulated upon the canvas and watched for what each novelty would declare him and his art to be.

Based on the phenomenon of conversion the new movement is, with the majority of the painters, essentially a religious movement. In every case, however, the conversion has been experienced in secular terms. The result has been the creation of private myths.

The tension of the private myth is the content of every painting of this vanguard. The act on the canvas springs from an attempt to resurrect the saving moment in his "story" when the painter first felt himself released from Value—myth of past self-recognition. Or it attempts to initiate a new moment in which the painter will realize his total personality—myth of future self-recognition.

Some formulate their myths verbally and connect individual works with their episodes. With others, usually deeper, the painting itself is the exclusive formulation, it is a Sign.

The revolution against the given, in the self and in the world, which since Hegel has provided European vanguard art with theories of a New Reality, has re-entered America in the form of personal revolts. Art as action rests on the enormous assumption that the artist accepts as real only that which he is in the process of creating. "Except the soul has divested itself of the love of created things . . ." The artist works in a condition of open possibility, risking, to follow Kierkegaard, the anguish of the aesthetic, which accompanies possibility lacking in reality. To maintain the force to refrain from settling anything, he must exercise in himself a constant No.

Apocalypse and Wallpaper

The most comfortable intercourse with the void is mysticism, especially a mysticism that avoids ritualizing itself.

Philosophy is not popular among American painters. For most, thinking consists of the various arguments that TO PAINT is something different from, say, to write or criticize: a mystique of the particular activity. Lacking verbal flexibility, the painters speak of what they are doing in a jargon still involved in the metaphysics of *things*: "My painting is not Art; it's an Is." "It's not a picture of a thing; it's the thing itself." "It doesn't reproduce Nature; it is Nature." "The painter doesn't think; he knows." Etc., etc. "Art is not, not not not not . . ." As against this, a few reply, art today is the same as it always has been.

Language has not accustomed itself to a situation in which the act itself is the "object." Along with the philosophy of TO PAINT appear bits of Vedanta and popular pantheism.

In terms of American tradition, the new painters stand somewhere between Christian Science and Whitman's "gangs of cosmos." That is, between a discipline of vagueness by which one protects oneself from disturbance while keeping one's eyes open for benefits; and the discipline of the Open Road of risk that leads to the farther side of the object and the outer spaces of the consciousness.

What made Whitman's mysticism serious was that he directed his "cosmic 'I'" toward a Pike's-Peak-or-Bust of morality and politics. He wanted the ineffable in *all* behavior—he wanted it *to win the streets*.

The test of any of the new paintings is its seriousness—and the test of its seriousness is the degree to which the act on the canvas is an extension of the artist's total effort to make over his experience.

A good painting in this mode leaves no doubt concerning its reality as an action and its relation to a transforming process in the artist. The canvas has "talked back" to the artist not to quiet him with Sibylline murmurs or to stun him with Dionysian outcries but to provoke him into a dramatic dialogue. Each stroke had to be a decision and was answered by a new question. By its very nature, action painting is painting in the medium of difficulties.

Weak mysticism, the "Christian Science" side of the new movement, tends in the opposite direction, toward *easy* painting—never so many unearned masterpieces! Works of this sort lack the dialectical tension of a genuine act, associated with risk and will. When a tube of paint is squeezed by the Absolute, the result can only be a Success. The painter need keeps himself on hand solely to collect the benefits of an endless series of strokes of luck. His gesture completes itself without arousing either an opposing movement within itself or his own desire to make the act more fully his own. Satisfied with wonders that remain safely inside the canvas, the artist accepts the permanence of the com-

346

monplace and decorates it with his own daily annihilation. The result is an apocalyptic wallpaper.

The cosmic "I" that turns up to paint pictures but shudders and departs the moment there is a knock on the studio door brings to the artist a megalomania that is the opposite of revolutionary. The tremors produced by a few expanses of tone or by the juxtaposition of colors and shapes purposely brought to the verge of bad taste in the manner of Park Avenue shop windows are sufficient cataclysms in many of these happy overthrows of Art. The mystical dissociation of painting as an ineffable event has made it common to mistake for an act the mere sensation of having acted—or of having been acted upon. Since there is nothing to be "communicated," a unique signature comes to seem the equivalent of a new plastic language. In a single stroke the painter exists as a Somebody—at least on a wall. That this Somebody is not he seems beside the point.

Once the difficulties that belong to a real act have been evaded by mysticism, the artist's experience of transformation is at an end. In that case what is left? Or to put it differently: What is a painting that is not an object nor the representation of an object nor the analysis or impression of it nor whatever else a painting has ever been—and that has also ceased to be the emblem of a personal struggle? It is the painter himself changed into a ghost inhabiting The Art World. Here the common phrase, "I have bought an O" (rather than a painting by O) becomes literally true. The man who started to remake himself has made himself into a commodity with a trademark.

Milieu: The Busy No-Audience

We said that the new painting calls for a new kind of criticism, one that would distinguish the specific qualities of each artist's act.

Unhappily for an art whose value depends on the authenticity of its mysteries, the new movement appeared at the same moment that Modern Art *en masse* "arrived" in America: Modern architecture, not only for sophisticated homes, but for corporations, municipalities, synagogues; Modern furniture and crockery in mail-order catalogues; Modern vacuum cleaners, can openers; beer ad "mobiles"—along with reproductions and articles on advanced painting in big-circulation magazines. *Enigmas for everybody.* Art in America today is not only nouveau, it's news.

The new painting came into being fastened to Modern Art and without intellectual allies—in literature everything had found its niche.

From this isolated liaison it has derived certain superstitions comparable to those of a wife with a famous husband. Superiorities, supremacies even, are taken for granted. It is boasted that modern painting in America is not only original but an "advance" in world art (at the same time that one says "to hell with world art").

347

Everyone knows that the label Modern Art no longer has any relation to the words that compose it. To be Modern Art a work need not be either modern or art; it need not even be a work. A three-thousand-year-old mask from the South Pacific qualifies as Modern and a piece of wood found on a beach becomes Art.

When they find this out, some people grow extremely enthusiastic, even, oddly enough, proud of themselves; others become infuriated.

These reactions suggest what Modern Art actually is. It is not a certain kind of art object. It is not even a style. It has nothing to do either with the period when a thing was made or with the intention of the maker. It is something that someone has had the power to designate as psychologically, aesthetically, or ideologically relevant to our epoch. The question of the driftwood is: *Who* found it?

Modern Art in America represents a revolution of taste—and serves to identify power of the caste conducting that revolution. Responses to Modern Art are primarily responses to claims to social leadership. For this reason Modern Art is periodically attacked as snobbish, Red, immoral, etc., by established interests in society, politics, the church. Comedy of a revolution that restricts itself to weapons of taste—and which at the same time addresses itself to the masses: Modern-design fabrics in bargain basements, Modern interiors for office girls living alone, Modern milk bottles.

Modern Art is educational, not with regard to art but with regard to life. You cannot explain Mondrian's painting to people who don't know anything about Vermeer, but you can easily explain the social importance of admiring Mondrian and forgetting about Vermeer.

Through Modern Art the expanding caste of professional enlighteners of the masses—designers, architects, decorators, fashion people, exhibition directors—informs the populace that a supreme Value has emerged in our time, the Value of the NEW, and that there are persons and things that embody that Value. This Value is a completely fluid one. As we have seen, Modern Art does not have to be actually new; it only has to be new to *somebody*—to the last lady who found out about the driftwood—and to win neophytes is the chief interest of the caste.

Since the only thing that counts for Modern Art is that a work shall be *new*, and since the question of its newness is determined not by analysis but by social power and pedagogy, the vanguard painter functions in a milieu utterly indifferent to the content of his work.

Unlike the art of nineteenth-century America, advanced paintings today are not bought by the middle class. Nor are they by the populace. Considering the degree to which it is publicized and feted, vanguard painting is hardly bought at all. It is *used* in its totality as material for educational and profit-

348

making enterprises: color reproductions, design adaptations, human-interest stories. Despite the fact that more people see and hear about works of art than ever before, the vanguard artist has an audience of nobody. An interested individual here and there, but no audience. He creates in an environment not of people but of functions. His paintings are employed not wanted. The public for whose edification he is periodically trotted out accepts the choices made for it as phenomena of The Age of Queer Things.

An action is not a matter of taste.

You don't let taste decide the firing of a pistol or the building of a maze.

As the Marquis de Sade understood, even experiments in sensation, if deliberately repeated, presuppose a morality.

To see in the explosion of shrapnel over No Man's Land only the opening of a flower of flame, Marinetti had to erase the moral premises of the act of destruction—as Molotov did explicitly when he said that Fascism is a matter of taste. Both M's were, of course, speaking the driftwood language of the Modern Art International.

Limited to the aesthetics, the taste bureaucracies of Modern Art cannot grasp the human experience involved in the new action paintings. One work is equivalent to another on the basis of resemblances of surface, and the movement as a whole a modish addition to twentieth-century picture making. Examples in every style are packed side by side in annuals and in the heads of newspaper reviewers like canned meats in a chain store—all standard brands.

To counteract the obtuseness, venality, and aimlessness of the Art World, American vanguard art needs a genuine audience—not just a market. It needs understanding—not just publicity.

In our form of society, audience and understanding for advanced painting have been produced, both here and abroad, first of all by the tiny circle of poets, musicians, theoreticians, men of letters, who have sensed in their own work the presence of the new creative principle.

So far, the silence of American literature on the new painting all but amounts to a scandal.

Harold Rosenberg

The Abstract Sublime*

By Robert Rosenblum

How Some of the Most Heretical Concepts of Modern American Abstract Painting Relate to the Visionary Nature-painting of a Century Ago

"It's like a religious experience!" With such words, a pilgrim I met in Buffalo last winter attempted to describe his unfamiliar sensations before the awesome phenomenon created by seventy-two Clyfford Stills at the Albright Art Gallery. A century and a half ago, the Irish Romantic poet, Thomas Moore, also made a pilgrimage to the Buffalo area, except that his goal was Niagara Falls. His experience, as recorded in a letter to his mother, July 24, 1804, similarly beggared prosaic response:

I felt as if approaching the very residence of the Deity; the tears started into my eyes; and I remained, for moments after we had lost sight of the scene, in that delicious absorption which pious euthusiasm alone can produce. We arrived at the New Ladder and descended to the bottom. Here all its awful sublimities rushed full upon me . . . My whole heart and soul ascended towards the Divinity in a swell of devout admiration, which I never before experienced. Oh! bring the atheist here, and he cannot return an atheist! I pity the man who can coldly sit down to write a description of these ineffable wonders: much more do I pity him who can submit them to the admeasurement of gallons and yards . . . We must have new combinations of language to describe the Fall of Niagara.

Moore's bafflement before a unique spectacle, his need to abandon measurable reason for mystical empathy, are the very ingredients of the mid-twentieth-century spectator's "religious experience" before the work of Still. During the Romantic Movement, Moore's response to Niagara would have been called an experience of the "Sublime," an aesthetic category that suddenly acquires fresh relevance in the face of the most astonishing summits of pictorial heresy attained in America in the last fifteen years.

Originating with Longinus, the Sublime was fervently explored in the later eighteenth and early nineteenth centuries and recurs constantly in the aesthetics of such writers as Burke, Reynolds, Kant, Diderot, and Delacroix. For them and for their contemporaries, the Sublime provided a flexible semantic container for the murky new Romantic experiences of awe, terror, boundlessness, and divinity that began to rupture the decorous confines of earlier aesthetic systems. As imprecise and irrational as the feelings it tried to name, the Sublime could be extended to art as well as to nature. One of its major expressions, in fact, was the painting of sublime landscapes.

* Reprinted from *Art News*, Vol. 59, No. 10 (February, 1961).

A case in point is the dwarfing immensity of Gordale Scar, a natural wonder of Yorkshire and a goal of many Romantic tourists. Re-created on canvas between 1811 and 1815 by the British painter James Ward (1769–1855), *Gordale Scar* [Fig. 1] is meant to stun the spectator into an experience of the Sublime that may well be unparalleled in painting until a work like Clyfford Still's *1957-D* [Fig. 2]. In the words of Edmund Burke, whose *Philosophical Enquiry into the Origin of Our Ideas of the Sublime and the Beautiful* (1757) was the most influential analysis of such feelings, "Greatness of dimension is a powerful cause of the sublime." Indeed, in both the Ward and the Still, the spectator is first awed by the sheer magnitude of the sight before him. (Ward's canvas is 131 by 166 inches; Still's, 113 by 159 inches.) At the same time, his breath is held by the dizzy drop to the pit of an abyss; and then, shuddering like Moore at the bottom of Niagara, he can only look up with what senses are left him and gasp before something akin to divinity.

Lest the dumbfounding size of these paintings prove insufficient to paralyze the spectator's traditional habits of seeing and thinking, both Ward and Still insist on a comparably bewildering structure. In the Ward, the chasms and cascades, whose vertiginous heights transform the ox, deer, and cattle into Lilliputian toys, are spread out into unpredictable patterns of jagged silhouettes. No laws of man or man-made beauty can account for these God-made shapes; their mysterious, dark formations (echoing Burke's belief that obscurity is another cause of the Sublime) lie outside the intelligible boundaries of aesthetic law. In the Still, Ward's limestone cliffs have been translated into an abstract geology, but the effects are substantially the same. We move physically across such a picture like a visitor touring the Grand Canyon or journeying to the center of the earth. Suddenly, a wall of black rock is split by a searing crevice of light, or a stalactite threatens the approach to a precipice. No less than caverns and waterfalls, Still's paintings seem the product of eons of change; and their flaking surfaces, parched like bark or slate, almost promise that this natural process will continue, as unsusceptible to human order as the immeasurable patterns of ocean, sky, earth, or water. And not the least awesome thing about Still's work is the paradox that the more elemental and monolithic its vocabulary becomes, the more complex and mysterious are its effects. As the Romantics discovered, all the sublimity of God can be found in the simplest natural phenomena, whether a blade of grass or an expanse of sky.

In his *Critique of Judgment* (1790), Kant tells us that whereas "the Beautiful in nature is connected with the form of the object, which consists in having boundaries, the Sublime is to be found in a formless object, so far as in it, or by occasion of it, *boundlessness* is represented" (I, Book 2, §23). Indeed, such a breathtaking confrontation with a boundlessness in which we also experience an equally powerful totality is a motif that continually links the painters of

351

1. James Ward: *Gordale Scar.* 1811–15. Oil on canvas. 131″ x 166″.
The Tate Gallery, London.

2. Clyfford Still: *1957-D No. 1.* 1957. Oil on canvas. 113″ x 159″.
The Albright–Knox Art Gallery, Buffalo, New York, Gift of Seymour H. Knox.

the Romantic Sublime with a group of recent American painters who seek out what might be called the "Abstract Sublime." In the context of two sea meditations by two great Romantic painters, Caspar David Friedrich's *Monk by the Sea* of about 1809 [Fig. 3] and Joseph Mallord William Turner's *Evening Star* [Fig. 4], Mark Rothko's *Light, Earth and Blue* of 1954 [Fig. 5] reveals affinities of vision and feeling. Replacing the abrasive, ragged fissures of Ward's and Still's real and abstract gorges with a no less numbing phenomenon of light and void, Rothko, like Friedrich and Turner, places us on the threshold of those shapeless infinities discussed by the aestheticians of the Sublime. The tiny monk in the Friedrich and the fisher in the Turner establish, like the cattle in *Gordale Scar,* a poignant contrast between the infinite vastness of a pantheistic God and the infinite smallness of His creatures. In the abstract language of Rothko, such literal detail—a bridge of empathy between the real spectator and the presentation of a transcendental landscape—is no longer necessary; we ourselves are the monk before the sea, standing silently and contemplatively before these huge and soundless pictures as if we were looking at a sunset or a moonlit night. Like the mystic trinity of sky, water, and earth that, in the Friedrich and Turner, appears to emanate from one unseen source, the floating, horizontal tiers of veiled light in the Rothko seem to conceal a total, remote presence that we can only intuit and never fully grasp. These infinite, glowing voids carry us beyond reason to the Sublime; we can only submit to them in an act of faith and let ourselves be absorbed into their radiant depths.

If the Sublime can be attained by saturating such limitless expanses with a luminous, hushed stillness, it can also be reached inversely by filling this void with a teeming, unleashed power. Turner's art, for one, presents both of these sublime extremes. In his *Snowstorm* of 1842 [Fig. 7], the infinities are dynamic rather than static, and the most extravagant of nature's phenomena are sought out as metaphors for this experience of cosmic energy. Steam, wind, water, snow, and fire spin wildly around the pitiful work of man—the ghost of a boat— in vortical rhythms that suck one into a sublime whirlpool before reason can intervene. And if the immeasurable spaces and incalculable energies of such a Turner evoke the elemental power of creation, other works of the period grapple even more literally with these primordial forces. Turner's contemporary, John Martin (1779–1854), dedicated his erratic life to the pursuit of an art which, in the words of the *Edinburgh Review* (1829), "awakes a sense of awe and sublimity, beneath which the mind seems overpowered." Of the cataclysmic themes that alone satisfied him, *The Creation,* an engraving of 1831 [Fig. 8], is characteristically sublime. With Turner, it aims at nothing short of God's full power, upheaving rock, sky, cloud, sun, moon, stars, and sea in the primal act. With its torrential description of molten paths of energy, it locates us once more on a near-hysterical brink of sublime chaos.

353

Robert Rosenblum

3. Caspar David Friedrich: *Monk by the Sea. ca.* 1809. Oil on canvas. 43″ x 67″.
Berlin, Palace collections.

4. J. M. W. Turner: *The Evening Star.* Oil on canvas. 36¼″ x 48¼″.
The National Gallery, London.

5. Mark Rothko: *Light, Earth and Blue.* 1954. Oil on canvas.
75¾″ x 67″. Collection of Lady D'Avigdor Goldsmid, London.

6. Barnett Newman: *Vir Heroicus Sublimis.* 1950–51. Oil on canvas.
96″ x 114½″. Collection of Ben Heller, New York.

7. J. M. W. Turner: *Snowstorm: Steamboat Off a Harbour's Mouth.* 1842.
Oil on canvas. 35½″ high. The National Gallery, London.

8. John Martin: *The Creation.* 1831. Engraving.

9. Jackson Pollock: *Number 1*. 1948. Oil on canvas. 68" x 104".
The Museum of Modern Art, New York.

That brink is again reached when we stand before a *perpetuum mobile* of Jackson Pollock, whose gyrating labyrinths re-create in the metaphorical language of abstraction the superhuman turbulence depicted more literally in Turner and Martin. In *Number 1, 1948* [Fig. 9], we are as immediately plunged into divine fury as we are drenched in Turner's sea; in neither case can our minds provide systems of navigation. Again, sheer magnitude can help produce the Sublime. Here, the very size of the Pollock—68 by 104 inches—permits no pause before the engulfing; we are almost physically lost in this boundless web of inexhaustible energy. To be sure, Pollock's generally abstract vocabulary allows multiple readings of its mood and imagery, although occasional titles (*Full Fathom Five, Ocean Greyness, The Deep, Greyed Rainbow*) may indicate a more explicit region of nature. But whether achieved by the most blinding of blizzards or the most gentle of winds and rains, Pollock invariably evokes the sublime mysteries of nature's untamable forces. Like the awesome vistas of telescope and microscope, his pictures leave us dazzled before the imponderables of galaxy and atom.

The fourth master of the Abstract Sublime, Barnett Newman, explores a realm of sublimity so perilous that it defies comparison with even the most

357

adventurous Romantic explorations into sublime nature. Yet it is worth noting that in the 1940s Newman, like Still, Rothko, and Pollock, painted pictures with more literal references to an elemental nature; and that more recently, he has spoken of a strong desire to visit the tundra, so that he might have the sensation of being surrounded by four horizons in a total surrender to spatial infinity. In abstract terms, at least, some of his paintings of the 1950s already approached this sublime goal. In its all-embracing width (114½ inches), Newman's *Vir Heroicus Sublimis* [Fig. 6] puts us before a void as terrifying, if exhilarating, as the arctic emptiness of the tundra; and in its passionate reduction of pictorial means to a single hue (warm red) and a single kind of structural division (vertical) for some 144 square feet, it likewise achieves a simplicity as heroic and sublime as the protagonist of its title. Yet again, as with Still, Rothko, and Pollock, such a rudimentary vocabulary creates bafflingly complex results. Thus the single hue is varied by an extremely wide range of light values; and these unexpected mutations occur at intervals that thoroughly elude any rational system. Like the other three masters of the Abstract Sublime, Newman bravely abandons the securities of familiar pictorial geometries in favor of the risks of untested pictorial intuitions; and like them, he produces awesomely simple mysteries that evoke the primeval moment of creation. His very titles (*Onement, The Beginning, Pagan Void, Death of Euclid, Adam, Day One*) attest to this sublime intention. Indeed, a quartet of the largest canvases by Newman, Still, Rothko, and Pollock might well be interpreted as a post-World-War-II myth of Genesis. During the Romantic era, the sublimities of nature gave proof of the divine; today, such supernatural experiences are conveyed through the abstract medium of paint alone. What used to be pantheism has now become a kind of "paint-theism."

Much has been written about how these four masters of the Abstract Sublime have rejected the Cubist tradition and replaced its geometric vocabulary and intellectual structure with a new kind of space created by flattened, spreading expanses of light, color, and plane. Yet it should not be overlooked that this denial of the Cubist tradition is not only determined by formal needs, but also by emotional ones that, in the anxieties of the atomic age, suddenly seem to correspond with a Romantic tradition of the irrational and the awesome as well as with a Romantic vocabulary of boundless energies and limitless spaces. The line from the Romantic Sublime to the Abstract Sublime is broken and devious, for its tradition is more one of erratic, private feeling than submission to objective disciplines. If certain vestiges of sublime landscape painting linger into the later nineteenth century in the popularized panoramic travelogues of Americans like Bierstadt and Church (with whom Dore Ashton has compared Still), the tradition was generally suppressed by the international domination of the French tradition, with its familiar values of reason, intellect, and objectivity. At times, the countervalues of the Northern Romantic tradition have been partially reasserted (with a strong admixture of French pictorial discipline) by such masters as van Gogh, Ryder, Marc, Klee, Feininger, Mondrian; but its most spectacular manifestations—the sublimities of British and German Romantic landscape—have only been resurrected after 1945 in America, where the authority of Parisian painting has been challenged to an unprecedented degree. In its heroic search for a private myth to embody the sublime power of the supernatural, the art of Still, Rothko, Pollock, and Newman should remind us once more that the disturbing heritage of the Romantics has not yet been exhausted.

Robert Rosenblum

After Abstract Expressionism*

By Clement Greenberg

Twenty-odd years ago all the ambitious young painters I knew in New York saw abstract art as the only way out. Rightly or wrongly, they could perceive no other way in which to go in order to say something personal, therefore new, therefore worth saying. Representational art confronted their ambition with too many occupied positions. But it was not so much representation *per se* that cramped them; rather it was illusion, the illusion of the three-dimensional. Schematic representation survived in the art of Matisse and Picasso (as today in Dubuffet's) and in that of Léger, Braque, Klee, and Miró, but nevertheless their art was felt to be virtually abstract. It was from these artists, in fact, along with Mondrian, that the young painters I am speaking of got their most important lessons in abstraction.

In those years serious abstract art seemed inseparable from the canons of Synthetic Cubism, which meant cleanly marked contours, closed and more or less regular shapes, and flat color. It may not have been necessary to observe these canons literally, but it did seem necessary to keep oriented to them. By the end of the 1930s this orientation began to be a constricting one. Despite the growing appreciation of Klee (whose influence freed at least Tobey, Ralph Rosenborg, and even Loren MacIver), and though the early abstract paintings of Kandinsky were beginning to be admired in New York, most of the young artists I have in mind continued to believe that the only way to real style in abstract art lay through trued and faired, silhouetted and flattened forms. Any other way seemed an evasion or, at best, too idiosyncratic for more than one artist to take at a time.

This was pretty much the plight of abstract art in New York up into the early 1940s—and I say "plight" advisedly. Good abstract art was being produced in New York at that time: not only by Stuart Davis, but also by Bolotowsky, Cavallon, Diller, Ferren, Glarner, Balcomb and Gertrude Green, George L. K. Morris, and a few others, all of whom adhered to "closed" Cubism. Some of Gorky's work of that period looks more independent now than it used to, and de Kooning was then doing what I think remain his supreme paintings, unshown though they were. Nevertheless, the sense of how confining closed Cubism had become betrayed itself in the feeling that Stuart Davis had to be surpassed rather than emulated. This was unfair, but in retrospect I can see why it was necessary. As good as he was—and still is—Davis remained a provincial artist, and there was a feeling abroad, however dim, that provincial-

* Originally published in *Art International*, Vol. VI, No. 8 (October, 1962); somewhat revised in 1969.

ism was what had most to be overcome. At the same time it seemed harder than ever to paint one's way out of provincialism, out of tutelage to Paris.

The cramping hold of Synthetic Cubism, as felt in the early 1940s, helps explain why Baziotes' Surrealist-influenced pictures of 1942 came as a breath of fresh air. Daring to hint at illusionist space, they somehow—unlike Matta's paintings of that time—got away with it. They did not strike me, for one, as taking the easy way out—at least not altogether. The real break-out came, however, with Pollock's and Hofmann's first one-man shows in New York, in October 1943 and March 1944 respectively. There I saw abstract pictures that were painterly (*malerisch*) in what impressed me as being for the first time a full-blown way. Kandinsky's abstract paintings of 1910–18 looked almost clean-shaven by comparison, and Klee like a tidy miniaturist: neither had been so loose or open, or extravagant, in his use of mauled paint. The only precedent lay in representational painting, and that neither Pollock nor Hofmann was completely abstract in these first shows of theirs had its significance.

Then it was like a general thaw. In 1943 and 1944 Gorky, too, became much more painterly, under the influence of landscape subjects and the early abstract Kandinsky. Several students and former students of Hofmann began to do abstract pictures under Bonnard's or Rouault's influence. De Kooning, whose abandonment of closed, if not exactly Synthetic, Cubism dates from around 1946, was in another few years accepting the influence of Soutine. In 1947 and 1948 the more conscious passage to Abstract Expressionism of such artists as Tworkov, Guston, Brooks, even of Tomlin in a sense, was a passage, precisely, to loose and painterly handling.

"Painterly" was not the word used, but what was really meant, as I see it, when Robert Coates called the new open abstract art in New York "Abstract Expressionism." Though a reaction against the tightness of Synthetic Cubism, it used the same vocabulary at first. Looser paint-handling, combined with what remained an essentially Cubist sense of design, drawing, layout, was what artists as different as Gorky and Pollock had in common during the mid-1940s. If the term "Abstract Expressionist" means anything verifiable, it means painterliness: loose, rapid handling, or the look of it; masses that blot and fuse instead of shapes that stay distinct; large, conspicuous rhythms; broken color; uneven saturations or densities of paint; exhibited brush, knife, finger, or rag marks—in short, a constellation of physical features like those defined by Wölfflin when he extracted his notion of the *Malerische* from Baroque art. As we can now see, the displacing of the "linear" and quasi-geometrical as the dominant mode in New York (and Parisian) abstract art after 1943 offers another instance of that cyclical alternation of non-painterly, or linear, and painterly which has marked the evolution of Western art since the sixteenth century.

Clement Greenberg

Painterly abstraction has tended to be less flat, or less taut in its flatness, than the "closed" or linear abstraction which preceded it. Above all, it contains many more velleities towards illusion. And I mean here illusion as distinct from representation or illustration; I mean the illusion of three-dimensional space with or without the bodying-forth of three-dimensional entities. The Kandinskys of 1910–18, so like landscapes, had already revealed this, and Abstract Expressionism again revealed, and continued to reveal, it. This should not have been surprising. The painterly in Western art had started out almost four hundred years ago as a means, first and foremost, to a heightened illusion of three-dimensional space; and in the course of painting and time uneven saturations of paint and color, and broken or blurred outlines, had come to evoke a bodily sense of space in depth almost as immediately and automatically as shading did, and more readily than perspective lines could. Three-dimensional space in the abstract and near-abstract painting of the 1920s and 1930s had been a matter mainly of "diagram" and association; in the painterly 1940s and 1950s it became again something closer to *trompe-l'oeil* illusion, atmospheric illusion. Not that it became *deeper*—not at all—but it did become more tangible as it were, more a thing of immediate perception and less a construct of "reading."

In June 1948 *Partisan Review* published a communication from George L. K. Morris in which he took me to task for, among other things, preferring what he called "behind-the-frame" painting. In my rejoinder I said that Mr. Morris had succumbed to the kind of dogmatism which held that in a given period one species of art must be the supreme one. All the same, his dogmatism did not take away from the acuteness of his "behind-the-frame" characterization, especially in its implications, as I only later came to recognize. Hofmann's and Pollock's and Gorky's pictures did stay further behind their frames than Mondrian's or than Picasso's post-1913 pictures did. This in itself said nothing about relative aesthetic value, and Mr. Morris was altogether wrong in inferring that it did. But he had a real point in his insinuation that painterly abstraction was headed backwards in terms of the evolution of style—even if going backwards in the literal sense of these terms was, at the time, almost the only way in which to go forwards in terms of major quality: that is, the only way in which to *maintain* major quality, not necessarily to *improve* on it.

Later, as the 1950s wore on, a good deal in Abstract Expressionist painting began fairly to cry out for a more coherent illusion of three-dimensional space; and to the extent that it did this it cried for representation, since such coherence can, as a rule, be created only through the tangible representation of three-dimensional objects. It was quite logical therefore that when painterly abstraction in New York finally crystallized into a set manner, it did so in a series of outspokenly representational works, namely de Kooning's "Women" pictures of 1952–55. This manner, as returned to abstract art by de Kooning himself and by the countless artists he has influenced, I call "homeless representation." By this I mean a plastic and descriptive painterliness that is applied to abstract ends but continues to suggest representational ones. In itself "homeless representation" is neither good nor bad, and maybe some of the best results of Abstract Expressionism earlier on were got by flirting with representation. Badness becomes endemic to a manner only when the latter hardens into mannerism. This happened with "homeless representation" in the mid-1950s, in de Kooning's and Guston's art, in the post-1953 art of Kline, and in the art of the many imitators of these painters. It is on the basis of actual results that I find fault with "homeless representation," not because of any *parti pris*. It's because what were merely its logical contradictions have turned into artistic ones too.

Something similar has happened with the two main tendencies of the European version of painterly abstraction (which likewise emerged during the war). In Europe too painterly abstraction presses towards the three-dimensional. But if one tendency leans, like our "homeless representation," towards the three-dimensionality of illusion, the other leans towards the literal, actual three-dimensionality of piled-on paint, and for its part could be called "furtive bas-relief." The latter tendency does happen to be more closely involved with representation than the former—even if it is largely schematic representation—because it started with Dubuffet and Fautrier, and came to a head—though not at all to an extreme—in the art of de Staël's last years. (By "schematic" representation I mean representation that depends mostly on linear handling or placing, without bodying forth what is represented through shading or atmospheric effects—i.e. without illusion.) Curiously enough, the other tendency in European painterly abstraction, the one closer to our "homeless representation," got its start from the very abstract works of Hartung and Mathieu, as well as from Wols, all three of whom are linear before they are anything else. (I do not profess to be able to explain the pictorial logic at work here, but I do think that one clue lies in the extent to which "furtive bas-relief," while employing the linear together with the protuberances and indentations of thick paint-matter for representation, is able at the same time to rely for pictorial unity on the kind of coherence provided automatically by literal, bodily, *real* three-dimensionality. There is, on the other hand, the more strictly pictorial kind of coherence that is automatically produced by the illusion of deep space—at least by now. I say "by now" because, after four-hundred-odd years of illusionist pictorial art, the devices of illusion tend to have a built-in unity and coherence.)

In Europe too painterly abstraction has degenerated into an affair largely of mannerisms, whether those of "homeless representation" or those of "furtive bas-relief." There too a vast quantity of bad abstract painting is relieved, within the orbit of the mannerisms, only by felicitous minor art. For our Johns and Diebenkorn, Europe has its Tápies and Sugai to show. This placing may be unfair to Diebenkorn, however, whose case is so exemplary that it is worth pausing over.

Diebenkorn's development has been what one might say that of Abstract Expressionism should have been. Earlier on he was the only *abstract* painter, as far as I know, to do anything substantially independent with de Kooning's touch (and it makes no difference that he did it with some help from Rothko's design). More recently, he has let the logic of that touch carry him back—with Matisse's help—to representational art, and one might say that this consistency of logic is partly responsible for his becoming at least as good a representational as he was an abstract painter. That de Kooning's touch remains as unmistakable as before in Diebenkorn's art does not take away anything from the success of the change. Uneven densities of paint, as produced by smearing, swiping, scrubbing, and scumbling, had in de Kooning's own hands created gradations of light and dark like those of conventional shading; though these were kept from actually modeling back into deep space by the declamatory abruptness with which they were juxtaposed, deep space is nevertheless increasingly suggested in almost everything de Kooning has done lately. By letting this suggestion become a forthright statement, Diebenkorn (along with another Californian, Elmer Bischoff) has in effect found a home for de Kooning's touch where it can fulfill itself more truthfully, and by the same token less pretentiously, than it has been able to so far in de Kooning's own art.

There are other painters, mainly in New York, who have begun to put de Kooning's manner to the uses of outright representational art, but until now their success has been less consistent or less significant. Jasper Johns should not be classed among these, however much he, too, takes from de Kooning, and however representational his art is. His case is another exemplary one; he brings de Kooning's influence to a head so to speak by suspending it vividly between abstraction and representation. The motifs of Johns's paintings and bas-reliefs, as William Rubin pointed out in *Art International* a few years ago, are always two-dimensional to start with, being taken from a repertory of man-made signs and images not too different in kind from that on which Picasso and Braque drew for the stenciled and affixed elements of their 1911–13 Cubism. Unlike them, Johns is interested in the literary irony that results from *representing* flat and artificial configurations which in actuality can be *reproduced;* yet the abiding significance of his art, as distinct from its journalistic one, lies mostly in the area of the formal or plastic. Just as the vivid possibility of deep space in photographs of signs or house-fronts, or in Harnett's and Peto's paintings of pin-up boards, sets off the native flatness of the objects shown, so the painterly paintedness of a Johns picture sets off, and is set off by, the ineluctable flatness of his number, letter, target, flag, and map images.

By means of this "dialectic" the arrival of Abstract Expressionism at representation, homeless and not homeless, is declared and spelled out. The original flatness of the picture surface, with a few outlines stenciled on it, is shown as sufficing to represent all that a picture by Johns really does represent. The covering of paint itself, with its de Kooningesque play of lights and darks, is shown as being completely superfluous to this end. Everything that usually serves representation and illusion is left to serve nothing but itself, that is abstraction; while everything that usually connotes the abstract or the decorative—flatness, bare outlines, all-over or symmetrical design—is put to the service of representation. And the more explicit this contradiction is made, the more effective in every sense the picture tends to be. When the image is too obscured the paint covering is liable to become less pointedly superfluous; conversely, when the image is left too prominent the whole picture is liable to dwindle to a mere image—an image on the order of Johns's sculptures, which, even when their bronze surfaces are left unpainted, amount to nothing more than what they really are: cast reproductions of man-made objects that, as far as three-dimensional art is concerned, could never be anything other than merely reproducible. The effect of a Johns painting is also weakened, often, when it is done in bright instead of neutral colors like black and gray, for the latter, being the shading colors *par excellence,* are just those that become the most exhibitedly and poignantly superfluous when applied to images of flatness.

I do not mean to imply that the effectiveness of Johns's paintings depends on a mere device. There is far more to them than that; otherwise I would not get the kind of effect from his art that I do. But the fact that as much of his art can be explained as has been explained here without the exertion of any particular powers of insight would indicate a certain narrowness. Johns sings the swan song of "homeless representation," and like most swan songs, it carries only a limited distance.

Echoes of Analytical Cubism and of its transition to Synthetic Cubism are not found in Johns alone among Abstract Expressionists, early and late (and Johns remains a kind of Abstract Expressionist even while pointing the way to Pop Art). Far from it. The whole evolution of Abstract Expressionism could, in fact, be described as the *de*volution from a Synthetic to an Analytical kind of abstract Cubism. By 1911 original Analytical Cubism had itself arrived at "homeless representation": a way of depicting objects in planar segments kept parallel to the picture plane that ended up by effacing the objects themselves, leaving only the illusion of the kind of space in which they were possible, along with a weaker illusion of the surfaces—the planar segments—that once clothed

365

them. In the all-over Pollocks and in the de Koonings of the last seven or eight years, analogous planar segments are analogously deployed (smaller in Pollock, larger in de Kooning), with the principal difference from Analytical Cubism lying in the articulation or jointing of the segments, which is no longer governed, as it still was in Braque and Picasso, by a model in nature. Yet, as I've already said more or less, de Kooning's large-ish facet-planes seem to grope for such a model—and off and on actually find it. Nor does the indeterminate space created by Pollock's webs and blotches always function as "abstract" space; it can also function as illusion. Whereas Analytical Cubism had arrived at the brink of outright abstraction by pursuing both art and nature, Abstract Expressionism returned to the verge of nature by pursuing, apparently, art alone. In several of his black and white pictures of 1951 Pollock actually signaled this return; de Kooning, in his "Women," which marked his real transition from Synthetic to Analytical Cubism, did more than signal it.

Meanwhile another kind of return was being made, though not under the auspices of Abstract Expressionism as defined so far. Abstract Expressionism was not, and is not, just painterly abstraction. Like all momentous tendencies in art, it exceeded any verbal or phenomenal definition of itself, making room for a variety of "deviations" and even "contradictions." Analytical Cubism, besides being a case of homeless representation, had embodied a synthesis of painterly and non-painterly. Synthetic Cubism and Mondrian had dissolved this synthesis in favor of the non-painterly, and Abstract Expressionism, as we have just seen, reacted violently in the opposite direction. But just before 1950 something like a new synthesis of painterly and non-painterly began to emerge in New York abstract art, as if to complete its inverted recapitulation of the original evolution of Cubism.

Actually, most of the New York painters first called Abstract Expressionists have not been painterly in a consistent or committed way. This is true even of Hofmann: the best things he has done in recent years—and they are among the best things he has ever done—move towards a personal synthesis in which the painterly is fused with the linear at the same time that Fauvism is married to Cubism. Kline turned painterly only after 1953, to the cost of his quality, as is negatively confirmed by the improvement his art showed whenever he reverted, as he did frequently in the last two years or so of his life, to his former sharp-edged manner. Motherwell has been painterly off and on, and several of his masterpieces of the late 1940s were quite so, but most of his successful pictures still tend towards the non-painterly. Gottlieb too wavers between the painterly and the non-painterly, and has done superb things in both manners.

Yet I feel that Gottlieb's wavering has the effect somehow of making him disloyal to his greatest gift, which is for color. In this respect he might have done well to take a hint from the example of three other New York painters who stand somewhat apart within Abstract Expressionism. I mean Newman, Rothko, and Still, who have renounced painterliness, or at least the kind associated with Abstract Expressionism, for the sake, precisely, of a vision keyed to the primacy of color.

Like so much of painterly art before it, Abstract Expressionism has worked in the end to reduce color's role. Unequal densities of paint become, as I have said, so many differences of light and dark, and these deprive color of both its purity and fullness. And though openness is supposed to be another quintessentially painterly aim, the slapdash application of paint ends by crowding the picture surface into a compact jumble—a jumble that, as we see it in de Kooning and his followers, is another version of academically Cubist compactness. Still, Newman, and Rothko turn away from the painterliness of Abstract Expressionism as though to save the objects of painterliness—color and openness—from painterliness itself. But rather than effecting a synthesis of painterly and non-painterly, their art could be said to transcend the differences between the two. A transcending, not a reconciliation—the latter belonged to Analytical Cubism, as it now belongs to Hofmann. These three painters take their lead from Impressionism as well as Cubism; and the fact that Impressionism was an epitome of painterly handling seems to have given an artist like Newman all the more insight into the whole question of painterly versus non-painterly as it affected abstract art.

Clyfford Still, who is one of the great innovators of Modernist art, is the leader and pioneer of this group with respect to the insistence on color. Setting himself against the immemorial emphasis on light-and-dark contrasts, he asserted color's capacity to act through the contrasts of pure hue more or less independently of value differences. Late Impressionism furnished the precedent here, and as with the later Monet, the suppression of light-and-dark contrasts made for a new kind of openness, a new expansiveness. The picture no longer divided itself into shapes, but rather into zones and areas and fields of color. This was the essential, but it was left to Newman and Rothko to drive this home. If Still's largest paintings, and especially those in which width exceeds height, fail so often to realize the grand openness they promise, it is not only because he will choose a surface too large for what he has to say; it is also because too many of his smaller color areas will fail to function as *areas*, and will remain merely patches—patches whose rustic-Gothic complications of outline interfere with and halt the flow of color-space.

With Newman and Rothko, temperaments that might strike one as natively far more painterly than Still's administer themselves copious antidotes in the form of the rectilinear. The latter is kept ambiguous, however; Rothko fuzzes all his dividing edges; Newman will insert a smudged edge as foil to his ruled

367

ones. Like Still, they both make a show of studiedness, as if to demonstrate their rejection of the mannerisms that have become inseparable by now from rapid brush or knife handling. Newman's occasional blurred edge, and the torn but exact one left by Still's knife, are there as though to advertise both their awareness and their repudiation of the plausible effects of spontaneity (*unconsideredness* would be the better word here perhaps). Still continues to invest in textures, and the tactile irregularities of his surfaces, with their contrasts of matt and shiny, paint coat and priming, contribute to the force of his art. But by eschewing tactility, and detail in drawing, Newman and Rothko reach what I find to be a more positive openness and more pungent effects of color. The rectilinear is "open" by definition as it were: it calls the least attention to drawing and design, gets least in the way of color-space. A thin paint surface likewise gets least in the way of color-space, simply by excluding tactile associations. (Here both Rothko and Newman seem to have taken their lead from Milton Avery, who took his from Matisse.) At the same time color is given more autonomy by being relieved of its localizing and denotative functions. It no longer specifies or *fills in* an area or plane, but speaks for itself by more or less dissolving definiteness of shape and distance. To this end—as Still was the first to show—it has to be warm color, or cool color infused with warmth. It also has to be uniform color, with only the subtlest variations of value if any at all; and it has, furthermore, to be spread over an absolutely, not relatively, large area. Size guarantees the purity as well as the intensity of hue needed to suggest indeterminate space: more blue being simply bluer than less blue. This too is why the picture has to be confined to but a few colors. Here again, Still pointed the way, the vision of the two- or three-color painting (as E. C. Goossen calls it) being his in the first place (whatever help towards it he may have got from the Miró of 1925–30).

It remains, however, that Newman and Rothko stand or fall by color more conspicuously than Still does. The right color in the right place can more readily redeem—at least in seeming—errors of spatial proportioning or configuration in their art. Similarly, the particular color key appears to decide everything in Monet's large "Lily Pad" pictures. But the converse is equally true: the right proportioning of spatial quantities of shapes can overcome the most refractory color or color relations. (It cannot be emphasized enough that art is entirely a matter of relativities and adjustments.)

The ultimate effect achieved in the art of all three of these painters has to be described as one of more than chromatic intensity. It is rather an effect of almost literal openness that embraces and absorbs color in the act of being created by it. Openness—and not only in pictorial art—is the quality that seems most to exhilarate the attuned eye of this time. Facile explanations suggest themselves here which I leave the reader to explore for himself. Let it suffice that I think that the new openness in Newman's Rothko's, and Still's painting shows the way to what I would risk saying is the only direction for high pictorial art in the near future.

That direction is also pointed to by their repudiation of virtuosity in execution or handling. Elsewhere I have written of the kind of self-critical process that I believe provides the infralogic of Modernist art ("Modernist Painting" in *Arts Yearbook 4*, 1961). The aim of the self-criticism, which is entirely empirical and not at all an affair of theory, is to determine the irreducible working essence of art and of the separate arts. Under the testing of this process more and more of the conventions of the art of painting have shown themselves to be dispensable, unessential. It has been established by now, it would seem, that the irreducibility of pictorial art consists in but two constitutive conventions or norms: flatness and the delimitation of flatness. In other words, the observance of merely these two norms is enough to create an object which can be experienced as a picture: thus a stretched or tacked-up canvas already exists as a picture—though not necessarily as a *successful one*. (The paradoxical outcome of this reduction has been not to contract, but actually to expand the possibilities of the pictorial. Much more lends itself now to being experienced pictorially or in meaningful relation to the pictorial: all sorts of large and small visual incidents and items that used to belong wholly to the realm of the aesthetically meaningless.)

As it looks to me, Newman, Rothko, and Still have swung the self-criticism of Modernist painting in a new direction by dint simply of continuing it far enough in its original one. The question now asked in their art is no longer what constitutes art, or the art of painting, as such, but what constitutes *good* art as such. What is the ultimate source of value or quality in art? And the worked-out answer appears to be: not skill, training, or anything else having to do with execution or performance, but conception alone. Culture or taste may be a necessary condition of conception, but the latter is alone decisive. Conception can be called invention, inspiration, or even intuition (which last is what it was called by Croce, who did anticipate theoretically what practice has just now discovered and confirmed for itself). On the other hand, it is true that skill used to be a vessel of inspiration and do some of the work of conception, but that was when the best pictorial art was, by and large, the most naturalistic. Skill, dexterity, is now revealed as no longer capable of generating quality because it has become too generalized, too accessible, and by the same token too patterned.

Inspiration, conception, alone belongs altogether to the individual; everything else can be acquired by anyone now. Inspiration or conception remains the only factor in the creation of a successful work that cannot be copied or imitated. It was left to artists like Mondrian and Newman to make this explicit (and it is really the only thing that Mondrian and Newman have in common). Newman's pictures look easy to copy, and maybe they are. But they are far from easy to conceive or invent, and their quality lies almost entirely in their conception. This should be self-evident, but even if it were not the frustrated efforts of Newman's imitators would reveal it. The onlooker who says his child could paint a Newman may be right, but Newman would have to be there to tell the child *exactly* what to do. The *exact* choices of medium, color, size, shape, and proportion—including the size and shape of the support—are what determine the success of the result, and these choices have to depend solely on inspiration (just as they did for Mondrian, despite much nonsense to the contrary). Like Rothko and Still, Newman happens to be a conventionally skilled artist—need I say it? But if he uses his skill, it is to suppress the evidence of it. And the suppression is part of the triumph of his art; next to it, most other contemporary painting begins to look fussy.

Because of this, the admiration of some of the strongest among the newer or younger American abstract artists goes out to Newman particularly. His rejection of virtuosity (of prestigious handwriting *à la* de Kooning, for instance) confirms them in what they themselves long to renounce, as it also confirms them in what they dare. It confirms painters like Louis and Noland all the more, precisely because they have not been directly influenced by Newman (or, for that matter, by Still or Rothko either). They may pursue a related vision of color and openness, but they do so all the more resolutely because it is not a derived vision. Not only do Louis and Noland *not* make two- or three-color pictures; they have also been more influenced in aim and means by Pollock than by anyone else. This takes nothing away from Newman, Rothko, or Still, and I stress the point only to clear up misconceptions circulated by journalists and curators. The fact that, so far, the direct influence of these three painters has been a crushing one—with Sam Francis being the only younger artist yet able to realize himself under it—may attest to the very power of their art.

The crux of the matter of the aftermath of Abstract Expressionism has, in any case, little to do with influence as such. Where artists divide in the last resort is where safe taste leaves off. This is as true in what begins to look like the aftermath of Abstract Expressionism as it ever was. Those who follow Newman, Rothko, or Still, individually or collectively, have become as safe by now in their taste as they would be following de Kooning, Gorky, or Kline. (I have the impression, anyhow, that some of the painters who have chosen to do the first instead of the second have been motivated more by *mere* frustration than by dissatisfaction or impatience with the going versions of Abstract Expressionism on Tenth Street.)

Nor do those other artists in this country who have gone in for "neo-Dada," or construction-collage, or ironic comments on the banalities of the industrial environment escape the jurisdiction of good safe taste—*they* almost least of all. (Johns is the sole exception.) For all the novel objects they represent or insert in their works, not one of these artists has taken a chance with color or design that the Cubists or the Abstract Expressionists did not take before them. (What happens when a real chance is taken with color can be seen from the shocked distaste that the "pure" painting of Jules Olitski provokes among New York artists.) Nor has any one of them, whether he harpoons stuffed whales to plane surfaces or fills watercloset bowls with diamonds, yet ventured to arrange these things outside the directional lines of the "all-over" Cubist grid. The results in every case have a conventional, Cubist prettiness that hardly entitles them to be discussed under the heading "After Abstract Expressionism." The same applies to those painters whose contribution lies in depicting plucked chickens instead of dead pheasants, or coffee cans and pieces of pastry instead of flowers in vases. Not that I do not find the clear and straightforward academic handling of their pictures refreshing and even intriguing after the turgidities of Abstract Expressionism; yet this effect is only momentary, since novelty, as distinct from originality, has no staying power.

Arshile Gorky, Surrealism, and the New American Painting*

By William Rubin

As critics and historians have brought into focus their views of painting in America during and just after World War II, a consensus has emerged regarding the quality of Arshile Gorky's art. Today no serious critic remains untouched by the beauty of his paintings; and if few would concede him the stature of Jackson Pollock, let alone that of Matisse, none would deny him a place among the masters of twentieth-century painting. However, this unanimity as to the quality of Gorky's art is in marked contrast to the divergence of opinion on the nature of his style and its historical position during the critical decade of the 1940s, or, more specifically, his possible role either as the last Surrealist or as a pioneer of the New American Painting.

The Surrealists themselves treat Gorky as a significant ornament of their movement, and he was, indeed, the last important painter accepted into their circle. His work attracted the attention of André Breton in 1943; two years later, when he exhibited at the Surrealist-oriented Julien Levy Gallery, he was considered a full-fledged member of the Surrealist group. The concluding section of Breton's 1945 edition of *Surrealism and Painting* is devoted to Gorky; he is also the last Surrealist to be dealt with in the quite different histories of Surrealist painting recently published by Patrick Waldberg and Marcel Jean. Painter-critic Robert Motherwell asserts that there is nothing in Gorky's work that cannot be understood within the context of Surrealism.

But there is also a considerable body of opinion that views Gorky as a pioneer of the New American Painting. His inclusion in the exhibition of that title, which The Museum of Modern Art circulated through Europe a few years ago, is symptomatic in this regard, as was the earlier (1950) exhibition of his work at the American Pavilion of the Venice Biennial along with Pollock and de Kooning. In a recent monograph Harold Rosenberg minimizes Gorky's relation to Surrealism and speaks of him as "a typical hero of Abstract Expressionism."

It is the coincidence in Gorky's art of elements usually associated with either Surrealism or recent American abstraction (far fewer of the latter, I believe) that provokes the divergence of opinion, and this dualism itself stems, to a large extent, from Gorky's unique historical position in a decade that saw both the end of Surrealism and the rise of the New American Painting. To view Gorky simply as the last Surrealist is to overlook certain qualities that differentiate his painting from that of all other Surrealists, qualities that are in fact contrary to

*Reprinted from *Art International*, Vol. VII, No. 3 (February, 1963). Portions of this article were delivered as a lecture at The Museum of Modern Art in connection with the Retrospective Exhibition of Gorky's work held there from December 19, 1962, through February 12, 1963.

the theory and practice of Surrealism. Yet to conceive of him primarily as a pioneer of the New American Painting necessitates gerrymandering one's image of his art so as to suppress not only its morphology, but its particular poetic sensibility and psychological disposition as well. Sufficient time has now elapsed for art historians to approach the decade of the forties, and the problem of Gorky's place in it, independently of the *partis pris*, both geographical and personal, which have converted much recent criticism of this period into polemic.

A proper assessment of Gorky's relationship to Surrealism requires that we reconsider certain aspects of that as yet imperfectly understood movement. The interwar period of the 1920s and 1930s, which Surrealism dominated, was clearly, it seems to me, a parenthetical phase of the great continuing revolution in style that had begun with Manet and the Impressionists. This revolution had reached a climax in the years immediately preceding the First World War, by which time the Cubists, Kandinsky, Delaunay, Mondrian, and others were producing non-figurative paintings or their approximations. The euphoria of those adventurous years—so movingly reflected in the tone of Apollinaire's *Cubist Painters*—was abruptly ended by the outbreak of the war.

In contrast to the galvanic speed with which the various "isms" followed one after the other from 1860 to 1914, the period from Sarajevo to Munich saw the rise of only two major avant-garde movements: Dada and Surrealism.[1] To be sure, most of the masters who had matured between 1905 and 1914 remained active, though frequently with less rewarding results, and more than one of the young painters who rallied around André Breton during Surrealism's pioneer years of the mid-twenties shared his view that Matisse was "an old lion, discouraged and discouraging."[2] Ludicrous as this sounds today, we must remember that Breton spoke at a time when the further development of "pure painting"—such as Mondrian, Kandinsky, and Delaunay had wrought from Fauvism and Cubism—no longer seemed possible *or even desirable*. The new art, or anti-art, of the Dada and Surrealist generations differed strikingly in its premises and character from that which had preceded it. For the first time the continuity of the plastic evolution, in which the generations of the first fifty years of Modern Painting were merged, was broken, to be resumed only with the advent of post-World War II abstraction.

The most salient aspect of the consecutive and interrelated movements called Dada and Surrealism, when we contrast them with Impressionism, Fauvism, and Cubism, is that neither of them emerged primarily from the evolution of art; rather, both began as broader revolutions in philosophical, literary, psychological, and political values. If, in other disciplines, Dada and Surrealism

[1] I consider the *Neue Sachlichkeit*, the Abstraction-Creation group, and the various Neoclassic reactions of secondary importance, *as movements*, to the history of painting.

[2] In fairness to Breton we must concede that the early and middle twenties constituted a relatively dry period in the work of such painters as Matisse, Bonnard, Picasso, and Kandinsky.

were truly radical and progressive, their posture led, paradoxically, to an attitude toward painting which—in terms of the history of art—turned out to be radical but reactionary. Though the apparent "new look" of the bulk of Dada and Surrealist art seemed to verify the avant-garde stance of the movements as a whole, this new look (which, like much of the pseudo-Dada of today, was not so new as it looked) not only argued the denial of many premises essential to earlier Modern Art, but, indeed, was only made possible by this denial. Thus, when Tzara called for an art "once again under the domination of man," and when Breton insisted that painting was only a window and all that mattered was "what it looks out upon," both were reacting against the advanced abstraction that had dominated the years of their youth. In the face of the crisis of World War I, such art seemed to them too hermetic, too incapable of direct and specific communication.

Their position, though infinitely more sophisticated, had something in common with that of the recent so-called New Humanist critics, who, in their turn, have reacted against history's next major advance in the direction of "pure painting," the American avant-garde in the late forties and fifties. For painting to be meaningful to Breton, it had to have subject matter in the Old Master sense and hence an iconography. But unlike the New Humanist critics, Breton was able to distinguish between a subject and a motif; Matisse's pot of flowers was as unacceptable to him as Delaunay's colored disks, in fact even more so, since to his mind it added a disturbingly trivial aspect to the picture. Breton had understood advanced abstraction as an assertion of the non-viability of the familiar subject matter of the phenomenological world and concluded that the artist would now have to replace such objective imagery with one drawn from the realm of his own psychology. This could be projected either through illusion (the "hand-painted dream photographs" of Dali and Magritte) or through allusion (the evocation of the artist's inner world by means of ambiguous signs, as in Miró, Arp, and Masson).

The Surrealist movement, which Breton's First Manifesto of 1924 formalized, continued for the next twenty years as the main embodiment of the avant-garde, a phenomenon unparalleled in the history of modern painting. Not that other movements have failed to last that long; some have lasted even longer, Impressionism for example. But in those cases, newer movements or individuals intervened at diminishing intervals to usurp the leadership of the avant-garde. This failed to happen, however, in the case of Surrealism. After 1929—by which time the most crucial work of Ernst, Miró, Masson, Tanguy, Arp, Magritte, and Dali had all been realized—Surrealism suffered a decade of relative dryness and indecision. And when, on the eve of the Second World War, the movement began to be revitalized, it still found itself unchallenged, if only by default, in its position as the avant-garde. The crises attendant upon the war—and particularly the flight of Breton, Ernst, Masson, Dali, Tanguy, Matta, and others to the Americas—seemed to have a quickening effect. Between 1938 and 1942 a number of young painters joined the Surrealist circle, though only two of them, Matta and Lam, were artists of consequence. This late flowering in exile was brought to a conclusion by the celebration of Gorky as a Surrealist in the last year of the war, the end of which was the signal for the hasty repatriation of the Surrealist exiles to France.

The vacuum left by the departure of the Surrealists from America—most were gone by 1947—was quickly filled by a group of American painters, many of whom had had contacts with the Surrealists and had exhibited with them in Peggy Guggenheim's gallery, Art of This Century. The end of the decade saw these artists established as painters of great force and originality, and by then Gorky's art was being looked at in a new context: not in terms of what had gone before, but of what had come after.

In attempting to bring into focus the historical picture of the remarkable transition that characterized the decade of the 1940s, we might start with the year 1947. If we accept Willem de Kooning's generous statement that it was "Jackson Pollock [who] broke the ice," the breakthrough surely dates from the winter of 1946–47, when Pollock first articulated his canvases with "all-over" webs of poured paint. Pollock had painted some beautiful pictures in the early forties, but, unlike his later work, they are not "world historical" in the Hegelian sense; despite their originality, they do not possess his full identity, containing perhaps too much of Picasso, Miró, and Masson, to allow this. De Kooning, Still, Motherwell, and Rothko, among others, also painted fine pictures in the early forties, but again, it was only during the period 1947–50 that they realized their more personal styles and painted what in some cases remain their best pictures.

The major influence on these American painters in the early forties was Picasso, but the most omnipresent and pervasive, though in generalized form, was Surrealism, mostly Miró, secondarily Masson and Matta, and marginally Ernst and Arp (the illusionistic side of Surrealist painting, as exemplified by Dali and Magritte, had no influence at all on these artists). But transcending the works of the Surrealist painters were certain Surrealist ideas relating picture-making to unconscious impulses and fantasies through the methods of automatism; these ideas—never fully realized in Surrealist painting itself—were very much in the air in the early and middle forties. Gorky was by no means the first to come in contact with them; as early as 1940 Motherwell was exploring ideas like these in discussions with Matta, with whom he was then quite friendly, and the former soon brought them to the attention of Pollock. Within a few years such diverse painters as Still, Rothko, Gottlieb, Baziotes, and Newman were working in a manner that might well be termed quasi-Surrealist (what the

375

French call *surrèalisant*). None were members of the Surrealist group (although Motherwell and Baziotes were shown in a major Surrealist exhibition), but the morphology of their work, its Freudianized mythological symbolism, and the flirtation with automatism, all seemed related to Surrealism. These were just the qualities (with the exception of automatism) that tended to be purged by the end of the decade.

The year 1947, which signaled the ripening of the New American Painting, also heralded the definite end of Surrealism. We know that historical movements do not instantly crystallize or dissolve and that periodicity always involves a set of abstractions. Nevertheless, there are significant events that clarify history by summarizing lengthy processes in their own brief moments. If the inception of Pollock's drip style was one such event, another was the International Exhibition of Surrealism held in Paris in 1947. Whereas the earlier and more lively exhibition that had been installed in the Reid Mansion on Fifth Avenue in 1942 had an air of "work in progress," the one in Paris was clearly a postmortem. Only one first-rate painter—Gorky—had been added to the roster in the interim, among a mass of mediocrities, and despite the title of the exhibition—Surrealism in 1947—not one good picture in the show was executed after 1945.[3]

The years 1942 through 1946 embrace the crucial period in which the conclusions of 1947 were being prepared. This, it seems to me, is essential to the understanding of Gorky's historical role; for his career as an independent painter, *and his alone*, spans exactly this critical period, Despite some vagueness and possible misrepresentation in the dates of his paintings through 1942, there is no question that he was working in his personal style by the end of that year, that he was creating masterpieces by the following year, and that he continued to produce them, if somewhat erratically, through 1947, the year before his death by suicide. Gorky's peculiar historical position sustains the impression that his style is hybrid and identifies him as what we may truly call a *transitional* painter. The idea that he is thus a link between the European tradition and present-day American abstraction finds favor with many critics, but Harold Rosenberg rightly cautions that

the "link" idea slips when it is applied to suggest that Gorky is nothing more than a transition to a body of painting more "advanced" and more "authentically American." . . . Those to whom Gorky represents a link to something newer and better should be reminded that in art, as elsewhere, a chain is nothing *but* links, and there is no particular virtue in being the one at the end.

[3] Unwilling to accept the fact that Surrealism has run its course, André Breton continues to stage Surrealist exhibitions, but the new work shown is generally abysmally bad, and when, rarely, it is not— as, for example, the Jasper Johns that figured prominently in the Surrealist International—it has had little to do with Surrealism.

We can sympathize with Rosenberg's reaction to the general tendency to confuse novelty and quality, to attribute to the word "advanced" the implications it would have if we were talking about technological progress. But the word "newer," which Rosenberg paired with the word "better," need not go down the drain with it, for American painting after Gorky is manifestly newer, and it is new in ways that differentiate it collectively from Gorky.

In any case, Rosenberg's image of art history as a chain with "nothing but links," that is, as a series of transitions, is as inadequate a critique of Gorky's position as it is of the general problem of periodicity. For Gorky is a transitional painter in the sense that very few painters in history have been. Cézanne, for example, synthesized much from Impressionism, and in its turn Cubism assimilated a great deal from Cézanne, but this does not make Cézanne a transitional painter. Moreover, the components of Cézanne's mature style do not have the hybrid character of Gorky's, neither does he occupy the peculiar position in history that was Gorky's. But even if we accept Rosenberg's metaphor, it should be pointed out that it is quite a different matter for a painter to be located in the middle of a link than precisely at the point at which it interlocks with the next one.

The nature of Gorky's unique and ambiguous relationship to Surrealism was unalterably conditioned by his earlier apprenticeship to pre-Surrealist European abstraction. This began in the late twenties with some very handsome pictures in the style of Cézanne, whom Gorky, significantly, considered the greatest painter of all time, and continued into the early and middle thirties with paraphrases of Picasso in both his Neoclassic and Synthetic Cubist phases. Subsequent influences—Miró, Masson, and Matta—were all drawn from Surrealism, except for Kandinsky, whose work became important for Gorky in 1943 and 1944.

Two things have consistently struck critics about the Cézannesque and Picassoid pictures: first, the frankness and lack of embarrassment with which Gorky imitated these masters; second, the surprisingly excellent quality of the results, given this fact of imitation. For Gorky, who never had any formal art-school education, the recapitulation of various stages of European painting was not simply a series of identifications, subsequently rejected, which allowed him to discover who he was by discovering who he was not; it was a series of lessons about the possibilities of painting. These possibilities were to remain part of his vocabulary long after the vehicles of their assimilation had disappeared.

Harold Rosenberg has advanced the theory that Gorky's work in the twenties and thirties was premised on *the deliberate rejection of originality.* If this is so, then his rejection of originality at the very time when Dada and Surrealism had consciously made it a goal of avant-garde painting constituted a kind of originality in reverse.

377

William Rubin

From the time of the Impressionists until the First World War neither artists nor critics placed a premium on originality *for its own sake*. Manet had set the tone with the statement that he "presumed neither to overthrow earlier painting nor to make it new," but "merely tried to be himself and not someone else." In the work of those pioneer generations, originality seemed a natural by-product—though by no means an inevitable concomitant—of making communicative, moving paintings. Bonnard, for example, was a painter with great prestige on the eve of World War I, despite the fact that his form of late Impressionism was much less "advanced" than the avant-garde art of the previous decade. The greatness of his painting was in no way diminished by the fact that its premises were hardly revolutionary.

→ It was with the Dada and Surrealist generations of the interwar period (and *not* recently in America, as some believe) that the situation changed. For the first time, originality—which was to become indistinguishable from novelty—was itself a goal. "Before all else," said Picabia, "we wanted to make something new. Something that nobody had ever seen before." Precisely at that moment the quality of avant-garde painting fell off. Genuine aesthetic invention gave way in large measure to an illusory originality in which the novelty depended on an increasing load of extra-plastic, often frankly literary, effects.

A not unrelated notion of originality held sway in America at that time; many painters believed that they could create a new and peculiarly American art by drawing their subjects from the "American Scene." This was not really very different from the run-of-the-mill Dada and Surrealist work being produced abroad, which, insofar as it *illustrated* the political, psychological, and literary ideas in vogue in the twenties and thirties, might well have been called the art of the "European Scene." But while the Europeans of the interwar generations incorporated elements of advanced painting into their description of the European Scene, the "American Scene" painters demonstrated their provincialism by the academic, art-school formulas they continued to employ.

There was, however, during the thirties, a small group of Americans, which included Gorky, de Kooning, Gottlieb, Rothko, and Pollock, who resisted the chauvinism of the painters of the "American Scene" and embraced the essentially international, pre-Surrealist tradition of modern painting. None was more resolute in this position than Gorky; in his commitment to Cézanne and Picasso he was much closer to the fountainhead of modern art than the painters of his own generation in Paris. This is what Meyer Schapiro was alluding to when he said that Gorky "belonged then to the School of Paris more surely than many painters living in France." An inveterate museum-goer, his attachment to the art in museums, rather than to the "scene" outside them (taken literally or figuratively) not only distinguished him from most of his European and American coevals, but *set him apart fundamentally from Surrealism* even when he later accepted much from it and was in turn accepted into its circles.

The first and still fragmentary traces of Surrealist influence in Gorky's art date from the middle and late thirties, when they were assimilated into the Picassoid type of Cubism he was imitating. We see the mark of early Surrealists Miró and Masson in a group of pictures that begin around 1935, such as *Image in Xhorkom* and *Enigmatic Combat.* The general organization of the picture surface here is Cubist; the touch, pigment texture, and contouring are still Picasso's; but the biomorphic forms, particularly in the *Image in Xhorkom,* belong to Surrealism and especially to Miró. These organic forms, which later became a pictorial and design cliché known as "free form," are particularly endowed with a power to evoke the subjective world of psychosexual associations; they are common to almost all Surrealist painting, from illusionists like Dali and Tanguy to more abtract painters like Miró and Masson.

Gorky's assimilation of Surrealist biomorphism into the context of firmly brushed, heavily impastoed Synthetic Cubism had already been anticipated by Picasso in such paintings as the *Girl Before the Mirror.* In this picture, which was shown at Valentine Dudensing's gallery in 1936 (four years after its execution) and which became part of the permanent collection of The Museum of Modern Art in 1938, Gorky had the model for the synthesis he was now to explore. In fact, we can see the specific influence of this painting in Gorky's *Enigmatic Combat,* which probably dates from 1936. As Harold Rosenberg has pointed out, some general aspects of design[4] as well as the title of the picture derive from a series of "Combats" painted by Masson from 1932 to 1935 and exhibited then in New York by Pierre Matisse. But the facture here is nevertheless Picasso's, and the circular "breast" on the lower left and the head on the lower right are quite clearly quotations from the *Girl Before the Mirror,* while the "liver" shape just left of center derives from Picasso's earlier *Artist and Model.* It was as if the dislocations of Masson's "Combats" had helped Gorky to break up the integrity of figuration still obtaining in Picasso's *Girl Before the Mirror,* leaving the elements strewn about the surface.

That it was possible for Gorky to synthesize Miró and Masson into his Cub-

---

[4] The relationship to Masson, particularly in the closing of the composition at the top, is evident only if we view the picture as it is reproduced here, which is upside down in relation to the way it is hung in The Museum of Modern Art exhibition. The Museum of Modern Art followed the practice of the San Francisco Museum, which owns the picture; the monograph by Schwabacher reproduces the picture in the same way. Rosenberg, in his monograph, turns the picture the other way, rightly, I believe. Good arguments can be made for both possibilities. However, Gorky saw the picture in California during his Retrospective there and presumably approved the way it was hung. At my suggestion, The Museum of Modern Art removed the present backing from the picture, uncovering the original labels. These indicate that the picture runs from top to bottom as reproduced here, suggesting that it was turned bottom end up by accident when the new backing was added. In any event, at this stage in his development, Gorky was given to turning his pictures bottom end up while working on them, which may account for the fact that one derives satisfaction from viewing this painting either way.

379

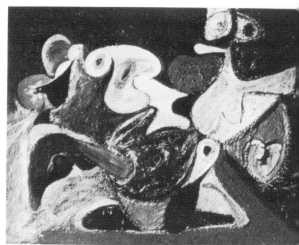

Arshile Gorky: *Image in Xhorkom. ca.* 1936.
Oil on canvas. 32⅞" x 43".
Collection of Maro Gorky and Natasha Gorky.

Arshile Gorky: *Still Life with Skull.*
ca. 1925. Oil on canvas. 33" x 26".
Estate of Arshile Gorky.
Courtesy of M. Knoedler & Co., Inc.,
New York, Paris, London.

Pablo Picasso: *Girl Before the Mirror.*
March, 1932. Oil on canvas. 63¾" x 51¼".
Collection of The Museum of Modern Art,
New York;
Gift of Mrs. Simon Guggenheim.

Arshile Gorky: *Enigmatic Combat. ca.* 1936.
Oil on canvas. 35¾" x 48".
Collection of The San Francisco Museum of Art,
Gift of Jeanne Reynal.

ism, whereas to do the same with Surrealists like Dali and Tanguy would have been unthinkable, makes sense if we recall that Miró and Masson alone among the Surrealists had earlier been convinced Cubists. While their organic forms strayed far from the morphology of Cubism, they rarely sacrificed the taste for shallow (as opposed to deep) space and for disposing the composition comfortably inside the frame, which they had learned during their Cubist apprenticeship.

Gorky's metamorphosis from an imitative painter, albeit an extraordinary one, into an independent painter began around 1940 and extended through 1942. This transformation, which took place under the sign of Surrealism in general and Miró in particular, can be traced in three pictures entitled *Garden in Sochi*. These three, the most important of at least six on the same theme, are something of a puzzle with respect to their specific dating and even to their sequence, and yet, it is only with the resolution of this problem that the history of Gorky's transformation can be clarified. The one quite certain date we have is 1941, that of the largest version, acquired by The Museum of Modern Art before Gorky's death. A smaller, more tightly painted, Miróesque version is dated 1940 by William Seitz in the catalogue-monograph for the museum exhibition; Schwabacher and Rosenberg have dated it between 1938 and 1941. A third version, loosely painted and not quite so small, has been dated "around 1941" in all publications. Since the historical problem involved here resists solution on the basis of the documentation we possess, we are forced to fall back mainly on the internal evidence of style in determining the order and dating; in my opinion, there is sufficient such evidence to warrant a far more specific account of this transitional series than now exists.

The image itself—the iconography, if you will—is common to all three versions. *Garden in Sochi* (Sochi is a Russian Black Sea resort) is the title Gorky gave to a vision actually derived from recollections of his father's farm on the shores of Lake Van in Armenia, where he grew up. In 1941 he recorded the following memories:

My father had a little garden with a few apple trees which had retired from bearing fruit. There was a patch of ground constantly in shade where grew incalculable amounts of wild carrots, and porcupines had made their nests. There was a blue rock half buried in the black earth with a few patches of moss placed here and there like fallen clouds. But from where came all the shadows in constant battle like the lancers in Paolo Uccello's painting? This garden was identified as the Garden of Wish Fulfillment, and I had often seen my mother and other village women opening their bosoms and taking their soft pendent breasts in their hands to rub them on the rock. Above all this stood an enormous tree completely bleached by the sun, the rain, the cold, and deprived of leaves. This was the Holy Tree. I myself don't know why this tree was holy, but I have witnessed many people, whoever passed by, who would voluntarily tear off a strip from their clothing and tie it to the tree.

381

André Masson: *Tormented Woman,*
from the series *Combats et Massacres.*
1933. Oil.

RIGHT, ABOVE. Arshile Gorky: *Garden in Sochi.* Oil
on canvas. 44¼″ x 62¼″. Collection of The Museum of Modern Art, New York, Purchase Fund
and gift of Wolfgang S. Schwabacher. (Painted in
1941 and previously considered Number III in the
series. I propose that it is Number 1.)

RIGHT, CENTER. Arshile Gorky: *Garden in Sochi.*
Oil on canvas. 25″ x 29″. Estate of Arshile Gorky.
Courtesy of M. Knoedler & Co., Inc., New York,
Paris, London. (Previously dated 1938–41 by
Schwabacher and 1940 by Seitz, this picture has
been considered Number 1 of the series. I propose
that it is Number II and was painted in 1941.)

RIGHT, BELOW. Arshile Gorky: *Garden in Sochi.*
Oil on canvas. 31″ x 39¾″. Estate of Arshile
Gorky. Courtesy of M. Knoedler & Co., Inc., New
York, Paris, London. (Previously dated "around
1941" and considered Number II of the series. I
propose that it is Number III and was painted late
in 1943.)

Thus, through many years of the same act, like a veritable parade of banners under the pressure of the wind all these personal inscriptions of signatures, very softly to my innocent ear used to give echo to the sh-h-h-sh-h of silver leaves of the poplars.

It would be idle to try to decipher literally the various *Gardens in Sochi* on the basis of this description, for the process of abstraction and the cross-fertilization of images from different sources produced hybrids that defy such limited readings. However, we can speculate as to whether the large vertical in the top center is not the trunk of the Holy Tree, with strips of tattered cloth waving around it in the breeze and a bird flying past on the right. Ethel Schwabacher, Gorky's friend and biographer, sees the shape of a crouching animal, probably one of Gorky's porcupines, on the lower right and, with more certainty, the blue rock and black earth on the lower left. This textual analysis, however, provides no clue to the image's most prominent form, occupying the center of all three versions, one that has been referred to variously as a boot, a shoe, and a slipper. (William Seitz observes that pointed slippers, birds, and similar paraphernalia can be found in Armenian manuscripts from Gorky's native region of Lake Van.) Whatever its original source, this is among the first of certain persistent shapes, indefinable but charged with evocative power, that illuminate Gorky's fantasy-world and endow his biomorphism with a specifically personal character.[5]

The three versions of *Garden in Sochi* show Gorky disengaging himself from the picture-making attitudes of Picasso's Cubism in favor of conceptions closer to Surrealism. The process involved a substitution of landscape for still life and a transformation of abstraction springing from immediate confrontation of the subject, that is, from visual perception, into a more subjective imagery pervaded with memories and fantasies. The temporal and geographical distance from the subject (his father's garden as against his studio props) permitted the aesthetic to fuse myriad associations from different levels of psychic experience into a hybrid image. The resultant type of ambiguity, a poetic device rendered possible by abstraction, is fundamental to the art of Miró, Arp, and the best of Masson and Matta; it contrasts with the more literal paradoxes of the "double image" exploited by Dali and Matta.

In this triad of *Gardens in Sochi* the Miróesque version is the pivotal picture. Contrary to the impressions given by Gorky's commentators, it is his *only* finished picture that may be called an imitation of Miró in something of the sense that most of his pictures of the twenties and thirties are imitations

[5] The flat and colorful Miróesque version of *Garden in Sochi* makes clearest the way in which all these recollections may have been merged (as in Gorky's description) with associations to the decorative patterns of Paolo Uccello's paintings. Long a favorite of Gorky's, Uccello held a special interest for the Surrealists, he was the only Old Master mentioned by Breton (in the First Manifesto) as a precursor of Surrealism. The Surrealist poet René Crevel wrote the earliest monograph devoted to him.

of Cézanne and Picasso. But even here there is much in the way Gorky scallops his forms for which there is no precedent in Miró, and the meandering contouring, almost oriental in its melismatic fluidity, anticipates the later very personal character of Gorky's line.

That Gorky should have used Miró to propel himself out of Cubism into imaginative, Surrealist biomorphism is logical; he was, in fact, reenacting the same transformation that had taken place in Miró's development during the early twenties. From 1919 (when he first visited Paris) through 1922, Miró had been occupied primarily with still-life and figure paintings realized in his own particularly decorative and schematized brand of Cubism; with *The Tilled Field* of 1923–24 his work moved toward fantasy, taking on interest for Breton and the Surrealists, whose acquaintance he had made shortly before. The overall schema of *The Tilled Field* is still obviously Cubist, as are many of the motifs, from the furrows to the printed newspaper letters. But strange things have happened: For example, a lizard wearing a dunce cap reads a newspaper, while a tree sprouts a giant eye and ear. Miró in Paris, like Gorky in New York, was weaving fantasies about the distant landscape of his youth.

Miró's disavowal of the rational world of Cubism in favor of synthesizing subjective, poetic images had its plastic counterpart in the introduction of curvilinear organic forms. This biomorphism soon triumphed completely in his art, as is demonstrated by his *Dutch Interior* of 1928, a picture that was constantly on view in the permanent collection of The Museum of Modern Art, and was probably a major influence on Gorky's *Garden in Sochi*.

It may be, however, that the unique affinity to Miró in the latter picture was catalyzed by a very particular event: the first Retrospective Exhibition of Miró in New York, held at The Museum of Modern Art in 1941. There Gorky could observe in detail Miró's conversion from Cubism to Surrealism. Among the pictures included were *The Tilled Field*, and one other which I believe may have left a particular impress on the *Garden in Sochi, The Still Life with Old Shoe* of 1937. (Apart from the shoe form—differently located in Gorky, to be sure—this painting also contains a strong vertical device in the top center around which the other forms cluster.) I do not insist on this possibility, though the synthesis of ideas from different Miró pictures is perfectly consistent with Gorky's methodology. But if the Miró Retrospective was a causal factor in the creation of the Miróesque version of *Garden in Sochi*, we would possess a new *terminus ante quem* for the execution of the picture, a date no earlier than 1941. I prefer this new date on internal stylistic evidence alone, and suggest that the painting is roughly contemporaneous with the version in The Museum of Modern Art and probably somewhat later in view of its thinner, less opaque paint film.

Where I really part company with previous Gorky critics is in the sequence

Joan Miró: *The Tilled Field*. 1932–4.
Oil on canvas. 26″ x 37″.
Collection of Mr. and Mrs. Henry Clifford,
Radnor, Pennsylvania.

Joan Miró: *Dutch Interior*. 1928.
36⅛″ x 28¾″.
Collection of The Museum of Modern Art,
New York, Mrs. Simon Guggenheim Fund.

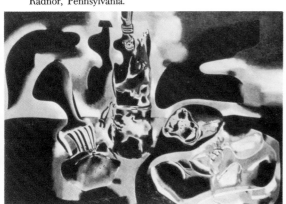

Joan Miró: *Still Life with Old Shoe*. 1937.
Oil on canvas. 32″ x 46″.
Collection of James Thrall Soby,
New Canaan, Connecticut.

Matta: *Psychological Morphology*. 1939.
Oil on canvas. 28″ x 36″.

of the two other versions. As we have seen, one of these, the green-ground version in The Museum of Modern Art collection, is definitely dated 1941. Schwabacher places the other—which I will call the painterly version—"around 1941," a dating concurred in by Seitz, who believes this picture precedes the museum's painting, which he considers the concluding and "most fully synthesized" version of the trio. I cannot accept this order and still make sense out of Gorky's development, for, as I see it, the painterly version (and I use this term in the sense of Wölfflin's *malerisch*) contains most of the elements of Gorky's mature style and is a more personal, if somewhat less imposing, picture than the one in The Museum of Modern Art.[6] While all three pictures contain Gorky's characteristic form language, the museum's version is realized with an opaque surface, a carry-over from his earlier Synthetic Cubist manner, even to the foreign substances—the Cubists had used sand and coffee grounds —mixed into the pigment to give it a raised, slightly abrasive look. Moreover, the Synthetic Cubist flatness is reinforced by the way the green ground is often applied *over* the figure elements, cutting into them and giving them the appearance of "reserve" shapes; this ambiguous overlapping of figure and ground entirely thwarts any tendency to read them three-dimensionally.

In contrast to such early characteristics evident in the museum's picture, the painterly version of *Garden in Sochi* displays some features as yet unseen in Gorky but common to his art *after 1942.* One of these is the suggestion of a shallow, slightly atmospheric space created by patchwork modeling, and the inherent illusionism of a loose, painterly style (much of this is lost in reproduction). Another is the advanced and exquisite draftsmanship. His fluent line, here taut or slightly brittle, there lyrical, is completely independent of the color patches whose contours it had previously delineated; these have retreated back from the line in a manner we see nowhere else in Gorky's art prior to 1943. Finally, the transparency and refinement of the surface, the delicacy of touch as compared with the other two versions, belong to Gorky's maturity.

These facts point inescapably to a later date for this picture: not 1941, but toward the end of 1943 in all probability, though 1946–47 is not impossible. (Gorky's style during the intervening years, 1944–45, rule out ascribing it to that period.) This would place the painting well after *The Pirate I* executed late in 1942, the first and most tentative of the loose, painterly canvases of Gorky's mature years[7] and one for which we have a sure date.[8] There the handling

[6] A small pendant to the series, known as *Garden in Sochi Motif,* is dated April, 1942. It is unthinkable that such an advanced picture as the painterly version of *Garden in Sochi* could antedate this.

[7] Certain pictures loosely dated in the late twenties and thirties, among them *The Artist and His Mother* (Whitney Museum) and a *Self-Portrait,* contain a number of soft painterly passages that adumbrate the touch and texture of Gorky's mature painting. It has been suggested that these passages are overpaintings done late in Gorky's life, but this seems to me unlikely.

[8] "Sure" to the extent that we can accept Gorky's own inscription. Elaine de Kooning has noted that Gorky was not above predating his pictures. *Art News,* V (January, 1951).

is much less assured than in the painterly version of *Garden in Sochi*, the drawing is uncertain, and the bipolarization of line and color-patch is in an incipient state. *Pirate I* and its mate *The Pirate II*, executed early in 1943, are the really exploratory pictures of the end of Gorky's transition, in which, with the help of Kandinsky, he was able to go beyond Picasso and Miró into his own loosely articulated, diaphanous world. What I regard as the last of the *Garden in Sochi* pictures unquestionably presupposes their existence.

It was during the crucial transitional moment in his art defined by the two versions of the *The Pirate* that Gorky turned to nature, not to imitate her but to stimulate inspiration. Some weeks in the Connecticut countryside in the summer of 1942 were followed a year later by a stay at the Virginia farm of his wife's father. The drawings made during these and the following summers served as the bases of paintings executed during the winters between. William Seitz relates how the conjunction of a new and happy marriage, the prospect of a family, and "the return to the bucolic environment he looked back to so nostalgically" seemed to realize the promise of the Garden of Wish Fulfillment.

Taking a worshiper's delight in the sun, Gorky produced some of [his] most original and sophisticated drawings. . . . he drew the life he saw "in the grass." But Gorky, as he once remarked, "never put a face on an image." While he scrutinized the botanical and biological organisms at close range, another vision was directed inward and backward, bringing into focus passages from the works of artists he admired, moments of past emotional experience or points of pain, fear or sexual desire. All these diverse levels and kinds of images joined in his mind the phenomena before him.

What Gorky had in fact done was to re-create the landscape as a theatre in which to project his own psychological drama. In so doing he was following in the footsteps of both Kandinsky and Matta (in this period the latter was one of Gorky's closest friends). Between 1938 and 1942 Matta had made a series of ambiguous biomorphic landscape pictures, which he called *Psychological Morphologies,* or *Inscapes,* whose hybrid forms were intended to dissolve the distinction between the subjective and objective, the mind and the senses, the painter and the world around him. The veiled identification of the human body with the landscape (*The Earth Is a Man* is a significant title) was expressed through ambiguous shapes that were meant to connote both while denoting neither. Though Matta provided the more immediate model for Gorky's "psychological landscapes," the latter surpass Matta's *Inscapes* in their range of feeling and in their poetry, to say nothing of their greater richness as paintings. This is partly due to the fact that Gorky was able to create a personal form of biomorphism that was less literal, less specific in its evocation, and hence more universal than even Miró's.

Arshile Gorky: *The Pirate I.* 1942.
Oil on canvas. 29¼″ x 40⅛″.
Collection of Mr. and Mrs. Julien Levy,
Bridgewater, Connecticut.

Matta: *Landscape.* 1940.
Pencil and crayon drawing.
Courtesy of Robert Elkon Gallery,
New York.

Arshile Gorky: *Landscape.* 1943.
Pencil and crayon drawing.
Collection of Walter Bareiss.

It is in Gorky's pencil and wax crayon drawings of 1943 that Matta's influence is most evident: he provided Gorky with a model of a more disjointed, loosely articulated surface than can be found even in the *Improvisations* of Kandinsky, whose influence was soon to become dominant. In comparing these Gorky drawings with Matta's work in the same media in previous years, we find common to both of them networks of lines that spread tenuously across the surface, completely obviating, through radiating patterns and other shorthand schemata of spatial notation, the flatness to which Gorky had previously subscribed. Here and there, too, in this implicitly deep space both artists summarily model little biomorphic animals or personages.

Kandinsky and Matta also furnished general precedents for the adoption of a painterly style, which emerges in Gorky's work at the end of 1942. However, with the exception of a few of Gorky's pictures from the winter of 1944–45, Matta's influence in this respect is clearly secondary, despite his more immediate presence in Gorky's world as both friend and painter. Matta had worked in a painterly manner from 1938, when he softened up the sculpturesque landscape of Tanguy, to 1944, when his semiautomatic veils, or washes, began to give way to harder, skeletonic forms that prophesied the later cybernetic monsters. To the extent that his style was abstract, his paintings represented a significant break with the flat, linear abstraction of Synthetic Cubist inspiration, which had dominated the thirties, particularly among the American abstract painters who constituted the avant-garde in New York. Matta's paintings pointed the way to a more informal, spontaneous, and lyrical abstraction, in which three-dimensional, illusionist space was again proposed as viable.

But despite the looseness of his painterly fabric—the paint was often applied with rags and allowed to drip or coagulate—an innate commitment to illustration tended to transform Matta's pigment into an illusion of something other than itself. At its most transparent, it suggested vaporous gases, and as it coagulated, it resembled molten rock and crystalline jewels. This was another form of the telluric fairyland of Surrealism, the inspiration of which reaches back through Max Ernst's decalcomania landscapes to the Byzantinism of Gustave Moreau.

Matta, like all Surrealist painters except Miró and Masson, had an inbred disdain for paint. Dali, Magritte, and Tanguy expressed this by the suppression of pigment inherent in their academic manner. Max Ernst and Matta preferred to exacerbate the medium by dripping, blotting, and rubbing it in a way that strained rather than explored its possibilities. Nothing could have been further from Gorky's taste. All his life Gorky nurtured a love for paint as an exquisite substance that had to be courted, cajoled, and tenderly assisted to its fullest blossoming. It is this remarkably refined sensibility to paint quality that invests the mature Gorky with a beauty that led Clement Greenberg to consider him

389

"in many ways . . . a better handler of brush and paint than anyone he was radically influenced by, including Picasso and Miró."

When, during the winter of 1942–43, Gorky went over into his loose, painterly manner, he did not resort to the paraphernalia of deep space as had Matta (though he employed it for some drawings), preferring only hints of modeling and atmospheric effects. His narrow frontal space, ultimately derived from the Cézannesque illusion of bas-relief taken over by Analytic Cubism, did not retreat from the picture plane to deep vanishing points, but was measured by half-modeled forms that seemed to project toward the spectator from a back

Matta: *Les grands transparents.*
1942.
Pencil and wax crayon drawing.
Collection of the artist.

Arshile Gorky: *Drawing.*
Pencil and wax crayon.
18½" x 24½".
Collection of
Mr. and Mrs. Stephen Hahn,
New York.

Wassily Kandinsky: *Sunday.* 1911.
Oil on canvas. 42⅜" x 37⅜".
Collection of Städtische Galerie, München,
Gabriele Münter Foundation.

Arshile Gorky: *Waterfall.*
Estate of Arshile Gorky.
Courtesy of M. Knoedler & Co., Inc.,
New York, Paris, London.

plane, which effectively closed the space. This was similar to the shallow space—also inspired by landscape painting—that we find in the Kandinskys of 1910 to 1914, and partially explains the affinity of such Gorky pictures as *Waterfall* with Kandinskys like *Sunday.*

The synthesis, in an entirely personal form, of the painterly language inspired by Kandinsky, the biomorphism of Miró, and the automatist Surreal "Inscape" of Matta was reached early in 1944 with one of Gorky's most stunning canvases, *The Liver Is the Cock's Comb.* Though confused and overcrowded in spots, and lacking the distilled perfection of later works like *The Diary of a Seducer* and *Agony, The Liver Is the Cock's Comb* contains some remarkable passages and recommends itself by its ambitiousness. The great plumes of color, probably inspired by Kandinskys on the order of *Black Lines* (1913), are potently seductive even though as a group their registration does not finally cohere. The general design, which subsequently was to be a favorite of Gorky's, involves a clustering of the slightly modeled forms above and below an implied horizontal that bisects the surface. These clusters thin out and disappear as

391

Arshile Gorky: *The Liver Is the Cock's Comb.* 1944. Oil on canvas. 72″ x 98″.
Collection of The Albright–Knox Art Gallery, Buffalo, New York, Gift of Seymour H. Knox.

Wassily Kandinsky: *Black Lines, No. 189.*
1913. Oil on canvas. 51¼″ x 51⅜″.
Collection of The
Solomon R. Guggenheim Museum, New York.

Kyle Morris: Untitled. 1959. 48″ x 72″.
Courtesy of The Kootz Gallery, New York.

we move to the top or the bottom of the field, where the ground color, which seems somewhat deeper in space than the plumes, shows through.[9]

The poetry of *The Liver Is the Cock's Comb* is more comprehensive, but also more self-conscious, than that of the *Gardens in Sochi,* and this must certainly be attributed to Gorky's close contacts with the Surrealists. One has only to compare the awkward but straightforward recollections of the Garden of Wish Fulfillment quoted earlier with the pretentious text with which he "describes" *The Liver Is the Cock's Comb:* "The song of a cardinal, liver, mirrors that have not caught reflection, the aggressively heraldic branches, the saliva of the hungry man whose face is painted with white chalk." As with the Surrealists, neither Gorky's title nor his description should be taken literally. One critic, misled by the title, interpreted the picture as "the successfully deceptive dismemberment of a rooster."

Another aspect of Surrealism synthesized in *The Liver Is the Cock's Comb* is the erotic, a concern already quite clear in the drawings of 1943 and one that later formed, as Ethel Schwabacher has observed, the core of his myth. Surrealism was the first movement in art to make sexuality central, a perfectly understandable development in view of its general commitment to Freud. Each painter handled the theme consistently with the character of his art as a whole. In Miró, for example, sex is always playful and whimsical; in Dali it is associated with voyeurism and impotence. But the two artists who gave the erotic the crucial role of catalyst to the imagination are Masson and Matta. Both understood the sexual paroxysm as the moment of the fusion of contraries: the conscious and unconscious, mind and body, the self and the "other";[10] and, hence, the moment of the liberation of the imagination. In Masson, sex has a robust quality that galvanizes the automatism of the methodology and binds all sorts of hybrid themes with its energy; in Matta, on the other hand, it developed in time an exceedingly aggressive and self-conscious character. In *The Liver Is the Cock's Comb* male and female genitalia (center left of the picture) are the only literal forms to emerge from the otherwise ambiguous context of shapes. But the sumptuous affirmation of the sexual in this picture was to give way to a context of nervous tension, suffering, and masochism in *The Diary of a Seducer* and, more notably, *Agony.*

It was during the winter of 1945–46 that Gorky's interest in spontaneousness carried him beyond the *Improvisations* of Kandinsky to the technique of automatism. This essay brought him nearer to Surrealism than he had yet been—or

[9] It is this design idea, combined with forms of a Motherwell-like profile realized in a de Kooning-esque manner, that we see in some paintings by Kyle Morris, one of the few American painters still influenced by Gorky.

[10] In the First Surrealist Manifesto, Breton had identified "Surreality" as an "absolute reality" achieved by the "resolution of the two states—in appearance so contradictory—of the dream and (consciously perceived) reality."

393

was ever to be afterward—and marks precisely the time of his greatest personal closeness to Breton and to Matta. Such pictures as *The Leaf of the Artichoke Is an Owl* and *One Year the Milkweed* were executed with a spontaneity far greater than anything we find in Kandinsky. The rapid drawing, the loose brushwork that encouraged spilling and dripping of the liquid paint, departed from Matta's automatism of 1938–42 and went beyond it. It was only natural that Breton should have encouraged Gorky in this excursion; in the First Surrealist Manifesto he had defined Surrealism primarily in terms of automatism.[11]

[11] *"Surrealism,* n.m. Pure psychic automatism by which one seeks to express, be it verbally, in writing, or in any other manner, the real workings of the mind. Dictated by the unconscious, in the absence of any control exercised by reason, and free from aesthetic or moral preoccupations."

Arshile Gorky:
The Diary of a Seducer. 1945.
Oil on canvas. 50″ x 62″.
Collection of
Mr. and Mrs. William A. M. Burden,
New York.

BELOW. Arshile Gorky:
Study for Agony. 1946–7.
Pencil, wax crayon, and wash.
22″ x 30″. Estate of Arshile Gorky.
Courtesy of M. Knoedler & Co., Inc.,
New York.

BELOW, LEFT. Arshile Gorky:
Agony. 1947.
Oil on canvas. 47″ x 50½″.
Collection of The Museum of Modern Art,
New York, A. Conger Goodyear Fund.

Julien Levy, Gorky's dealer at the time, writes that "automatism was a redemption" for Gorky, an emotional "liberation." Surrealism, he continues, had "made Gorky dig himself deep into his work . . . bring himself to the surface," so that "his most secret doodling could become central."

Pierre Naville used the last phrase of this definition to support his contention that Surrealist art involved a contradiction in terms. The "Naville Crisis" divided Surrealists briefly during the mid-twenties but was resolved by the *de facto* presence of works by Ernst, Miró, and Masson of generally Surrealist nature. Breton converted this into *de jure* recognition with short essays on these and other painters in *Le Revolution surréaliste*, which later appeared together as a book, *Le Surréalisme et la peinture*.

Needless to say, automatism in artmaking was no longer "pure," since to some degree there was a conscious organization of the picture surface.

Arshile Gorky:
The Leaf of the Artichoke Is an Owl.
1944. Oil on canvas. 24″ x 36″.
Collection of Mrs. Ethel K. Schwabacher,
New York.

Arshile Gorky:
One Year the Milkweed. 1944.
Oil on canvas. 37″ x 47″.
Estate of Arshile Gorky.
Courtesy of M. Knoedler & Co., Inc.,
New York.

But there is an essential difference between Gorky's automatism and that of the Surrealists, and it was to this that Breton alluded when he singled out Gorky as the "only Surrealist" who kept "in direct contact with nature, placing himself *before her* to paint." (Not that the pictures in question had been inspired by drawings made from nature.) This fundamental distinction between Surrealist techniques and those of abstract painting is made clear in a memorable exchange that took place in the 1930s between Matisse and Masson (who was then spending a few weeks as Matisse's guest in Grasse). Masson was explaining his manner of working:

"I begin without an image or plan in mind, but just draw or paint rapidly according to my impulses. Gradually, in the marks I make, I see suggestions of figures or objects. I encourage these to emerge, trying to bring out their implications even as I now consciously try to give order to the composition."

"That's curious," Matisse replied, "with me it's just the reverse. I always start with something—a chair, a table—but as the work proceeds, I become less conscious of it. By the end I am hardly aware of the subject with which I started."

Even when it appears most abstract, Surrealist art is thus moving, to use Breton's phrase, *in favor of the subject*. Although automatist Massons, such as the sand painting illustrated here, appear less figurative and hence apparently more abstract than Matisse's pictures (despite the "figure" emerging in the Masson), the image evolves in a manner that tends to clarify a subject and is thus opposite to the abstracting process of Matisse (or Picasso, or Kandinsky). And while the employment of one or another of these contrary approaches neither assures nor precludes quality, it nevertheless leaves a particular imprint on the expressive character of the work.

The methodological divergence revealed in the Matisse-Masson conversation holds, with some modifications, for the difference between Gorky's and Matta's automatism. Matta began by unpremeditatedly spreading washes of color (usually with rags) and then "provoked" the image, which became more particularized, more illustrative, as he proceeded. In contrast, the drawings that constituted Gorky's starting points are more illustrative than the paintings that derive from them. This is perfectly understandable, given the fact that Gorky began his drawings from nature, that is, in direct contact with his motif; as these were transformed into paintings, the elements became less literal, more abstract. Gorky's painterliness does not—like Matta's—harden or dissolve into illusion, but constantly affirms—even when it is most airy—its own material character as pigment resting on the surface of a canvas. In this sense it is related more to European abstract painting (and the extension of that art in the New American Painting) than to Surrealism.

Curiously enough, Breton's observation that Gorky worked from nature did not restrain him from formally identifying Gorky as a Surrealist, even though,

André Masson:
Painting. 1927.
Oil and sand on canvas.

as he noted, this was true of no other Surrealist painter. This inconsistency is sharpened by my recollection of a conversation in which Breton explained that Picasso was never really a Surrealist, notwithstanding his many fantasy pictures and his participation in the activities of the Surrealist group, "because he always started with something he saw, something in nature, whereas the Surrealist always starts with his imagination."

Despite the beauty of a few of these automatist Gorkys, *One Year the Milkweed* in particular, most of them are confused and overcomplicated (*How My Mother's Embroidered Apron Unfolds in My Life,* for example). Others, like *The Unattainable,* contain excessively suave drawing that degenerates into emotionally shallow linear figure skating. By the end of 1945, however, Gorky returned to his more personal style, with a new delicacy and transparency in the backgrounds (not unrelated to Baziotes) for which his automatist wash pictures were very likely responsible. By then he had been an independent painter for three years, though during that time he had still found it necessary to explore the ideas of others. Now he had literally experienced everything, and he was ready to produce his most individual works. One of them, *The Diary of a Seducer,* executed late in 1945, is probably his masterpiece. The most sorrowful aspect of the studio fire of January, 1946, was that the greater number of the twenty-seven pictures destroyed (as well as numerous drawings) came from this most perfect moment of his art.

In 1947, the tragedies that were to lead to Gorky's suicide the following year—the fire, cancer, sexual impotence, a broken neck—were taking their toll, and his work reflects this. Already for a year his biomorphism had been marked

William Rubin

by extremes of pathos and aggression. The new profiles of his shapes suggested emotions that were being exacerbated, literally drawn out almost beyond the point of endurance. In the center right of *Betrothal II* (see detail) is one of these new biomorphic shapes. Its contour is pinched together and drawn upward in a more and more fragile line—like a nerve that is being stretched tight—until, just before it snaps, it is resolved into another plane. The four corners of this plane are in turn tortuously pulled outward so that its sides appear scalloped, a painful distortion that is set off boldly by the more regular rectangular plane on which it is superimposed. Precedent for this type of transmutation of the entire contour of a plane into an independent line may be found in Mirós like *Fratellini* (1926). But there the drawing is relaxed; Miró's line never attains the tautness and ductility of Gorky's.

In the drawings of 1946 and 1947 cruel and monstrous personages, of the type that had entered Matta's art in 1945, manifested themselves through a kind of hard and summary modeling that Gorky had never used before. But, as we observe in comparing the drawing for *Agony* with the finished work, these specters were rendered less descriptive when converted into painting, where the gentle, though deeply poignant, touch dissolved them into the surface design.

With the pictures of 1947 Gorky's contribution to modern painting ends. The few canvases of the last tormented months of his life are understandably overwrought and add nothing.

The year of *Agony* (1947) was, as we have seen, the year when Pollock "broke the ice"; from then until the end of the decade a large number of New York painters were to integrate moving and highly original styles of their own. Nobody, and least of all Gorky in view of his attachment to European art and culture, could have, in 1947, grasped the full extent of the native movement that was emerging. But Gorky had been particularly close to at least one major painter of that movement, Willem de Kooning, and it was through him that a few aspects of Gorky's art found their way into the New American Painting. In his works of the early forties de Kooning had created a highly personal amalgam out of elements of Miró and Picasso, and such pictures as *Pink Angels* (*ca.* 1945), with its distant organic forms laced together by a tangle of angular and mordant lines, show his extraordinary draftsmanship already fully developed. In 1948 his language of forms was temporarily inflected by Gorky's biomorphism. *Painting* of that year (Museum of Modern Art) develops a cluster of such forms slightly in front of the vestiges of a rectilinear ground, like a still life seen against architecture. It is in such black paintings of 1948 and 1949 that Gorky is painted into de Kooning's pictures. But he is painted right out again; and in the process his symbolic forms are reduced to signs and finally to marks.

Gorky had discovered himself by building upon his sources; de Kooning

The Bethrothal II. (detail).

Arshile Gorky: *The Bethrothal II.* 1947.
Oil on canvas. 50¾″ x 38″.
Collection of The Whitney Museum of
American Art, New York.

Joan Miró: *Fratellini.* 1927.
Oil on canvas. 51¾″ x 38″.
Collection of
Mr. and Mrs. Harry Lewis Winston,
Birmingham, Michigan.

Willem de Kooning: *Painting.* 1948.
Collection of The Museum of Modern Art,
New York, Purchase Fund.

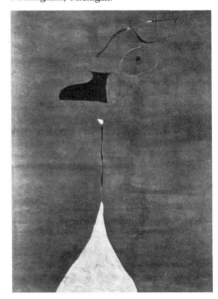

affirmed himself by annihilating them. Even in *Painting*, the Gorkyesque bio-morphism is rendered with an Expressionist roughness and directness that has no antecedent in Gorky or, for that matter, anywhere in the European tradition, including Van Gogh and the 1910–14 Kandinsky. De Kooning smothered Gorky's morphology in a rude painterliness—scumbled, dry-brushed, blotted—which was to become the characteristic manner of most New York Painting for a decade; in pictures like *Night Square* the biomorphism is so flayed and torn open as to be virtually unrecognizable. In making Gorky's morphology his own, de Kooning obliterated it, and with it went the tradition of *peinture-poésie* which variants of that morphology had served from the time of the early Arp reliefs through Miró to Matta and Gorky.

It can be said for Gorky that his was one of the first truly painterly styles to emerge after World War I. And since Abstract Expressionism, "if it means anything, means painterliness," as Clement Greenberg has observed, then Gorky is one of the godfathers of the new abstraction. But Gorky was painterly (i.e., *malerisch*) in the manner of earlier European painting, even as he expanded this manner, while de Kooning was painterly in a new and prophetic way. There was a bludgeoning forthrightness to the passion of the de Kooning manner; Gorky's exquisite anguish always retained that emotional fragility tinged with masochism, which had been the common denominator of the Symbolist-Surrealist tradition.[12]

To the limited extent that Gorky was to influence subsequent American painting, de Kooning was the primary channel. As a matter of fact, the Gorky component in de Kooning's morphology is sometimes more manifest in the work of de Kooning's followers, like Marca-Relli, than it is in his own. In charting the relationship of Gorky's painting to that of the younger generation, the case of Joan Mitchell is perhaps the most illustrative. Her paintings of around 1950 are an amalgam of Kandinsky and Gorky, though larger, blander, and more vigorously executed than the work of either. In the course of the fifties these sources were assimilated into a de Kooningesque manner, within which she soon found her own profile (contrary to the development of the majority of Tenth-Street painters who, in recapitulating a similar progression, remained mere imitators). It was clear that one could operate more freely and more personally in the *manner* of de Kooning than in the *morphology* of Gorky, the adoption of which (like that of the "drip" Pollock) led to an appearance of slavish imitation. The few painters who committed themselves to that morphology, like Seong Moy, whose painting drew momentary critical attention just after 1950, soon found themselves its prisoners. Even today allusions to Gorky are difficult to assimilate. In the work of Hassel Smith, for example, the morphology is Gorky's, while the manner is de Kooning's, and it is the Gorky that is obtrusive.

[12] How many times had supplice been rhymed with delice in such poetry!

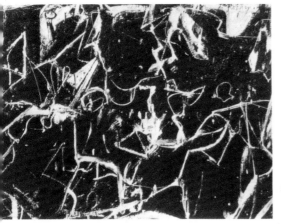

Willem de Kooning: *Night Square*. 1948.
Oil on masonite. 30″ x 40″.
Collection of Mrs. Martha Jackson,
New York.

Conrad Marca-Relli. *Battle Theme*. 1957.
Oil and collage. 52″ x 60″.
Courtesy of The Kootz Gallery, New York.

Joan Mitchell: *Harbour December*. 1956.
Oil on canvas. 80″ x 80″.
Courtesy of The Stable Gallery, New York.

Joan Mitchell: *Abstraction*. 1950. Oil on canvas.
Collection of the Vassar College Art Museum.

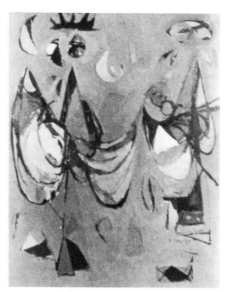

Hassel Smith: *Number 6, 1960.*
Oil on canvas. 68″ x 69½″.
Collection of the Washington University Gallery of Art, St. Louis, Missouri.

Seong Moy: *The King and His Paramour.*
1950. Oil.

The mere fact that Gorky had no immediate followers among younger American painters is no measure of his quality or his historical position, for the same is true of Pollock (contrary to popular misconceptions). The styles of these painters resisted transformation and assimilation, whereas de Kooning's did not. But there the similarity ends, for Pollock's style shared, as Gorky's did not,[13] certain broader characteristics with the styles of such painters as de Kooning, Kline, Rothko, Still, Motherwell, and Newman. None of these characteristics (which include handling of scale, drawing, chiaroscuro and color, touch, and impasto) were common to all these painters, but every one of those generally identified as "the first generation" of the New York School shared some of them with a few others. Clyfford Still, for example, relates to Rothko and Newman as a "color painter," and to de Kooning, Pollock, and Kline in the impastoed character of his surface. As one went from room to room in The Museum of Modern Art's New American Painting exhibition, it was interesting to see how, for all their differences of style, some underlying identity ran through the works of these artists. With the partial exception of Baziotes, only Gorky's paintings seemed out of place, despite their beauty, or perhaps because of their very nature. One felt that if Gorky was indeed a Janus figure facing backward to the European tradition and forward to the New American Painting, then only the eyes that looked back were in focus.

[13] Only with Baziotes can we find any extensive affinities, and his case rather proves the point, for unlike that of the rest of that generation, his style has remained essentially within the character of the middle forties.

Shape as Form: Frank Stella's New Paintings*
By Michael Fried

The craving for simplicity. People would like to say: "What really matters is only the colors." You say this mostly because you wish it to be the case. If your explanation is complicated, it is disagreeable, especially if you don't have strong feelings about the thing itself.   —WITTGENSTEIN

I

Frank Stella's new paintings investigate the viability of shape as such. By *shape as such* I mean not merely the silhouette of the support (which I shall call literal shape), not merely that of the outlines of elements in a given picture (which I shall call depicted shape), but shape as a medium within which choices about both literal and depicted shapes are made, and made mutually responsive. And by the viability of shape, I mean its power to hold, to stamp itself out, and *in*— as verisimilitude and narrative and symbolism used to impress themselves— compelling conviction. Stella's undertaking in these paintings is therapeutic: to restore shape to health, at least temporarily, though of course its implied "sickness" is simply the other face of the unprecedented importance shape has assumed in the finest Modernist painting of the past several years—most notably, in the work of Kenneth Noland and Jules Olitski. It is only in their work that shape as such can be said to have become capable of holding, or stamping itself out, or compelling conviction—as well as, so to speak, capable of failing to do so. These are powers or potentialities—not to say responsibilities—which shape never until now possessed, and which have been conferred upon it by the development of Modernist painting itself. In this sense shape has become something different from what it was in traditional painting or, for that matter, in Modernist painting until recently. It has become, one might say, an object of conviction, whereas before it was merely . . . a kind of object. Stella's new pictures are a response to the recognition that shape itself may be lost to the art of painting as a resource able to compel conviction, precisely because—as never before—it is being called upon to do just that.

The way in which this has come about is, in the fullest sense of the word, dialectical, and I shall not try to do justice to its enormous complexity in these rough notes. An adequate account of the developments leading up to Stella's new paintings would, however, deal with the following:

1. The emergence of a new, exclusively visual mode of illusionism in the work of Pollock, Newman, and Louis. No single issue has been as continuously

* Somewhat revised version of an article first published in *Artforum*, Vol. V, No. 3 (November, 1966).

fundamental to the development of Modernist painting as the need to acknowledge the literal character of the picture-support. Above all, this has tended to mean acknowledging its flatness or two-dimensionality. There is a sense in which a new illusionism was implicit in this development all along. As Clement Greenberg has remarked:

> The flatness toward which Modernist painting orients itself can never be an utter flatness. The heightened sensitivity of the picture plane may no longer permit sculptural illusion, or *trompe-l'oeil*, but it does and must permit optical illusion. The first mark on a surface destroys its virtual flatness, and the configurations of a Mondrian still suggest a kind of illusion of a kind of third dimension. Only now it is a strictly pictorial, strictly optical third dimension.[1]

But the universal power of any mark to suggest something like depth belongs not so much to the art of painting as to the eye itself; it is, one might say, not something that has had to be established so much as something—a perceptual limitation—that cannot be escaped,[2] whereas the dissolution of traditional drawing in Pollock's work, the reliance on large and generally rather warm expanses of barely fluctuating color in Newman's, and the staining of thinned (acrylic) pigment into mostly unsized canvas in Louis' were instrumental in the creation of a depth or space accessible to eyesight alone which, so to speak, specifically belongs to the art of painting.[3]

   2. *The neutralizing of the flatness of the picture-support by the new, exclusively optical illusionism.* In the work of Pollock and Newman, but even more in that of Louis, Noland, and Olitski, the new illusionism both subsumes and dissolves the picture-surface—opening it, as Greenberg has said, from the rear[4]—while simultaneously preserving its integrity. More accurately, it is the *flatness* of the picture-surface, and not that surface itself, that is dissolved, or at least neutralized, by the illusion in question. The literalness of the picture-surface is not denied; but one's experience of that literalness is an experience of the properties of different pigments, of foreign substances applied to the sur-

[1] "Modernist Painting," *The New Art: A Critical Anthology,* ed. Gregory Battcock (New York: E. P. Dutton, 1966), p. 107.

[2] Mondrian, in his paintings of the 1920s and after, often seems to be attempting to combat just this minimal illusionism. Sometimes, for example, he stops his black lines short of the framing-edge, thereby emphasizing their paintedness, i.e., the fact that they are marks on a flat surface. In other paintings he takes the more radical step of *continuing* the black lines and even the blocks of color *past* the edge onto the sides of the canvas (which appears to have been meant to be exhibited with its sides visible). The result is that one tends to see these paintings as solid *slabs,* which helps to counteract—though it cannot efface—their minimal illusionism.

[3] For discussions of these developments see Greenberg's essay "Louis and Noland," *Art International,* IV:5, pp. 26–29, and my *Three American Painters* (Cambridge: Harvard University Press, 1965). The latter also discusses in some detail the emergence of what I have called "deductive structure," a development I adumbrate here.

[4] Greenberg says this of Noland's paintings in his "Louis and Noland," p. 28.

face of the painting, of the weave of the canvas, above all of color—but not, or not in particular, of the flatness of the support. (One could say that here the literalness of the picture-surface is not an aspect of the literalness of the support.) Not that literalness here is experienced as competing in any way with the illusionistic presence of the painting as a whole; on the contrary, one somehow *constitutes* the other. And in fact there is no distinction one can make between attending to the surface of the painting and to the illusion it generates: to be gripped by one is to be held, and moved, by the other.

3. *The discovery shortly before 1960 of a new mode of pictorial structure based on the shape, rather than the flatness, of the support.* With the dissolution or neutralizing of the flatness of the support by the new optical illusionism, the shape of the support—including its proportions and exact dimensions—came to assume a more active, more explicit importance than ever before. The crucial figures in this development are Frank Stella and Kenneth Noland. In Stella's aluminum stripe paintings of 1960, for example, 2½-inch-wide stripes begin at the framing-edge and reiterate the shape of that edge until the entire picture is filled; moreover, by actually shaping each picture—the canvases are rectangles with shallow (one-stripe deep) notches at two corners or along the sides or both—Stella was able to make the fact that the literal shape determines the structure of the entire painting completely perspicuous. That is, in each painting the stripes appear to have been generated by the framing-edge and, starting there, to have taken possession of the rest of the canvas, as though the whole painting self-evidently followed from, not merely the shape of the support, but its actual physical limits. Noland, on the other hand, cannot be said to have come into contact with the physical limits of the support until his first chevron paintings of 1962. His initial breakthrough to major achievement in the late 1950s came when he began to locate the center of concentric or radiating motifs at the exact center of square canvases. This related depicted shape to literal shape through a shared focus of symmetry. Whether or not Noland recognized that *this* was the significance of centering his rings and armatures of color is less important than that he experienced the centering itself as a discovery: a constraint in whose necessity he could believe, and in submission to which his magnificent gifts as a colorist were liberated. His shift to chevron motifs a few years later was, I believe, inspired in part by the need to achieve a more active or explicit relation between depicted and literal shape than the use of concentric rings, none of which actually made contact with the framing-edge, allowed. Within a few months Noland discovered that suspending his chevrons from the upper corners of the support (the bottom edge of the lowest chevron running into each corner) empowered him, first, to prize loose the point of the bottommost chevron from the midpoint of the bottom framing-edge, and second, to pull all the chevrons away from the central axis of the

405

painting—besides enabling him to work with rectangular formats other than the square. In these paintings—the asymmetrical chevrons of 1964—the exact dimensions of the support become important in this sense: that if the edge of the bottommost chevron did not *exactly* intersect the upper corners of the canvas, the relation of *all* the chevrons—that is, of depicted shape—to the shape of the support became acutely problematic and the ability of the painting as a whole to compel conviction was called into question. Since that time, apparently in an attempt to make depicted shape relate more generally to the shape of the support in its entirety, Noland too has shaped his pictures. (His recent work includes a number of narrow diamond-shaped pictures that I will discuss further on.) It cannot be emphasized too strongly, however, that Noland's chief concern throughout his career has been with color—or rather, with feeling *through* color—and not with structure: which makes the role that structural decisions and alterations have played in his development all the more significant. This is not to say that Noland's colorism has had to maintain itself in the teeth of his forced involvement with structural concerns. On the contrary, it is precisely his deep and impassioned commitment to making color yield major painting that has compelled him to discover structures in which the shape of the support is acknowledged lucidly and explicitly enough to compel conviction.

4. *The primacy of literal over depicted shape.* In both Noland's and Stella's (stripe) paintings the burden of acknowledging the shape of the support is borne by the depicted shape, or perhaps more accurately, by the relation between it and the literal shape—a relation that declares the primacy of the latter. And in general the development of Modernist painting during the past six years can be described as having involved the progressive assumption by literal shape of a greater—that is, more active, more explicit—importance than ever before, and the consequent subordination of depicted shape. It is as though depicted shape has become less and less capable of venturing on its own, of pursuing its own ends; as though unless, in a given painting, depicted shape manages to participate in—by helping to establish—the authority of the shape of the support, conviction is aborted and the painting fails. In this sense depicted shape may be said to have become dependent upon literal shape—and indeed unable to make itself felt as shape except by acknowledging that dependence.

II

Let this stand as the general background of concerns from which Stella's new paintings emerge. A fuller delineation of their immediate context is still required, however, if the concentrated and radical exploration of shape which they undertake is meaningfully to be described.

Although Noland has found it necessary to develop structures in which the shape of the support plays a determining role, his continuing ambition to liberate feeling through color has made him reluctant to call attention to the physical limits of the support—the way, for example, Stella's stripe paintings call attention to them. In the latter, Stella identifies the shape of a given picture with its framing-edge, thereby assimilating the first to the second. Noland, on the other hand, is anxious to keep this from happening; or rather, the same concerns that, in effect, compel him to acknowledge the shape of the support also compel him to try to keep our awareness of its physical limits to an absolute minimum. Above all Noland is anxious to keep us from experiencing the shape of his paintings as *edge*, hence as something literal and nonillusive; and in order to make sure this does not happen, he tries to keep us from experiencing the shape at all. It is as though, for Noland, to experience the shape of a painting is inescapably to experience the painting itself as something literal, as a kind of object; and this would compromise its presence as visual illusion. And in general the shapes of his paintings are never experienced as acutely as the limits of and boundaries between the depicted elements within them.

That Noland's paintings avoid calling attention to their physical limits does not mean that those limits are not still there—and there to be felt. What *put* them there to be felt is the acknowledgment of literal shape that the paintings themselves make—and which, as it were, exerts upon the edge a kind of pressure, or inquisition, from which it cannot escape. If Noland's paintings offered some alternative to our experiencing their shapes as an aspect of their literalness —either by positively identifying literal shape with illusion, or by repudiating it altogether—their efficacy as illusion or presence would not be, as I sometimes find them to be, threatened by, or at, the edges. (The suggested alternatives are those explored in Olitski's spray paintings and Stella's new pictures respectively.) This is not to deny that throughout Noland's masterful paintings of the past several years the literal shape of the support is made to seem the *outcome*, or *result*, of the depicted shapes—rather than, as in Stella's stripe paintings, the other way around. But the fact remains that a painting by Noland cannot be said to *hold* as shape—it cannot be said to need to either—but merely to *have* one, like any solid object in the world. Or rather, it is as though the shape were *itself* a kind of object in the world—an object that has been prized loose from the illusionistic presence of the painting by its very importance to the structure of that painting. One is made to feel, that is, that in these paintings the distinction between depicted and literal shape marks a difference, not simply between two kinds of *shape*—each, so to speak, conceived of as a pictorial entity—but between two utterly distinct and different kinds of entities. The first of these, depicted shape, is powerless to make itself felt except by acknowledging the primacy of the other, while that other—literal shape—does not *hold* as shape. It *is* a shape, but what this suddenly seems to mean is only that it is an object in

407

the world—an object whose relevance to our experience of the painting is not clear.

The fact that in some of his recent paintings Noland has not been content simply to minimize the shape of the support, but has instead begun actively to subvert it, suggests that his previous paintings may have come to seem problematic to him for the sorts of reasons I have been discussing. For example, his last show at the Emmerich Gallery included four 8-by-2-foot diamond-shaped paintings in each of which four relatively broad bands of color run parallel to one or the other pair of sides, thereby acknowledging the shape of the support. At the same time, however, the extreme attenuation of these pictures makes them unable to contain within the limits of the support their own extraordinary presences as color and illusion. In the grip of the sheerly visual illusion generated by the interaction of the colored bands, the acute-angled corners of the supports appear to vibrate and shimmer, to erode both from within and without, to become even more attenuated and needle-like than they are, while the obtuse-angled corners tend to round off, to appear dull or blunt. The result is that the physical limits of the supports are overrun, indeed all but dissolved, by the painting's illusionistic presences. At the same time an effect like that of simultaneous contrast between the colored bands makes them appear to overlap one another physically, like shingles. So that, while the physical limits of the support are assaulted by illusion, the (depicted) boundaries between the bands are the more acutely felt—as if absorbing the literalness or objecthood given up by the support. Moreover, because some sort of progressive sequence (e.g., of value) among the bands appears to be required for the illusionistic overlapping I have just described, one's actual experience, or sensation, of these paintings is *directional*. One is aware, that is, of being held and moved by a progression or sequence—a resource until now foreign to Modernist painting—and this further intensifies the assault these paintings make on their own static, literal shapes. In several other paintings in the same show—long horizontal rectangles with a few parallel bands of color, again arranged progressively, running their entire lengths—Noland achieved an equal subversion by somewhat simpler means: the rectangles are too long, and proportionally too narrow, to be experienced as discrete shapes. Instead, confronted head on, they seem to extend almost beyond the limits of our field of vision, to become nothing but extension, to *end up* only being rectangular; approached from the side (their length makes this inviting) what is striking is not their rectangularity but the speed with which that rectangle—or rather, the speed with which the colored bands—appears to diminish in perspective recession.[5] Here, again, although

[5] That Noland's long horizontal paintings make their own shapes ungraspable in this way was observed by Rosalind Krauss in her article "Allusion and Illusion in Donald Judd," *Artforum*, IV:9, p. 26. In the same issue Mrs. Krauss discusses Stella's new paintings, pp. 47–49.

Kenneth Noland: *Up Cadmium*. 1966. Acrylic paint on canvas. 6' x 18'.
Photograph courtesy of André Emmerich Gallery, New York.

the relation of depicted to literal shape within each painting acknowledges in
the simplest possible way the primacy of the latter, the actual limits of the
support do not quite manage to constitute a single, definite shape, while the
boundaries between the colored bands seem almost tactile or *stepped* by comparison.

I have argued elsewhere that the desire to oppose the kind of structure at
work in Noland's and Stella's paintings provided much of the motivation behind
Jules Olitski's first spray paintings of 1965.[6] These pictures are completely devoid of depicted shape, and in fact represent what is almost certainly the most
radical and thoroughgoing attempt in the history of Modernism to make major
art out of nothing but color. At the same time, no paintings have ever depended
so completely or so nakedly for their success on the shape (and in particular
the proportions) of their supports, experienced, one might say, in relation both
to nothing particular within each painting and to everything it contains.[7] It is,
I think, true of these paintings—and of no others—that they succeed as paintings just so far as they succeed, or hold, or stamp themselves out, as shapes.
And in fact no shapes, depicted or literal, have ever stamped themselves out
more compellingly or more feelingly. In the sense in which I have been using
the word, it is not true to say that these paintings *acknowledge* the shape of the
support; but their relative quality depends even more intimately upon it. (In
this respect they differ sharply from Noland's paintings, whose success or failure
as art does not depend on their efficacy as shapes.) So that while they were made
in opposition to a mode of pictorial organization which established the primacy
of literal over depicted shape, in these paintings literal shape's assumption of

[6] In my essay "Jules Olitski's New Paintings," *Artforum*, IV:3, pp. 36–40.

[7] In his brief remarks on Olitski's work, published in the catalogue to the United States pavilion at
the last Biennale, Clement Greenberg wrote, "The degree to which the success of Olitski's paintings
depends on proportion of height to width in their enclosing shapes is, I feel, unprecedented." Greenberg goes on to note the relative superiority of the pictures with tall, narrow formats.

authority has become not merely relative but absolute: as though it alone were capable of performing the office of shape, of being felt as shape.

The very success of Olitski's paintings as shapes lays bare the conditions that make this success possible—conditions it is hard to imagine any paintings but Olitski's being able to fulfill. It is, to begin with, clearly central to their potency as shapes that they are wholly devoid of depicted shape; but it is also clear that two paintings equally devoid of depicted shape may succeed unequally as shapes—and, therewith, as works of art. Moreover, virtually all the best early spray paintings belong to a single format—the narrow vertical rectangle—and the more any painting departs from this format toward the horizontal or square the more likely it is to fail. This is connected with the fact that when the early spray paintings fail—relatively speaking—we tend to see the framing-edge as marking the limits of a spatial *container,* and the sprayed canvas itself as something like *background* in traditional painting. The narrow vertical format somehow keeps this from happening: not by denying the illusion but, so to speak, by making it self-sufficient, a presence, like that of a human figure, instead of a void waiting to be filled. In the best narrow vertical paintings the framing-edge does not appear to contain the illusion; on the contrary, it is the illusion that contains the limits of the support. So that whereas the relatively square paintings can often be seen as receptacles which may happen to be empty but which could be filled, could contain objects, the best of the narrow vertical pictures *already contain* their object, namely, the edges of the painting, its outermost and tactile limits. (In this connection it is significant that, in the paintings in question, all relatively well-defined bursts of color and variations in value are restricted to the vicinity of the edges and corners of the canvas.) One might say that whereas in traditional painting the illusion of a tactile space commences at the inside of the framing-edge, in the best early spray paintings the illusion of something like depth or space accessible to eyesight alone ends at the outside of that edge. And that whereas traditional illusionism begins at the surface of the canvas, the strictly visual mode of illusionism of the Olitskis in question ends there.

In recent paintings, such as those exhibited at the Biennale [of 1966], Olitski has taken to masking out all but thin bands around two or three sides of the sprayed canvas, spraying some more and then removing the masking. The result is a clear difference between the previously masked and unmasked areas, a difference that can be subtle or blatant, and can vary enormously from place to place along the boundary between the bands and the rest of the picture which they partly frame. Further, this internal "frame" is not strictly parallel to the edges of the canvas; sometimes its long vertical component is inflected slightly away from the perpendicular. Both these developments can be understood, at least in part, as undermining or mitigating the absoluteness of the primacy

410

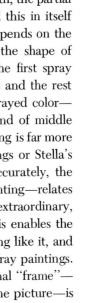

Jules Olitski: *Prinkep*. 1966.
Acrylic paint on canvas. 94″ x 48″.
Photograph courtesy of
André Emmerich Gallery, New York.

which literal shape assumes in his first spray paintings. To begin with, the partial internal "frame" amounts to something like depicted shape; and this in itself means that the quality of individual paintings no longer solely depends on the almost unanalyzable relation between the sprayed canvas and the shape of the support that apparently governs the success or failure of the first spray paintings. But because the boundary between the framing bands and the rest of the painting consists of the same pictorial stuff—the same sprayed color— as the areas it delimits, the role of the internal "frame" as a kind of middle term between the shape of the support and the rest of the painting is far more complex than that played by depicted shape in Noland's paintings or Stella's stripe paintings. To be sure, the internal "frame"—or, more accurately, the boundary between the "framing"-bands and the rest of the painting—relates structurally to the shape of the support. But it also establishes an extraordinary, and indeed unprecedented, continuity *across* that boundary. This enables the paintings in question both to contain depicted shape, or something like it, and yet be seen as pictorially seamless and integral—like the early spray paintings. Moreover, the fact that the long vertical component of the internal "frame"— or the vertical boundary between that "frame" and the rest of the picture—is sometimes inflected away from the perpendicular further reduces the perspicuity of literal shape's primacy at the same time that it acknowledges, or is made possible by, this primacy. That is, in these paintings the primacy of literal shape is such that even a slight departure from verticality within the painting makes itself felt with an intensity of expression I, for one, find astonishing. But it is precisely the strength of this primacy that enables the paintings in question both to tolerate the departure and to move us by it. The very acuteness, even poignancy, of our experience of what is, after all, an extremely slight inflection, acknowledges the strength, and more than that, the *depth*, of the norm from which that inflection departed—in this case, the shape of the support. But the fact remains that what we actually feel, and are inexplicably moved by, is the inflection from the norm rather than the norm itself. All these differences between his early and later spray paintings have enabled Olitski to realize his ambitions across a considerably wider range of formats. And if it is true, as I believe it is, that none of the later spray paintings (none that I have seen at any rate) stamps itself out as shape quite as powerfully as the best of the early ones, part of what these differences have meant is that the quality of a given picture no longer depends entirely on its success or failure as shape.

There is, then, a sense in which the conflict between a sheerly visual or optical mode of illusionism and the literal character of the support is central both to Noland's and Olitski's paintings. In Olitski's pictures—at any rate, the early spray pictures—the conflict is naked and direct. It is, for example, felt in the threat that the illusion will seem almost to come detached from the framing-edge, to leave the literal shape hanging on the wall and situate itself indefinitely further back. This is not to say that when this does *not* happen the illusion is properly described as *attached* to the edge of the support. Rather, the physical limits of the support mark, or declare, or simply *are*, the limits of the illusion itself. We become aware of the conflict in question only when, in relatively less successful paintings, illusion and literal shape actually part company—despite the fact that when this happens, the illusion can no longer be described as sheerly visual, any more than background in traditional painting can be characterized in these terms. In Noland's paintings, on the other hand, opticality and the physical limits of the support are not juxtaposed against one another as in Olitski's paintings. Instead, it is the structure of his paintings—the relation between depicted and literal shape in them—that *brings* the two into conflict with one another. This is what makes the fact that his paintings do not stamp themselves out as shapes feel like a failure or refusal to do so—a failure or refusal that, especially in the light of Olitski's spray paintings, leaves the literalness, or *objecthood*, of the limits of the support there to be felt. I said earlier that Noland himself seems to have become increasingly troubled by this, and in his recent narrow diamond and long horizontal rectangle paintings appears to have tried to subvert their shapes. But it should be remarked that this does not resolve the conflict between opticality and the literal character of the support that, I have claimed, is central to both Noland's and Olitski's work; if anything, it intensifies it.

III

It is only in the presence of this conflict that the question of whether or not a given painting holds or stamps itself out as shape makes full sense—or rather, only here that the issue of "the viability of shape as such" characterizes a specific stage in resolving, or unfolding, problems of acknowledgment, literalness, and illusion which, as I said at the beginning of these notes, have been among the issues of Modernism from its beginning. In Stella's stripe paintings, for example, the reiteration by the stripes of the irregular shapes of the support makes the dependence of depicted on literal shape far more explicit than Noland's paintings ever allow it to seem. But if one asks whether Stella's paintings hold better or make themselves felt more acutely as shapes than Noland's paintings, the answer, I think, is not just that they do not, but that the whole issue of holding or failing to hold is much less relevant to them. That is, because they are not illusive in anything like the way Noland's and Olitski's paintings are, there is nothing for them to hold as shapes *against*.[8]

I must emphasize that in defining this conflict between visual illusionism and literal shape in Noland's and Olitski's paintings I have not meant to imply an adverse criticism either of the quality of their best paintings or of the general level of their respective achievements. This is worth stressing precisely because there are certain younger artists to whose sensibilities all conflict between the literal character of the support and illusion of any kind is intolerable, and for whom, accordingly, the future of art lies in the creation of works that, more than anything else, are *wholly literal*—in this respect *going beyond* painting. It should be evident that what I think of as literalist sensibility is itself a product, or by-product, of the development of Modernist painting itself—more accurately, by the increasingly explicit acknowledgment of the literal character of the support that has been central to that development. But it ought also to be observed that the literalness isolated and hypostatized in the work of artists like Donald Judd and Larry Bell is by no means the *same* literalness as that acknowl-

[8] The aluminum paintings of 1960 are an exception to this. Although not illusionistic, they can, I think, be said to hold as shape—chiefly by virtue of the fact that their supports depart from the rectangular only by a few shallow notches at the corners and sides. As a result the paintings are seen as restrained or held back by these notches by completing the rectangles they all but occupy. This gives the shapes of these paintings something to hold against—i.e., the pressure from within each painting toward the rectangle it almost is—and, in effect, makes the question of whether or nor they make themselves felt as shapes a real one.

413

edged by advanced painting throughout the past century: it is not the literalness *of the support*. Moreover, hypostatization is not acknowledgment. The continuing problem of *how* to acknowledge the literal character of the support—of *what counts* as that acknowledgment—has been at least as crucial to the development of Modernist painting as the fact of its literalness; and this problem has been eliminated, not solved, by the artists in question. Their pieces cannot be said to acknowledge literalness; they simply *are literal*. And it is hard to see how literalness as such, divorced from the conventions which, from Manet to Noland, Olitski and Stella, have *given* literalness value and have *made* it a bearer of conviction, can be experienced as a *source* of both of these—and what is more, one powerful enough to generate new conventions, a new art.[9]

Because Frank Stella's stripe paintings, especially those executed in metallic paint, represent the most unequivocal and conflictless acknowledgment of literal shape in the history of Modernism, they have been crucial to the literalist view I have just adumbrated, both because they are seen as extreme instances of a putative development within Modernist painting—i.e., the increasingly explicit acknowledgment of literalness per se—and because they help to make that development visible, or arguable, in the first place. They are among the last paintings that literalists like Judd are able to endorse more or less without reservation: largely because the ambition to go beyond them—to pursue their apparent implications—was instrumental in the abandonment of painting altogether by these same artists.

In Stella's new paintings, however, the relation between depicted and literal

[9] Judd, almost certainly the foremost ideologist of the literalist position, has claimed—in "Specific Objects," *Arts Yearbook*, No. 8 (1965)—that "a work needs only to be interesting." It is hard to know exactly what this means, because some work, such as Noland's, Olitski's, and Stella's paintings, is *more* than just interesting. It is, I want to say, *good*—more accurately, good *painting*. And in fact—despite the proliferation of work that is neither painting nor sculpture, and despite the pervasiveness of the facile notion that the arts in our time are at last heading toward synthesis—what Modernism has come increasingly to mean is that, more than ever, *value* or *quality* can persuasively be predicated of work that lies only *within*, not *between*, the individual arts. (Though it has also come to mean that that work must challenge, in characteristic ways, what we are prepared to *count* as belonging more than trivially to the art in question.) The circularity of this state of affairs will be repugnant to many, and it is certainly harrowing, but I do not think that it is self-condemning. The crucial question, after all, is not so much whether anything artistically valuable lies outside the circle, as whether a meaningful concept of artistic value or a significant experience of it can reside anywhere but in its coils.

My own impulse is to say that interest is basic to art—but not to either *making* or *judging* it. And if it is objected that what we ought to try to do is enjoy art rather than judge it, I would simply say that that may have been possible once but isn't anymore. This, however, is not to *contrast* enjoyment with judging—it is rather to insist that there is no *real* enjoyment, or no enjoyment of what is *really there*, apart from judging. One can still enjoy Olitski's paintings simply as color, if one wants, but that is not to enjoy them, or be moved by them, or see them as *paintings*. And this means that there is an important sense in which one is not seeing them *at all*. But to experience painting as painting is inescapably to engage with the question of quality. This, too, is the work of Modernism, and if one does not like it one ought to face the fact that what one does not like is painting, or at least what painting has become.

414

shape seems nowhere near as straightforward in its declaration of the latter as in the stripe paintings—or, for that matter, in Noland's work. Rather, there is a new and even somewhat startling freedom both in the variety of shapes used in a given picture and in their disposition relative to one another and to the support. This is not to say that the shape of the support is either ignored or denied. On the contrary, it is very clearly taken into account; but the way in which this is accomplished does not affirm the dependence of depicted on literal shape so much as it establishes an unprecented *continuity* between them. In *Moultonboro III*, for example, the shape of the support is an irregular polygon formed by superimposing a triangle and a square, the first apparently having come slanting down from the upper right to wedge itself deeply into the second. (In *Chocorua III* a triangle is superimposed on a rectangle; the same is true of *Tuftonboro III* except that the rectangle is missing its upper right corner; while in *Conway III* a parallelogram is superimposed on another, this time more horizontal, rectangle. These are the only formats among the eleven Stella has used for his new paintings that have been arrived at by superimposition, pure and simple.[10]) The triangle itself comprises two elements—an eight-inch-wide light yellow band around its perimeter and the smaller triangle, in Day-Glo yellow, bounded by that band—both of which seem to be acknowledging, by repeating, the shape of the support. For that reason it is almost startling to realize that only a relatively small segment of the triangle coincides with, is part of, the shape of the support. Most of the triangle lies wholly inside the picture and, in the terms proposed at the outset, exists only as depicted shape. Even more surprising, however, is the fact that realizing this does not in itself undermine the triangle's efficacy as shape. It is as though that segment which coincides with the literal shape of the painting somehow implies the rest of the triangle—the merely depicted portion of it—strongly enough for the latter to succeed as shape despite its failure to relate self-evidently to any other segment of the framing-edge. But it would, I think, be just as true to one's experience of *Moultonboro III* to claim that what enables the relatively small segment of the triangle that coincides with the shape of the support to make itself felt as shape is what might be called the implicative power, in this context, of the merely depicted portion of the triangle. The yellow triangular band and the Day-Glo triangle within it are, after all, what make that segment intelligible: without them, and without another largely internal shape—the blue Z-form in which the triangular band (and hence the triangle as a whole) rests—the upper-right-hand segment of the support would not be part of a triangle but would belong instead to the literal shape of the painting perceived in its entirety as an

[10] Stella made four paintings in each of the eleven formats. There are, then, eleven subseries within which not only the shape of the support but the configurations on the surface of the canvas are identical.

415

Frank Stella: *Moultonboro III.* 1966.
110″ x 120″.
(The media for all the paintings,
unless otherwise noted,
is fluorescent alkyd and epoxy
paint on canvas.)
Collection of Carter Burden, New York.
Photograph courtesy of
Leo Castelli Gallery, New York.

Frank Stella: *Chocorua III.* 1967.
120″ x 128″.
Collection of Leo Castelli Gallery, New York.

Frank Stella: *Tuftonboro III.* 1966.
100½″ x 109″.
Collection of Leo Castelli Gallery, New York.

Frank Stella: *Conway III.* 1966.
80″ x 122″.
Collection of Leo Castelli Gallery, New York.

416

irregular seven-sided polygon, whereas in the painting as it stands roughly the opposite is the case. The beholder is, in effect, compelled *not* to experience the literal shape in its entirety—as a single entity—but rather to perceive it segment by segment, each of which is felt to belong to one or another of the smaller shapes that constitute the painting as a whole.

This last point is important. For one thing it indicates a crucial difference between Stella's new paintings on the one hand and Noland's and Olitski's pictures, as well as Stella's own previous work, on the other. In this respect Noland's paintings in general are closer to Olitski's spray pictures than to Stella's new work, despite the fact that—unlike Olitski—both he and Stella work with nonrectangular supports and discrete areas of color. It also suggests that, confronted by Stella's new paintings, the distinction between depicted and literal shape becomes nugatory. It is as though in a painting like *Moulton-boro III* there *is* no literal shape and, therefore, no depicted shape either; more accurately, because none of the shapes that we experience in that painting is wholly literal, there is none that we are tempted to call merely depicted. There *are* shapes that lie entirely inside the picture limits—that do not make contact with those limits—just as there are others that partly coincide with the edge of the support. But neither enjoys precedence over the other—in particular, neither sponsors nor guarantees the other's efficacy as shape—any more than either the depicted or the literal limits of a shape that partly coincides with the edge of the support is experienced as more fundamental to that shape's efficacy than the other. Both types of shape succeed or fail on exactly the same grounds—grounds that do not concern the relation of a given shape to the shape of the support seen in its entirety. Each, one might say, is implicated in the other's failure and strengthened by the other's success. But the failure and success of individual shapes cannot be understood in terms of the distinction between depicted and literal shape with which I have been working until now.

The relation between depicted and literal shape that holds in the stripe paintings no longer holds in these, not because the relation has been altered or defied but because the distinction is defeated by the paintings themselves. Nothing, apparently, is more central to their conception than the desire to establish all shapes on an equal footing—to make pictures that comprise nothing but individual shapes, each of which is felt to stand or fall without reference, or appeal, to a single master shape, the support seen as a single entity. In fact, because in most of the new pictures the physical limits of the support are not perceived as constituting a single shape, there is even a sense in which—despite the nonrectangularity of their supports—the pictures in question are *not shaped*: if being shaped implies having an *enclosing* shape, the term is less applicable to Stella's nonrectangular pictures than, for example, to Olitski's rectangular ones. (In this same sense the physical limits of the support can be

417

said not to constitute a *framing* edge.) It should be remarked, however, that Stella could not have made paintings of which this is true except by using irregular supports—that is, by avoiding not only the rectangle but geometrically regular figures of any kind—in order to prevent the eye from instantly perceiving the shape of the support as a single entity. Moreover, the fact that in perhaps the three most successful subseries of the new paintings—the *Union, Effingham,* and *Wolfeboro* pictures—Stella has not used regular geometric shapes at all seems to me to have something to do with their success. In certain other of the new paintings, the eye pounces on a shape of this kind and only then takes in the rest of the painting. When this happens, the rest of the painting is put under enormous pressure by the geometrically regular shape to match its own sheer perspicuousness—which, inevitably, it cannot do. In other words, regularity of shape seems to be enough in itself to disturb the parity among shapes on which the success of Stella's new pictures seems largely to depend. In *Moultonboro III*—as in the *Chocorua* and *Tuftonboro* paintings mentioned earlier—the desire for parity manifests itself in the implied juxtaposition of two equally regular and hence equally perspicuous shapes (i.e., a triangle and a rectangle). But in each painting the two shapes compete for one's attention, almost as though they were juxtaposed to one another within a larger conventional painting—with the result that one tends to pull back, to distance the pictures in question and, as it were, to surround each of them with an imaginary rectangular frame large enough to contain the painting and some space around it besides, whereas in the *Union, Effingham,* and *Wolfeboro* paintings there is no competition for one's attention. None of the elements they comprise is in any way perspicuous, or even particularly interesting in itself; one does not, so to speak, *recognize* any of them—except perhaps the trapezoid at the bottom of *Wolfeboro* (and then, as we shall see, it is an open question what one recognizes it *as*). And far from being inclined to distance or frame these pictures, I for one feel strongly that—more than any pictures I have ever seen—they ought not to be framed at all.

Moreover, the fact that the physical limits of the support do not make themselves felt as a single entity but, in effect, belong segment by segment to individual shapes the remainder of whose limits do not coincide with those of the support implies a strong and, I think, unprecedented continuity between the "outside" of a given painting (its physical limits) and its "inside" (everything else). The eight-inch-wide colored bands deployed throughout the new paintings are a kind of paradigm for this continuity. In general one such band begins by running along at least one side of the support—in *Union III* the same band runs along four or five sides—until, at some point or other, it encounters another shape whose "merely" depicted portion it follows into the heart of the canvas, taking the beholder with it. That is, a particular stretch of the edge

418

Frank Stella: *Effingham III.* 1966.
128″ x 132″.
Collection of Ferus Gallery, Los Angeles.
Photograph courtesy of
Leo Castelli Gallery, New York.

Frank Stella: *Wolfeboro III.* 1966.
160″ x 100″.
Collection of Ferus Gallery, Los Angeles.
Photograph courtesy of
Leo Castelli Gallery, New York.

of the painting is, in effect, first isolated from the rest of that edge—the band,
as it were, broadens and usurps the office of the edge—and is then carried into
the interior of the painting. The result is both that the paintings are infused
with an extraordinary and compelling directionality, and that one is made to
feel that the important difference in them is not between "inside" and "outside" but between *open* and *closed*. The side or sides along which the bands
run are experienced as closed (or closed *off*) while the others are felt as open—
and when, as in *Union III* and *Effingham III*, the open side or sides are at the
top of the painting, the effect can be one of an astonishing vertical acceleration,
or soaring, or release. There is, one might say, no more "outside" or "inside"
to the best of Stella's new paintings than to the individual shapes they comprise; and to the extent that a given shape can be said to have an "outside" and
"inside" the relation between the two is closer to that, say, between the edge
of a tabletop and the rest of that tabletop than to the relation between the
edge of a Noland or an Olitski or even a Stella stripe painting and the rest of
that painting. This is not to say that Stella's new pictures are *nothing more* than
objects. Unlike Judd's constructions, for example, or Bell's glass boxes, they

419

do not isolate and hypostatize literalness as such. At the same time, however, literalness in them is no longer experienced as the exclusive property of the support. Rather, it is suffused more generally and, as it were, more *deeply* throughout them. It is as though literalness in these pictures does not belong to the support *at all* except by coincidence—specifically, the coincidence between the limits of the individual shapes that constitute a given painting and the physical limits of the support; as though, that is, one's experience of literalness is above all an experience of the literalness of the *individual shapes themselves*. Though of course what I have just called their literalness is identical with their success as shapes—and *that*, while not a direct function of the literalness of the support, is at any rate inconceivable apart from that literalness.

The dissociation of literalness from the support that I have just tried to describe is intimately related to another aspect of Stella's new paintings, namely, their extraordinary, and sheerly visual, illusiveness. This is not to say that, in a given picture, each shape seems to lie in a definite or specifiable depth relation to every other. On the contrary, nothing is more fundamental to the nature of the new paintings' illusiveness than the extreme ambiguity, indeterminacy, and multivalence of the relations that appear to obtain among the individual shapes, as well as between those shapes and the surface of the picture (or, at any rate, the *plane* of that surface). In *Moultonboro III*, for example, although one is not made to feel that the light yellow triangular band stands in any single or definite spatial relation to the turquoise blue Z-shaped band into which it fits, one nevertheless experiences their juxtaposition somewhat as though both were objects in the world, not simply or even chiefly shapes on a flat surface— objects, moreover, whose relation to one another, and indeed whose actual character, are ineluctably ambiguous. This is most salient in the case of the Z-shaped turquoise band, largely because—or so it seems—its top and bottom segments are not parallel to one another. (The first, running as it does along the upper edge of the square, is horizontal, while the second, flush with the lowest side of the triangle, slants from the lower left toward the upper right.) That is, one tends to see the bottom segment, or the bottom two segments, as though somewhat from above and in perspective—while at the same time one is not given enough data to locate them in a definite spatial context, in relation either to contiguous shapes or to some ground plane. Moreover, because the top segment of the Z-form runs across the upper edge of the square and is therefore horizontal, one tends to experience that segment as frontal. But this would mean that the Z-form is not only irregular in two dimensions but bent or warped in three—though it is not at all clear which segment or segments are bent or warped and which, if any, are to be taken as normative. The beveled ends of the Z-form, each parallel to nothing else in the painting, compound the ambiguity by implying that the respective planes of both the bottom and top

420

segments are warped away from, or are oblique to, that of the picture-surface—though, of course, they might *not* be. (Almost all the bands in Stella's new paintings are beveled in this way—a factor that adds immeasurably to the illusionistic power, and general complexity, of the paintings in question. In fact its absence from *Conway III* is partly responsible for the relatively flat and conventional appearance of that picture.) The result is that the Z-form is seen as participating in a wide range of equally ambiguous and indeterminate spatial situations—more accurately, an entire gamut of such situations each of which is simultaneously not merely compatible with but continuous with or transparent to every other. But it is not just the situations in which the Z-form finds itself or the relationships into which it enters that continually escape one but—more than anything else—its "real" shape. (Similarly, when one "recognizes" the shape at the bottom of *Wolfeboro III*, does one recognize it as a trapezoid—its configuration on the surface of the canvas—or as a rectangle seen in perspective?) It is as though across the entire gamut of illusionistic possibilities the "real" Z-form—flat or warped, regular or irregular, partly or wholly parallel or oblique to the picture-surface—lies somewhere out there, beyond the painting, waiting to be known. There is, of course, a "real" Z-form on the surface of the canvas. But the configuration on that surface of the individual shapes that constitute a given picture is no more definitive in this regard than their possible configurations in illusionistic space: above all because, as I have claimed, literalness in these paintings is primarily experienced as the property, not of the support, but of the shapes themselves. All this makes Stella's new paintings as radically illusive and intractably ambiguous as any in the history of Modernism. Radically illusive in that what is rendered illusive in them is nothing less than literalness itself; and intractably ambiguous in that the shapes they comprise are experienced as embracing an entire gamut of existential possibilities—including their juxtaposition on the surface of the canvas—each of which is simultaneously continuous with every other, and none of which is sufficiently privileged to make one feel that it, at any rate, is really *there*. There is, one might say, no *it* at all.

Stella's new paintings, then, depart from his stripe paintings in two general respects—first, by not acknowledging literal shape, and second, by resorting to illusion—both of which ought to make them unpalatable to literalist sensibility. And indeed I want to suggest that it is one of the most significant facts about his new pictures that Stella seeks in them to repudiate—not literalist taste or sensibility exactly—but the literalist implications which, in the grip of a particular conception of the nature of Modernist painting, his stripe paintings appear to carry. This is not to claim that his new pictures are chiefly a response to the drawing of those implications by others—Judd, for example. Rather, I am suggesting that it was in *his own* unwillingness, even inability, to pursue beyond painting what were *to him as well*—if not indeed before anyone— his stripe paintings' apparent implications in that direction that Stella discovered both the depth of his commitment to the enterprise of painting, and the irreconcilability with that commitment of what may be called a reductionist conception of the nature of that enterprise.[11] At the same time it is hard not to see their relation to Noland's and Olitski's paintings as issuing, at least in part, from a dissatisfaction, or anyway an uneasiness, with their work that— to my mind, at any rate—has much in common with that which literalist sensibility appears to feel. Moreover, it is tempting to regard this in turn as evidence in favor of the suggestion that the impulse behind the work of literalists like Judd and Bell is anything but alien to Stella. Because if it is true that, unlike Noland and Olitski, Stella has actually *felt* a reductionist conception of his undertaking urge toward the isolation and hypostatization of literalness, it would be surprising if there were not at least some agreement between his response to painting other than his own and the literalist attitude toward that same painting. And in fact Stella's new paintings can, I believe, be seen as responding critically to the same aspect of Noland's and Olitski's paintings that, I suggested earlier, literalist taste finds unacceptable, though here again the differences between Stella and the literalists lie deeper than their apparent agreement. From a literalist point of view the aspect in question is experienced as a conflict between pictorial illusion of any kind on the one hand and literalness as such on the other; this conflict is unacceptable because it compromises the latter; and its elimination entails making works of art (or putative works of art) that are nothing but literal—works in which illusion, to the extent that it may be said to exist at all, is itself literal. Whereas Stella's new paintings, by

---

[11] I take a reductionist conception of Modernist painting to mean this: that painting roughly since Manet is seen as a kind of cognitive enterprise in which a certain quality (e.g., literalness), set of norms (e.g., flatness and the delimiting of flatness) or core of problems (e.g., how to acknowledge the literal character of the support) is progressively revealed as constituting the *essence* of painting—and, by implication, of having done so all along. This seems to me gravely mistaken, not on the grounds that Modernist painting is *not* a cognitive enterprise, but because it radically misconstrues the *kind* of cognitive enterprise Modernist painting is. What the Modernist painter can be said to discover in his work—what can be said to be revealed to him in it—is not the irreducible essence of *all* painting, but rather that which, at the present moment in painting's history, is capable of convincing him that it can stand comparison with the painting of both the Modernist and pre-Modernist past whose quality seems to him beyond question. (In this sense one might say that Modernist painting discovers the essence of all painting to be *quality*.) The object of his enterprise is therefore *both* knowledge and conviction—knowledge *through*, or better still, *in*, conviction. And this knowledge is simultaneously knowledge of *painting* (i.e., what it must be in order to elicit conviction) and of *himself* (i.e., what he finds himself convinced by)—apprehended not as two distinct entities, but in a single, inextricable fruition. It should be clear that the conception of Modernist painting that I have just adumbrated is not only anti-reductionist, but anti-positivist; in this respect I believe it has significant affinities with the persuasive account of the enterprise of science put forward by Thomas S. Kuhn in *The Structure of Scientific Revolutions* (Chicago: University of Chicago Press, 1962). The further exploration of these affinities would, I am sure, prove rewarding. But a footnote is not the best place to begin.

making literalness illusive, not only come to grips with but actually resolve what I characterized earlier as the conflict in Noland's and Olitski's paintings between a particular kind of pictorial illusionism—i.e., addressed to eyesight alone—and the literal character of the support. And by so doing they unmake —at least in the event and for the moment—the distinction between shape as a fundamental property of objects and shape as an entity belonging to painting alone that emerges for the first time in Noland's and Olitski's paintings.

IV

In closing I want merely to touch on another aspect of Stella's new paintings—namely, what seems to me their intimate and profoundly significant relation to the finest Modernist *sculpture* of the recent past. (I am thinking chiefly of the work of English sculptor Anthony Caro.) Almost any of the remarks and observations I have made about the new pictures could, I think, lead to an obvious comparison with Caro's sculptures: what, for example, do pieces like *Bennington* and *Yellow Swing* do if not make literalness illusive? Moreover, the relation between Stella and contemporary sculpture is far from superficial or coincidental. Rather, it has to do with the problematic character

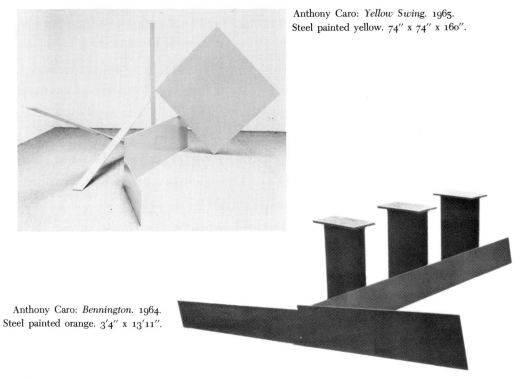

Anthony Caro: *Yellow Swing.* 1965.
Steel painted yellow. 74″ x 74″ x 160″.

Anthony Caro: *Bennington.* 1964.
Steel painted orange. 3′4″ x 13′11″.

of shape in the most advanced painting of our time—even, I want to say, with the nature of shape itself, with what shape is. In any case, I am suggesting that one result of the development within Modernist painting discussed in these notes is that for the first time since the late eighteenth century sculpure is in a position to inspire painting; and that in Stella's recent paintings this has actually begun to happen. At the same time, however, painting is in a position not simply to be inspired by advanced sculpture, but in certain respects fundamental to that sculpture actually to have an advantage—though not of quality—over it. I will mention three: (1) The intractable ambiguity of the visual illusionism in Stella's new pictures goes beyond advanced sculpture in the direction of the opticality and illusiveness—of seeming a kind of mirage—that, as Greenberg was the first to remark, is basic to it.[12] Because sculpture is literal it can, in the end, be *known;* whereas the shapes that constitute Stella's new paintings, and the new paintings as experienced wholes, cannot. (2) The fact, or the convention, that paintings hang on a wall means that Stella's new paintings *begin off the ground;* whereas advanced sculpture—which, as Greenberg has again remarked, is illusively weightless—has to begin at ground level and literally *climb* to whatever height it reaches. This "advantage" is perhaps most strikingly evident in *Effingham III,* largely because that painting as a whole is most like a *ground* plan. *Union III,* as well, profits from it immensely. And in general Stella can float or suspend elements as though without visible means of support. (3) There is no *general* difficulty about the use of color in Stella's paintings; but the problem of color in contemporary sculpture is in important respects acute. And by this I mean not simply the propriety of *applied* color but the fact that all sculpture—like all solid, opaque objects—*is* colored, or *has* color, or anyway has *surface.* It is as though, finally, the opticality toward which advanced sculpture aspires brings one up short, not against its literalness exactly, but against the fact that when we perceive a solid object eyesight makes contact with no more than its surface (and then only part of that). That is to say, advanced sculpture, such as Caro's, makes this fact a disturbing one, and in effect thrusts it into our awareness. It makes us *note* it, whereas painting, one wants to say, in comparison with sculpture, is all *surface.*[13] (Which is not at all the same as saying that it is done on a flat and *very thin* surface; an element of equal thinness in a Caro is experienced as solid.) Stella's paintings, by the very closeness of their relation to advanced sculpture, make this difference more salient than it has ever been.

[12] See "The New Sculpture," *Art and Culture* (Boston, 1961), p. 144. I also want to call attention to Greenberg's essay on the sculpture of Anthony Caro in *Arts Yearbook,* No. 8 (1965). The relevance to Stella's paintings of many of Greenberg's observations about Caro's work seems to me striking.

[13] See Thompson Clarke's essay, "Seeing Surfaces and Physical Objects," in *Philosophy in America,* ed. Max Black (London, 1966). The fact that eyesight touches only the surface of solid objects, and then only part of that surface, has traditionally played an important role in philosophical skepticism.

Postscript

I wrote this essay in August and September, 1966. It was the first of four essays written between then and April, 1967, the last of which, "Art and Objecthood," builds explicitly on conclusions reached in "Shape as Form." In readying these pages for republication here, I have made various changes for the sake of clarity and form. However, I have let the argument stand as it was—not because I believe it to be correct in all particulars (for example, I would not now characterize Stella's undertaking as "therapeutic"; and Noland's paintings of 1965–66 are not seen to receive justice), but because if I had tried to fix everything that now seems to me to need fixing I would have ended up writing a new essay.

In closing I want to thank Stanley Cavell who read this essay in manuscript and made suggestions that I have used. I have also put to use remarks and observations made in my presence by Noland, Olitski, and Stella.

—Michael Fried
July, 1969

Biographical Data

JOSEF ALBERS

Born in Bottrop, Germany, 1888
Came to the United States, 1933
Lives in New Haven, Connecticut

Selected one-man exhibitions:
1936 New Art Circle, J. B. Neumann, New York City
1938 New Art Circle, J. B. Neumann
       Artists Gallery, New York City
1940 The San Francisco Museum of Art, San Francisco, California
1942 The Baltimore Museum of Art, Baltimore, Maryland
       Museum of New Mexico, Santa Fe, New Mexico
1944 Mint Museum of Art, Charlotte, North Carolina
1947 California Palace of the Legion of Honor, San Francisco, California
1949 Cincinnati Art Museum, Cincinnati, Ohio
       Museum of Fine Arts, Richmond, Virginia
       Yale University Art Gallery, New Haven, Connecticut
1950 J. B. Speed Art Museum, Louisville, Kentucky
1951 Contemporary Art Society, Sydney, Australia
1953 Wadsworth Atheneum, Hartford, Connecticut
       The San Francisco Museum of Art
1954 Honolulu Academy of Arts, Honolulu, Hawaii
1955 Hayden Gallery, Massachusetts Institute of Technology, Cambridge, Massachusetts
1956 Kunsthaus, Zurich, Switzerland
       Yale University Art Gallery
1957 Museum der Stadt Ulm, Ulm, Germany
       Karl-Ernst-Osthaus-Museum, Hagen, Germany
1958 Kunstverein, Münster, Germany
       Kunstverein, Freiburg, Germany
1959 Landesmuseum, Münster, Germany
       Museum am Ostwall, Dortmund, Germany
1961 Stedelijk Museum, Amsterdam, The Netherlands
1963 Mint Museum of Art
       Kunsthaus, Hamburg, Germany
       Museum Folkwang, Essen, Germany
1965 Dallas Museum of Fine Arts, Dallas, Texas
       The San Francisco Museum of Art
1965–67 The Museum of Modern Art, New York City (circulated in the United States, South America, and Mexico)
Sidney Janis Gallery, New York City, 1949, 1952, 1955, 1958, 1959, 1961, 1963, 1964, 1968

MILTON AVERY

Born in Altmar, New York, 1893
Died in New York City, 1965

Selected one-man exhibitions:
1928 Opportunity Gallery, New York City
1932 Gallery, 144 West 13th Street, New York City
1935 Valentine Gallery, New York City

1936 Valentine Gallery
1938 Valentine Gallery
1943 Phillips Gallery, Washington, D.C.
1944 Phillips Gallery
     Arts Club of Chicago, Chicago, Illinois
1946 Colorado Springs Fine Arts Center, Colorado Springs, Colorado
1947 Portland Art Museum, Portland, Oregon
1952 The Baltimore Museum of Art, Baltimore, Maryland
     Institute of Contemporary Art, Boston, Massachusetts
     Joe and Emily Lowe Gallery, Coral Gables, Florida
     Phillips Gallery
     Wadsworth Atheneum, Hartford, Connecticut
1956 Mills College, Oakland, California
     Houston Museum of Fine Arts, Houston, Texas
     Santa Barbara Museum of Art, Santa Barbara, California
     Art Gallery, University of Nebraska, Lincoln, Nebraska
1959 Art Alliance, Philadelphia, Pennsylvania
1960 The Whitney Museum of American Art, New York City (circulated in the United States)
1965–66 The Museum of Modern Art, New York City (circulated in the United States)
1966 Arkansas Art Center, Little Rock, Arkansas
     Art Gallery, University of Nebraska
1969 National Collection of Fine Arts, Smithsonian Institution, Washington, D.C.
Grace Borgenicht Gallery, New York City, 1951, 1952, 1954, 1956, 1957, 1958, 1959, 1960, 1963, 1964, 1968

ALEXANDER CALDER

Born in Philadelphia, Pennsylvania, 1898
Lives in Roxbury, Connecticut, and Saché, France

Selected one-man exhibitions:
1928 Weyhe Gallery, New York City
1934 Pierre Matisse Gallery, New York City
1938 George Walter Vincent Smith Art Museum, Springfield, Massachusetts
1940 Willard Gallery, New York City
1943 The Museum of Modern Art, New York City
1944 Buchholz Gallery, New York City (first of several)
1946 Galerie Louis Carré, Paris, France
1948 Ministry of Education, Rio de Janeiro, Brazil
     Museum of Art, São Paulo, Brazil
1949 Museum of Fine Arts, Richmond, Virginia
1950 Galerie Maeght, Paris, France (first of several)
     Hayden Gallery, Massachusetts Institute of Technology, Cambridge, Massachusetts
1953 The Walker Art Center, Minneapolis, Minnesota
1955 Museo de Arte, Caracas, Venezuela
1956 Perls Galleries, New York City (first of several)
     Galleria dell'Obelisco, Rome, Italy
     Galerie Weill, Paris, France
1959 Museu de Arte Moderno, Rio de Janeiro, Brazil
1962 Tate Gallery, London, England
     Musée des Beaux-Arts, Rennes, France

1964–65 The Solomon R. Guggenheim Museum, New York City
        Milwaukee Art Center, Milwaukee, Wisconsin
        Washington University Art Gallery, St. Louis, Missouri
        Des Moines Art Center, Des Moines, Iowa
        The National Gallery of Canada, Ottawa, Canada
        Musée National d'Art Moderne, Paris, France
1967 Akademie der Kunst, Berlin, Germany
1968 Musée des Augustins, Toulouse, France
1969 Fondation Maeght, Saint Paul, France

JOHN CHAMBERLAIN

Born in Rochester, Indiana, 1927
Lives in New York City

One-man exhibitions:
1957 Wells Street Gallery, Chicago, Illinois
1958 Davida Gallery, Chicago, Illinois
1960 Martha Jackson Gallery, New York City
1962 Leo Castelli Gallery, New York City
     Dilexi Gallery, Los Angeles, California
1964 Galerie Ileana Sonnabend, Paris, France
     Pace Gallery, Boston, Massachusetts
     Leo Castelli Gallery
1965 Leo Castelli Gallery
1966 Dwan Gallery, Los Angeles, California
1967 The Cleveland Museum of Art, Cleveland, Ohio
1968 Leo Castelli Gallery
     Contemporary Arts Center, Cincinnati, Ohio
1969 Leo Castelli Warehouse, New York City

JOSEPH CORNELL

Born in Nyack, New York, 1903
Lives in Flushing, New York

One-man exhibitions:
1939 Julien Levy Gallery, New York City
1940 Julien Levy Gallery
1942 Wakefield Gallery, New York City
1946 Hugo Gallery, New York City
1948 Copley Galleries, Beverly Hills, California
1949 Egan Gallery, New York City
1950 Egan Gallery
1953 Egan Gallery
     Allan Frumkin Gallery, Chicago, Illinois
1955 Stable Gallery, New York City
1956 Wittenborn, New York City
1957 Stable Gallery

431

1959 Bennington College, Bennington, Vermont
1962 Ferus Gallery, Los Angeles, California
1963 New York University Art Collection, Loeb Student Center, New York City
1965 The J. L. Hudson Gallery, Detroit, Michigan
1966 Robert Schoelkopf Gallery, New York City
1967 Pasadena Art Museum, Pasadena, California
      The Solomon R. Guggenheim Museum, New York City

STUART DAVIS

Born in Philadelphia, Pennsylvania, 1894
Died in New York City, 1964

Selected one-man exhibitions:
1917 Sheridan Square Gallery, New York City
1918 Ardsley Gallery, Brooklyn, New York
1925 Newark Museum, Newark, New Jersey
1929 Whitney Studio Galleries, New York City
1941 Cincinnati Modern Art Society, Cincinnati, Ohio
      Indiana University, Bloomington, Indiana
1945 The Museum of Modern Art, New York City
1946 The Baltimore Museum of Art, Baltimore, Maryland
1952 American Pavilion, XXVI Biennale, Venice, Italy
1957 The Walker Art Center, Minneapolis, Minnesota
      Des Moines Art Center, Des Moines, Iowa
      The San Francisco Museum of Art, San Francisco, California
      The Whitney Museum of American Art, New York City
1965 National Collection of Fine Arts, Smithsonian Institution, Washington, D.C.
      The Art Institute of Chicago, Chicago, Illinois
      The Whitney Museum of American Art
      Art Galleries of the University of California, Los Angeles, California
The Downtown Gallery, New York City, 1927, 1932, 1943, 1946, 1952, 1954, 1956, 1958, 1960, 1962, 1963

WILLEM DE KOONING

Born in Rotterdam, The Netherlands, 1904
Came to the United States, 1926
Lives in The Springs, Long Island

Selected one-man exhibitions:
1948 Egan Gallery, New York City
1951 Egan Gallery
1953 Sidney Janis Gallery, New York City
      School of the Museum of Fine Arts, Boston, Massachusetts
      Workshop Art Center, Washington, D.C.
1955 Martha Jackson Gallery, New York City
1956 Sidney Janis Gallery
1959 Sidney Janis Gallery
1961 Paul Kantor Gallery, Beverly Hills, California
1962 Sidney Janis Gallery
      Alan Stone Gallery, New York City (with Barnett Newman)

1964 James Goodman Gallery, Buffalo, New York
Alan Stone Gallery
1965 Smith College, Northampton, Massachusetts
1967 M. Knoedler & Company, Inc., New York City
1968 M. Knoedler & Cie., Inc., Paris, France
1968–69 Stedelijk Museum, Amsterdam, The Netherlands
Tate Gallery, London, England
The Museum of Modern Art, New York City
The Art Institute of Chicago, Chicago, Illinois
Los Angeles County Museum of Art, Los Angeles, California
1969 M. Knoedler & Company, Inc.

BURGOYNE DILLER

Born in New York City, 1906
Died in New York City, 1965

Selected one-man exhibitions:
1933 Contemporary Arts Gallery, New York City
1946 Pinacotheca Gallery, New York City
1949 Pinacotheca Gallery
1951 Rose Fried Gallery, New York City
1961 Galerie Chalette, New York City
1962 Galerie Chalette
1963 Galerie Chalette
1964 Galerie Chalette
1966 New Jersey State Museum, Trenton, New Jersey
1968 Noah Goldowsky Gallery, New York City
Los Angeles County Museum of Art, Los Angeles, California

MARK DI SUVERO

Born in Shanghai, China, 1933
Came to the United States, 1941
Lives in New York City

One-man exhibitions:
1960 Green Gallery, New York City
1965 Dwan Gallery, Los Angeles, California
1966 Park Place Gallery, New York City
1968 Lo Giudice Gallery, Chicago, Illinois

DAN FLAVIN

Born in New York City, 1933
Lives in Cold Spring, New York

One-man exhibitions:
1961 Judson Gallery, New York City
1964 Kaymar Gallery, New York City
Green Gallery, New York City
1965 Ohio State University, Columbus, Ohio

433

1966 Galerie Rudolf Zwirner, Cologne, Germany
      Nicholas Wilder Gallery, Los Angeles, California
1967 Kornblee Gallery, New York City
1968 Museum of Contemporary Art, Chicago, Illinois
      Galleria Sperone, Turin, Italy
      Galerie Heiner Friedrich, Munich, Germany
1969 Konrad Fischer Gallery, Düsseldorf, Germany
      Irving Blum Gallery, Los Angeles, California
      The National Gallery of Canada, Ottawa, Canada

HELEN FRANKENTHALER

Born in New York City, 1928
Lives in New York City

One-man exhibitions:
1951–58 Tibor de Nagy Gallery, New York City
1959 André Emmerich Gallery, New York City
1960 The Jewish Museum, New York City
      André Emmerich Gallery
1961 Everett Ellin Gallery, Los Angeles, California
      André Emmerich Gallery
      Galerie Lawrence, Paris, France
1962 André Emmerich Gallery
      Bennington College, Bennington, Vermont
      Galleria dell'Ariete, Milan, Italy
1963 André Emmerich Gallery
      Galerie Lawrence
1964 Kasmin Ltd., London, England
1965 André Emmerich Gallery
      The David Mirvish Gallery, Toronto, Canada
1966 André Emmerich Gallery
1968 André Emmerich Gallery
1969 The Whitney Museum of American Art, New York City
      Whitechapel Gallery, London, England

ARSHILE GORKY

Born in Khorkom Vari Haiyotz, Armenia, 1904
Came to the United States, 1920
Died in Sherman, Connecticut, 1948

Selected one-man exhibitions:
1934 Mellon Galleries, Philadelphia, Pennsylvania
1938 Boyer Galleries, New York City
1941 The San Francisco Museum of Art, San Francisco, California
1945 Julien Levy Gallery, New York City
1946 Julien Levy Gallery
1947 Julien Levy Gallery
1948 Julien Levy Gallery
1951 The Whitney Museum of American Art, New York City
      The Walker Art Center, Minneapolis, Minnesota
      The San Francisco Museum of Art

1952 The Art Museum, Princeton University, Princeton, New Jersey
1962 The Museum of Modern Art, New York City
     Washington Gallery of Modern Art, Washington, D.C.

ADOLPH GOTTLIEB

Born in New York City, 1903
Lives in New York City

One-man exhibitions:
1930 Dudensing Galleries, New York City
1934 Uptown Gallery, New York City
     Theodore A. Kohn & Son, New York City
1940 Artists Gallery, New York City
1942 Artists Gallery
1944 Wakefield Gallery, New York City
1945 Gallery 67, New York City
     Nierendorf Galleries, New York City
1947 Kootz Gallery, New York City
     Kootz Gallery
1949 Jacques Seligmann Galleries, New York City
1950 Kootz Gallery
1951 Kootz Gallery
1952 Kootz Gallery
1953 Kootz Gallery
     Area Arts, San Francisco, California
1954 Kootz Gallery
     Bennington College, Bennington, Vermont
     Lawrence Art Museum, Williams College, Williamstown, Massachusetts
     Kootz Gallery, Provincetown, Massachusetts
1957 Martha Jackson Gallery, New York City
     HCE Gallery, Provincetown, Massachusetts
     The Jewish Museum, New York City
1958 André Emmerich Gallery, New York City
1959 André Emmerich Gallery
     Galerie Rive Droite, Paris, France
     Institute of Contemporary Arts, London, England
     Paul Kantor Gallery, Beverly Hills, California
1960 French and Company, New York City
     Sidney Janis Gallery, New York City
1961 Galleria dell'Ariete, Milan, Italy
     Galerie Handschin, Basel, Switzerland
1962 Sidney Janis Gallery
1963 The Walker Art Center, Minneapolis, Minnesota,
     American Section of VII Bienal de São Paulo, São Paulo, Brazil
1964 Marlborough-Gerson Gallery, New York City
1966 Marlborough-Gerson Gallery
     Hayden Gallery, Massachusetts Institute of Technology, Cambridge, Massachusetts
1967 Arts Club of Chicago, Chicago, Illinois
1968 The Whitney Museum of American Art, New York City
     The Solomon R. Guggenheim Museum, New York City
     The Corcoran Gallery of Art, Washington, D.C.
     Rose Art Museum, Brandeis University, Waltham, Massachusetts

PHILIP GUSTON

Born in Montreal, Canada, 1913
Came to the United States, 1919
Lives in Woodstock, New York

One-man exhibitions:
1944 University of Iowa, Iowa City, Iowa
1945 Midtown Galleries, New York City
1947 School of the Museum of Fine Arts, Boston, Massachusetts
     Munson-Williams-Proctor Institute, Utica, New York
1950 University of Minnesota, Minneapolis, Minnesota
1952 Peridot Gallery, New York City
1953 Egan Gallery, New York City
1956 Sidney Janis Gallery, New York City
1958 Sidney Janis Gallery
1959 V Bienal, São Paulo, Brazil
1960 XXX Biennale, Venice, Italy
     Sidney Janis Gallery
1961 Sidney Janis Gallery
1962 The Solomon R. Guggenheim Museum, New York City
     Stedelijk Museum, Amsterdam, The Netherlands
     Musée des Beaux-Arts, Brussels, Belgium
1963 Whitechapel Gallery, London, England
     Los Angeles County Museum of Art, Los Angeles, California
1966 The Jewish Museum, New York City

HANS HOFMANN

Born in Weissenburg, Bavaria, Germany, 1880
Came to the United States, 1933
Died in New York City, 1966

Selected one-man exhibitions:
1931 California Palace of the Legion of Honor, San Francisco, California
1941 Isaac Delgado Museum of Art, New Orleans, Louisiana
1944 Art of This Century, New York City
     Arts Club of Chicago, Chicago, Illinois
1946 Mortimer Brandt Gallery, New York City
1947 Betty Parsons Gallery, New York City
1948 Addison Gallery of American Art, Andover, Massachusetts
1949 Galerie Maeght, Paris, France
1954 The Baltimore Museum of Art, Baltimore, Maryland
1955 Bennington College, Bennington, Vermont
1956 Art Alliance, Philadelphia, Pennsylvania
     Rutgers University, New Brunswick, New Jersey
1957 The Whitney Museum of American Art, New York City
1958 Des Moines Art Center, Des Moines, Iowa
     The San Francisco Museum of Art, San Francisco, California
     Art Galleries of the University of California, Los Angeles, California
     Seattle Art Museum, Seattle, Washington
     The Walker Art Center, Minneapolis, Minnesota
     Munson-Williams-Proctor Institute, Utica, New York
     The Baltimore Museum of Art

1962 Frankische Galerie am Marientor, Nuremberg, Germany
      Kölnischer Kunstverein, Cologne, Germany
      Kongresshalle, Berlin, Germany
1963 Santa Barbara Museum of Art, Santa Barbara, California
      The Museum of Modern Art, New York City
1964 Worth Ryder Art Gallery, University of California, Berkeley, California
1966 Stanford Art Museum, Stanford University, Stanford, California
1969 Everson Museum of Art, Syracuse, New York
Between 1947 and 1966 he showed annually or biannually with Kootz Gallery, New York City

EDWARD HOPPER

Born in Nyack, New York, 1882
Died in New York City, 1967

Selected one-man exhibitions:
1933 The Museum of Modern Art, New York City
1934 Arts Club of Chicago, Chicago, Illinois
1937 Carnegie Institute, Pittsburgh, Pennsylvania
1950 The Whitney Museum of American Art, New York City
      Museum of Fine Arts, Boston, Massachusetts
      The Detroit Institute of Arts, Detroit, Michigan
1959 Rhode Island School of Design, Providence, Rhode Island
1960 Wadsworth Atheneum, Hartford, Connecticut
1962 Philadelphia Museum of Art, Philadelphia, Pennsylvania
      Worcester Art Museum, Worcester, Massachusetts
1963 University of Arizona Art Gallery, Tucson, Arizona
1964 Munson-Williams-Proctor Institute, Utica, New York
      The Whitney Museum of American Art
1965 The Art Institute of Chicago, Chicago, Illinois
      The Detroit Institute of Arts
      City Art Museum of St. Louis, St. Louis, Missouri

JASPER JOHNS

Born in Augusta, Georgia, 1930
Lives in New York City

One-man exhibitions:
1958 Leo Castelli Gallery, New York City
1959 Galleria d'Arte del Naviglio, Milan, Italy
      Galerie Rive Droite, Paris, France
1960 Tweed Gallery, Minneapolis, Minnesota
      Columbia Museum of Art, Columbia, South Carolina
      Leo Castelli Gallery
1961 Galerie Rive Droite
      Leo Castelli Gallery
1962 Galerie Ileana Sonnabend, Paris, France
      Everett Ellin Gallery, Los Angeles, California
1963 Leo Castelli Gallery
1964 Whitechapel Gallery, London, England
      The Jewish Museum, New York City
1965 Pasadena Art Museum, Pasadena, California

437

1965 Ashmolean Museum, Oxford, England
American Embassy, London, England
Minami Gallery, Tokyo, Japan
1966 Leo Castelli Gallery
National Collection of Fine Arts, Smithsonian Institution, Washington, D.C. (drawings)
1968 Leo Castelli Gallery
The Museum of Modern Art, New York City (circulating exhibition, lithographs)
Galerie Buren, Stockholm, Sweden
1969 Castelli-Whitney, New York City
David Whitney Gallery, New York City
Castelli Graphics, New York City

DONALD JUDD

**Born in Excelsior Springs, Missouri, 1928
Lives in New York City**

One-man exhibitions:
1964 Green Gallery, New York City
1966 Leo Castelli Gallery, New York City
1968 The Whitney Museum of American Art, New York City
Irving Blum Gallery, Los Angeles, California
1969 Leo Castelli Gallery
Galerie Ileana Sonnabend, Paris, France
Galerie Rudolf Zwirner, Cologne, Germany

ELLSWORTH KELLY

**Born in Newburgh, New York, 1923
Lives in New York City**

One-man exhibitions:
1951 Galerie Arnaud, Paris, France
1956 Betty Parsons Gallery, New York City
1957 Betty Parsons Gallery
1958 Galerie Maeght, Paris, France
1959 Betty Parsons Gallery
1961 Betty Parsons Gallery
1962 Tooth Gallery, London, England
1963 Betty Parsons Gallery
Gallery of Modern Art, Washington, D.C.
1964 Galerie Maeght
Institute of Contemporary Art, Boston, Massachusetts
1965 Sidney Janis Gallery, New York City
Ferus Gallery, Los Angeles, California
Galerie Maeght
Knull International, Düsseldorf, Germany
1967 Sidney Janis Gallery
Irving Blum Gallery, Los Angeles, California
1968 Sidney Janis Gallery
Irving Blum Gallery

FRANZ KLINE

Born in Wilkes-Barre, Pennsylvania, 1910
Died in New York City, 1962

Selected one-man exhibitions:
1950 Egan Gallery, New York City
1951 Egan Gallery
1952 Margaret Brown Gallery, Boston, Massachusetts
1954 Institute of Design, Chicago, Illinois
    Allan Frumkin Gallery, Chicago, Illinois
    Egan Gallery
1956 Sidney Janis Gallery, New York City
1958 Galleria La Tartaruga, Rome, Italy
    Galleria d'Arte del Naviglio, Milan, Italy
    Sidney Janis Gallery
1960 Sidney Janis Gallery
1961 Sidney Janis Gallery
    Collector's Gallery, New York City
    New Arts Gallery, Atlanta, Georgia
    Arts Club of Chicago, Chicago, Illinois
1962 Gallery of Modern Art, Washington, D.C.
    Rose Art Museum, Brandeis University, Waltham, Massachusetts
    The Baltimore Museum of Art, Baltimore, Maryland
1968 The Whitney Museum of American Art, New York City
1969 Dallas Museum of Fine Arts, Dallas, Texas
    The San Francisco Museum of Art, San Francisco, California
    Museum of Contemporary Art, Chicago, Illinois

GABE KOHN

Born in Philadelphia, Pennsylvania, 1910
Lives in Los Angeles, California

Selected one-man exhibitions:
1948 Atelier Mannuci, Rome, Italy
1950 Galleria dello Zodiaco, Rome, Italy
1958 Tanager Gallery, New York City
1959 Leo Castelli Gallery, New York City
1961 Otto Gerson Gallery, New York City
1963 David Stuart Galleries, Los Angeles, California
    La Jolla Museum of Art, La Jolla, California
1966 David Stuart Galleries

ROY LICHTENSTEIN

Born in New York City, 1923
Lives in New York City

One-man exhibitions:
1951 Carlebach Gallery, New York City
1952 John Heller Gallery, New York City
1953 John Heller Gallery

439

1954 John Heller Gallery
1957 John Heller Gallery
1962 Leo Castelli Gallery, New York City
1963 Ferus Gallery, Los Angeles, California
       Galerie Ileana Sonnabend, Paris, France
       Leo Castelli Gallery
1964 Il Punto, Turin, Italy
       Leo Castelli Gallery
       Ferus Gallery
1965 Galerie Ileana Sonnabend
       Leo Castelli Gallery
1966 The Cleveland Museum of Art, Cleveland, Ohio
1967 Pasadena Art Museum, Pasadena, California
       The Walker Art Center, Minneapolis, Minnesota
       Leo Castelli Galley
       Contemporary Arts Center, Cincinnati, Ohio
       Stedelijk Museum, Amsterdam, The Netherlands
1968 Tate Gallery, London, England
       Kunsthalle, Bern, Switzerland
       Kestner-Gesellschaft, Hannover, Germany
       Irving Blum Gallery, Los Angeles, California
1969 Irving Blum Gallery

MORRIS LOUIS

Born in Baltimore, Maryland, 1912
Died in Washington, D.C., 1962

One-man exhibitions:
1957 Martha Jackson Gallery, New York City
1959 French and Company, New York City
1960 French and Company
       Institute of Contemporary Arts, London, England
       Galleria dell'Ariete, Milan, Italy
       Galerie Lawrence, Paris, France
       Bennington College, Bennington, Vermont
1961 Galerie Neufville, Paris, France
       André Emmerich Gallery, New York City
1962 Galerie Schmela, Düsseldorf, Germany
       Galerie Müller, Stuttgart, Germany
       Galerie Lawrence
       André Emmerich Gallery
1963 Kasmin Ltd., London, England
       The Solomon R. Guggenheim Museum, New York City
1964 Galerie Renée Ziegler, Zurich, Switzerland
       André Emmerich Gallery
1965 Staatliche Kunsthalle, Baden, Germany
       André Emmerich Gallery
1966 Washington Gallery of Modern Art, Washington, D.C.
       André Emmerich Gallery
1967 The Cleveland Museum of Art, Cleveland, Ohio
       Seattle Art Museum, Seattle, Washington
       Los Angeles County Museum of Art, Los Angeles, California
       Museum of Fine Arts, Boston, Massachusetts

1967 City Art Museum of St. Louis, St. Louis, Missouri
  André Emmerich Gallery
1968 André Emmerich Gallery
1969 André Emmerich Gallery
  Lawrence Rubin Gallery, New York City

ROBERT MORRIS

Born in Kansas City, Missouri, 1931
Lives in New York City

One-man exhibitions:
1957 Dilexi Gallery, San Francisco, California
1958 Dilexi Gallery
1963 Green Gallery, New York City
1964 Galerie Schmela, Düsseldorf, Germany
  Green Gallery
1965 Green Gallery
1966 Dwan Gallery, Los Angeles, California
1967 Leo Castelli Gallery, New York City
1968 Stedelijk van Abbemuseum, Eindhoven, The Netherlands
  Galerie Ileana Sonnabend, Paris, France (spring)
  Galerie Ileana Sonnabend (fall)
  Leo Castelli Gallery
1969 Leo Castelli Gallery
  Galleria Enzo Sperone, Turin, Italy
  Irving Blum Gallery, Los Angeles, California

ROBERT MOTHERWELL

Born in Aberdeen, Washington, 1915
Lives in New York City

Selected one-man exhibitions:
1944 Art of This Century, New York City
1946 Kootz Gallery, New York City
  The San Francisco Museum of Art, San Francisco, California
  Arts Club of Chicago, Chicago, Illinois
1949 Kootz Gallery
1952 Kootz Gallery
1953 Allen Memorial Art Museum, Oberlin College, Oberlin, Ohio
1957 Sidney Janis Gallery, New York City
1959 Bennington College, Bennington, Vermont
  Sidney Janis Gallery
1961 Sidney Janis Gallery
  Galerie Berggruen, Paris, France
1962 Pasadena Art Museum, Pasadena, California
  Galleria Odyssia, Rome, Italy
  Galerie del Spiegel, Cologne, Germany
1963 Smith College, Northampton, Massachusetts
  Hayden Gallery, Massachusetts Institute of Technology, Cambridge, Massachusetts
1965 Phillips Gallery, Washington, D.C.
  The Museum of Modern Art, New York City

1966 Contemporary Art Museum, Houston, Texas
The Baltimore Museum of Art, Baltimore, Maryland
Stedelijk Museum, Amsterdam, The Netherlands
Whitechapel Gallery, London, England
Volkswang Museum, Essen, Germany
Civic Museum, Turin, Italy
1967 The San Francisco Museum of Art
1968 The Whitney Museum of American Art, New York City
1969 Marlborough-Gerson Gallery, New York City
Virginia Museum of Art, Richmond, Virginia
Marlborough Galleria d'Arte, Rome, Italy

BARNETT NEWMAN

Born in New York City, 1905
Lives in New York City

One-man exhibitions:
1950 Betty Parsons Gallery, New York City
1951 Betty Parsons Gallery
1958 Bennington College, Bennington, Vermont
1959 French and Company, New York City
1962 Alan Stone Gallery, New York City (with Willem de Kooning)
1965 Nicholas Wilder Gallery, Los Angeles, California
1966 The Solomon R. Guggenheim Museum, New York City
1969 M. Knoedler & Company, Inc., New York City

ISAMU NOGUCHI

Born in Los Angeles, California, 1904
Lives in Long Island City, New York

One-man exhibitions:
1929 Eugene Schoen Gallery, New York City
1930 Marie Sterner Gallery, New York City
Harvard Society for Contemporary Art, Cambridge, Massachusetts
Arts Club of Chicago, Chicago, Illinois
1931 Albright Art Gallery, Buffalo, New York
Rochester Memorial Art Gallery, Rochester, New York
Becker Gallery, New York City
1932 Becker Gallery
Demotte Gallery, New York City
Reinhardt Galleries, New York City
1933 Mellon Galleries, Philadelphia, Pennsylvania
1934 Honolulu Academy of Arts, Honolulu, Hawaii
Sidney Burney Gallery, London, England
Western Association of Art Museum Directors *touring show*
1935 Marie Harriman Gallery, New York City
1939 Honolulu Academy of Arts
1942 The San Francisco Museum of Art, San Francisco, California
1948 Egan Gallery, New York City
1951 Mitsukoshi Department Store, Tokyo, Japan
1952 Kamakura Modern Museum, Kamakura, Japan

1953 Stable Gallery, New York City
1955 Stable Gallery
1959 Stable Gallery
1961 Daniel Cordier & Michel Warren Galleries, New York City
   Fort Worth Art Center, Fort Worth, Texas
1963 Cordier & Ekstrom, Inc., New York City
1964 Claude Bernard Gallery, Paris, France
1965 Cordier & Ekstrom, Inc.
1967 Cordier & Ekstrom, Inc.
1968 The Whitney Museum of American Art, New York City
   Cordier & Ekstrom, Inc.

KENNETH NOLAND

Born in Asheville, North Carolina, 1924
Lives in New York City

One-man exhibitions:
1956 Tibor de Nagy Gallery, New York City
1958 Tibor de Nagy Gallery
1959 French and Company, New York City
1960 Galleria dell'Ariete, Milan, Italy
   André Emmerich Gallery, New York City
   Galerie Lawrence, Paris, France
1961 Bennington College, Bennington, Vermont
   Galerie Neufville, Paris, France
   André Emmerich Gallery
1962 Galerie Schmela, Düsseldorf, Germany
   Galerie Charles Lienhard, Zurich, Switzerland
   André Emmerich Gallery
1963 Galerie Lawrence
   Kasmin Ltd., London, England
   André Emmerich Gallery
1964 Galerie Schmela
   The Jewish Museum, New York City
1965 Kasmin Ltd.
   The David Mirvish Gallery, Toronto, Canada
1966 André Emmerich Gallery
1967 André Emmerich Gallery
1968 The David Mirvish Gallery
   Kasmin Ltd.
1969 Lawrence Rubin Gallery, New York City

CLAES OLDENBURG

Born in Stockholm, Sweden, 1929
Came to the United States, 1936
Lives in New York City

One-man exhibitions:
1959 Judson Gallery, New York City
1960 Reuben Gallery, New York City
1961 The Store, New York City (sponsored by Green Gallery)

443

1962 Green Gallery, New York City
1963 Dwan Gallery, Los Angeles, California
1964 Sidney Janis Gallery, New York City
Pace Gallery, Boston, Massachusetts
1966 Sidney Janis Gallery
Galerie Ileana Sonnabend, Paris, France
Robert Fraser Gallery, London, England
Moderna Museet, Stockholm, Sweden
1967 Sidney Janis Gallery
1969 The Museum of Modern Art, New York City

JULES OLITSKI

Born in Gomel, Russia, 1922
Came to the United States, 1924
Lives in New York City

One-man exhibitions:
1950 Galerie Huit, Paris, France
1958 Iolas Gallery, New York City
1959 French and Company, New York City
1960 French and Company
1961 Poindexter Gallery, New York City
1962 Poindexter Gallery
1963 Poindexter Gallery
Bennington College, Bennington, Vermont
Galleria d'Arte, Santa Croce, Florence, Italy
Galleria Travestere di Topazia Alianta, Rome, Italy
Toninelli Arte Moderna, Milan, Italy
1964 Poindexter Gallery
Richard Gray Gallery, Chicago, Illinois
Galerie Lawrence, Paris, France
Kasmin Ltd., London, England
The David Mirvish Gallery, Toronto, Canada
1965 Poindexter Gallery
Kasmin Ltd.
The David Mirvish Gallery
1966 Kasmin Ltd.
The David Mirvish Gallery
Nicholas Wilder Gallery, Los Angeles, California
André Emmerich Gallery, New York City
1967 The Corcoran Gallery of Art, Washington, D.C.
Pasadena Art Museum, Pasadena, California
The San Francisco Museum of Art, San Francisco, California
André Emmerich Gallery
1968 Kasmin Ltd.
Nicholas Wilder Gallery, Los Angeles, California
André Emmerich Gallery
Institute of Contemporary Art, University of Pennsylvania, Philadelphia, Pennsylvania
Hayden Gallery, Massachusetts Institute of Technology, Cambridge, Massachusetts
1969 The Metropolitan Museum of Art, New York City

JACKSON POLLOCK

Born in Cody, Wyoming, 1912
Died in Easthampton, Long Island, 1956

Selected one-man exhibitions:
1943 Art of This Century, New York City
1945 Arts Club of Chicago, Chicago, Illinois
      Art of This Century
      The San Francisco Museum of Art, San Francisco, California
1946 Art of This Century
1947 Art of This Century
1948 Betty Parsons Gallery, New York City
1949 Betty Parsons Gallery (Jan.–Feb. and Nov.–Dec.)
1950 Museo Correr, Venice, Italy
      Galleria d'Arte del Naviglio, Milan, Italy
      Betty Parsons Gallery
1951 Hilltop Theatre Art Room, Lutherville, Maryland
      Betty Parsons Gallery
1952 Studio Paul Facchetti, Paris, France
      Sidney Janis Gallery, New York City
      Bennington College, Bennington, Vermont
      Lawrence Art Museum, Williams College, Williamstown, Massachusetts
1954 Sidney Janis Gallery
1955 Sidney Janis Gallery
1956–57 The Museum of Modern Art, New York City
1967 The Museum of Modern Art

LARRY POONS

Born in Tokyo, Japan, 1937
Came to the United States, 1938
Lives in New York City

One-man exhibitions:
1963 Green Gallery, New York City
1964 Green Gallery
1965 Green Gallery
1967 Leo Castelli Gallery, New York City
1968 Kasmin Ltd., London, England
      Leo Castelli Gallery

ROBERT RAUSCHENBERG

Born in Port Arthur, Texas, 1925
Lives in New York City

One-man exhibitions:
1951 Betty Parsons Gallery, New York City
1953 Stable Gallery, New York City
      Galleria d'Arte Contemporanea, Florence, Italy
      Galleria del Obelisco, Rome, Italy

445

1955 Egan Gallery, New York City
1958 Leo Castelli Gallery, New York City
1959 Galleria La Tartaruga, Rome, Italy
     Galerie 22, Düsseldorf, Germany
     Leo Castelli Gallery
1960 Leo Castelli Gallery
1961 Galerie Daniel Cordier, Paris, France
     Galleria dell'Ariete, Milan, Italy
     Leo Castelli Gallery
1962 Dwan Gallery, Los Angeles, California
1963 Galerie Ileana Sonnabend, Paris, France
     The Jewish Museum, New York City
     Leo Castelli Gallery
1964 Whitechapel Gallery, London, England
     Galerie Ileana Sonnabend
     Arte Moderna, Turin, Italy
1965 Amerika House, Berlin, Germany
     Contemporary Arts Society, Houston, Texas
     The Walker Art Center, Minneapolis, Minnesota
     Moderna Museet, Stockholm, Sweden
     Leo Castelli Gallery
1966 The Museum of Modern Art, New York City
1967 Leo Castelli Gallery
     Douglas Gallery, Vancouver, British Columbia, Canada
1968 Stedelijk Museum, Amsterdam, The Netherlands
     Peale House, Pennsylvania Academy of the Fine Arts, Philadelphia, Pennsylvania
     Kolnischer Kunstverein, Cologne, Germany
     Musée d'Arte Moderne de la Ville de Paris, Paris, France
     The Museum of Modern Art
     Leo Castelli Gallery
1969 Leo Castelli Gallery
     Fort Worth Art Center, Fort Worth, Texas

AD REINHARDT

Born in Buffalo, New York, 1913
Died in New York City, 1967

One-man exhibitions:
1943 Columbia University, New York City
1944 Artists Gallery, New York City
1946 Art School Gallery, Brooklyn Museum, Brooklyn, New York
     Mortimer Brandt Gallery, New York City
1960 Galerie Iris Clert, Paris, France
1964 Dwan Gallery, Los Angeles, California
     Galerie Iris Clert
     I.C.A. Gallery, London, England
1965 Graham Gallery, New York City
     Stable Gallery, New York City
1967 The Jewish Museum, New York City
Betty Parsons Gallery, New York City—1946, 1947, 1948, 1949, 1950, 1951, 1952, 1953, 1955, 1956,
     1959, 1960, 1965

JAMES ROSENQUIST

**Born in Grand Forks, North Dakota, 1933
Lives in Easthampton, Long Island**

One-man exhibitions:
1962 Green Gallery, New York City
1963 Green Gallery
1964 Green Gallery
      Dwan Gallery, Los Angeles, California
1965 Arte Moderna, Turin, Italy
      Galerie Ileana Sonnabend, Paris, France
      Leo Castelli Gallery, New York City
1966 Leo Castelli Gallery
      Moderna Museet, Stockholm, Sweden
      Stedelijk Museum, Amsterdam, The Netherlands
      Kunsthalle, Bern, Switzerland
      Louisiana Museum, Humlebaek, Denmark
      Baden-Baden Museum, Baden-Baden, Germany
1968 National Gallery of Canada, Ottawa, Canada
      Galerie Ileana Sonnabend
1969 Leo Castelli Gallery

MARK ROTHKO

**Born in Dvinska, Russia, 1903
Came to the United States, 1913
Lives in New York City**

One-man exhibitions:
1933 Art Museum, Portland, Oregon
      Contemporary Arts Gallery, New York City
1945 Art of This Century, New York City
1946 Museum of Art, Santa Barbara, California
      Betty Parsons Gallery, New York City
1947 Betty Parsons Gallery
1948 Betty Parsons Gallery
1949 Betty Parsons Gallery
1950 Betty Parsons Gallery
1951 Betty Parsons Gallery
1954 Rhode Island School of Design, Providence, Rhode Island
      The Art Institute of Chicago, Chicago, Illinois
1955 Sidney Janis Gallery, New York City
1957 Contemporary Arts Museum, Houston, Texas
1958 Sidney Janis Gallery
1960 Phillips Gallery, Washington, D.C.
1961 The Museum of Modern Art, New York City
      Whitechapel Gallery, London, England
      Stedelijk Museum, Amsterdam, The Netherlands
1962 Palais des Beaux-Arts, Brussels, Belgium
      Kunsthalle, Basel, Switzerland
1962–63 Museum of Modern Art, Paris, France
1963 The Solomon R. Guggenheim Museum, New York City
1964 Marlborough Fine Art Ltd., London, England

447

GEORGE SEGAL

Born in New York City, 1924
Lives in South Brunswick, New Jersey

One-man exhibitions:
1956 Hansa Gallery, New York City
1957 Hansa Gallery
1958 Hansa Gallery
     Rutgers University, New Brunswick, New Jersey
1959 Hansa Gallery
1960 Green Gallery, New York City
1962 Green Gallery
1963 Galerie Ileana Sonnabend, Paris, France
     Gallery Schmela, Düsseldorf, Germany
     Douglass College, New Brunswick, New Jersey
1964 Green Gallery
1965 Sidney Janis Gallery, New York City
1967 Sidney Janis Gallery
1968 Museum of Contemporary Art, Chicago, Illinois
     Sidney Janis Gallery
1969 Galerie Darthea Speyer, Paris, France

DAVID SMITH

Born in Decatur, Indiana, 1906
Died near Bennington, Vermont, 1965

Selected one-man exhibitions:
1939 Skidmore College, Saratoga Springs, New York
1941 Kalamazoo Institute of Art, Kalamazoo, Michigan
     St. Paul Gallery and School of Art, St. Paul, Minnesota
     University of Minnesota, Minneapolis, Minnesota
     Sculptor's Guild, Outdoor Exhibition, New York City
1942 The Walker Art Center, Minneapolis, Minnesota
1943 Skidmore College
     The Walker Art Center
1946 Skidmore College
1947 Munson-Williams-Proctor Institute, Utica, New York
1951 Bennington College, Bennington, Vermont
1952 Bennington College
     Deerfield Academy, Deerfield, Massachusetts
     Lawrence Art Museum, Williams College, Williamstown, Massachusetts
     The Walker Art Center
1954 Cincinnati Art Museum, Cincinnati, Ohio
     The San Francisco Museum of Art, San Francisco, California
1957 The Museum of Modern Art, New York City
1959 French and Company, New York City
     New Gallery, Bennington College
1960 French and Company
     Everett Ellin Gallery, Los Angeles, California

1961 Carnegie Institute, Pittsburgh, Pennsylvania
1961–63 The Museum of Modern Art (circulated in the United States—sculptures)
1963 The Museum of Modern Art (circulated in the United States and Canada—drawings)
1964 Institute of Contemporary Art, University of Pennsylvania, Philadelphia, Pennsylvania
1965 Los Angeles County Museum of Art, Los Angeles, California
1966 The Museum of Modern Art (circulated in Europe—retrospective)
     Fogg Art Museum, Harvard University, Cambridge, Massachusetts
1967 Washington Gallery of Modern Art, Washington, D.C.
1969 The Solomon R. Guggenheim Museum, New York City
     Dallas Museum of Fine Arts, Dallas, Texas
     The Corcoran Gallery of Art, Washington, D.C.

TONY SMITH

Born in South Orange, New Jersey, 1912
Lives in South Orange, New Jersey

One-man exhibitions:
1966 Wadsworth Atheneum, Hartford, Connecticut
1967 Institute of Contemporary Art, University of Pennsylvania, Philadelphia, Pennsylvania
     Bryant Park, New York City
     The Walker Art Center, Minneapolis, Minnesota
     Galerie Müller, Stuttgart, Germany
1968 Galerie Renée Ziegler, Zurich, Switzerland
     Fischbach Gallery, New York City
     University of Southern Illinois, Carbondale, Illinois
1969 Donald Morris Gallery, Detroit, Michigan
     The Museum of Modern Art, New York City (circulating exhibition)
     University of Hawaii, Honolulu, Hawaii

FRANK STELLA

Born in Malden, Massachusetts, 1936
Lives in New York City

One-man exhibitions:
1960 Leo Castelli Gallery, New York City
1961 Galerie Lawrence, Paris, France
1962 Leo Castelli Gallery
1963 Ferus Gallery, Los Angeles, California
1964 Leo Castelli Gallery
     Galerie Lawrence
     Kasmin Ltd., London, England
1965 Ferus Gallery
1966 Leo Castelli Gallery
     The David Mirvish Gallery, Toronto, Canada
     Pasadena Art Museum, Pasadena, California
     Kasmin Ltd.
1967 Seattle Art Museum, Seattle, Washington
     Galerie Bischofberger, Zurich, Switzerland

1967 Douglas Gallery, Vancouver, British Columbia, Canada
  Leo Castelli Gallery
1968 Washington Gallery of Modern Art, Washington, D.C.
  The David Mirvish Gallery
  Irving Blum Gallery, Los Angeles, California
  Bennington College, Bennington, Vermont
  Kasmin, Ltd.
1969 University of Puerto Rico, Mayagüez, Puerto Rico
  Rose Art Museum, Brandeis University, Waltham, Massachusetts

CLYFFORD STILL

Born in Grandin, North Dakota, 1904
Lives in Westminster, Maryland

One-man exhibitions:
1943 The San Francisco Museum of Art, San Francisco, California
1946 Art of This Century, New York City
1947 Betty Parsons Gallery, New York City
  California Palace of the Legion of Honor, San Francisco, California
1950 Betty Parsons Gallery
  Metart Gallery, San Francisco, California
1951 Betty Parsons Gallery
1959 Albright-Knox Art Gallery, Buffalo, New York
1963 Institute of Contemporary Art, University of Pennsylvania, Philadelphia, Pennsylvania
1966 Albright-Knox Art Gallery

BRADLEY WALKER TOMLIN

Born in Syracuse, New York, 1899
Died in New York City, 1953

One-man exhibitions:
1922 Skaneateles and Cazenovia, New York
1923 Anderson Galleries, New York City
1926 Montross Gallery, New York City
1927 Montross Gallery
1931 Frank K. M. Rehn Galleries, New York City
1944 Frank K. M. Rehn Galleries
1950 Betty Parsons Gallery, New York City
1953 Betty Parsons Gallery
1955 Phillips Gallery, Washington, D.C.
1957–58 The Whitney Museum of American Art, New York City
  North Carolina Museum of Art, Raleigh, North Carolina
  Colorado Springs Fine Arts Center, Colorado Springs, Colorado
  Art Galleries of the University of California, Los Angeles, California
  Pasadena Art Museum, Pasadena, California
  Fine Arts Gallery of San Diego, San Diego, California
  The San Francisco Museum of Art, San Francisco, California
  Munson-Williams-Proctor Institute, Utica, New York

ANDY WARHOL

Born in Philadelphia, Pennsylvania, 1930
Lives in New York City

One-man exhibitions:

1962 Ferus Gallery, Los Angeles, California
Stable Gallery, New York City
1963 Ferus Gallery
1964 Galerie Ileana Sonnabend, Paris, France
Stable Gallery
Leo Castelli Gallery, New York City
1965 Morris International Gallery, Toronto, Canada
Galerie Ileana Sonnabend
Gian Enzo Sperone Arte Moderna, Turin, Italy
Galleria Rubbers, Buenos Aires, Argentina
Institute of Contemporary Art, University of Pennsylvania, Philadelphia, Pennsylvania
Galerie Buren, Stockholm, Sweden
1966 Leo Castelli Gallery
Institute of Contemporary Art, Boston, Massachusetts
Galerie Hans R. Nuendorf, Hamburg, Germany
1967 Galerie Ileana Sonnabend
Galerie Rudolf Zwirner, Cologne, Germany
1968 Moderna Museet, Stockholm, Sweden
Rowan Gallery, London, England
1969 Castelli-Whitney, New York City

Selected Bibliography

JOSEF ALBERS

On Albers:

Thwaites, J., and Thwaites, M. "Albers and De Monda at the Katherine Kuh Gallery," *Magazine of Art*, vol. 30 (November, 1937), 682–683.

"Abstractionist Albers' Glass Pictures," *Baltimore Museum News*, vol. 5 (December, 1942), 1.

de Kooning, Elaine. "Albers Paints a Picture," *Art News*, vol. 49 (November, 1950), 40–43.

Bill, Max. *Josef Albers, Fritz Glarner, Friedrich Vordemberge-Gildewart*. Zurich: Kunsthaus, 1956.

Charlot, J. "Nature and the Art of Josef Albers," *College Art Journal*, vol. 15, no. 3 (1956), 190–196.

Hamilton, G. H. *Josef Albers*. New Haven: Yale University Art Gallery, 1956.

Loew, M. "Albers, Impersonalization in Perfect Form," *Art News*, vol. 55 (April, 1956), 28–29.

Catalogue on Albers. Articles on Albers by Arp, W. Grohmann, F. Roh. Paris: Denise René Galerie, 1957.

Grohmann, Will. "Zum 70 Geburtstag von Josef Albers," *Frankfurter Allgemeine Zeitung* (March 19, 1958). Also in *Yale University Art Bulletin*, 1958.

Bill, Max. "Josef Albers," *Werk*, Switzerland (April, 1958).

Tillim, Sidney. "What Happened to Geometry? An Inquiry into Geometrical Painting in America," *Arts*, vol. 33 (June, 1959), 38–44.

Hopkins, Henry. "Josef Albers," *Artforum*, vol. 2 (February, 1964), 26–27.

Josef Albers: The American Years. Washington, D.C.: Washington Gallery of Modern Art, 1965.

Coplans, J. "Albers as a Printmaker," *Art News*, vol. 63 (February, 1965), 51.

Josef Albers: White Line Squares. Los Angeles: Los Angeles County Museum of Art, 1966.

Gomringer, Eugen. *Josef Albers*. New York: Wittenborn, 1968.

By Albers:

"Interview," *Art Digest*, vol. 19 (January, 1945), 15.

"On Art and Expression," "On Enunciation," "On Articulation," "Seeing Art," *Yale Literary Magazine*, New Haven, 1960.

Bucher, François. *Despite Straight Lines*. Contains explanatory text by Albers. New Haven: Yale University Press, 1961.

"The Color in My Painting," *Josef Albers*. Raleigh: North Carolina Museum of Art, 1962.

Interaction of Color. Explanatory text by Albers. New Haven: Yale University Press, 1963.

Statements in *Josef Albers: Homage to the Square*. New York: The Museum of Modern Art, Under Auspices of the International Council, 1964.

"Op Art and/or Perceptual Effects," *Yale Scientific Magazine* (November, 1965).

Statements in *Josef Albers: White Line Squares*. Los Angeles: Los Angeles County Museum of Art, 1966.

MILTON AVERY

On Avery:

Frost, Rosamund. "American Fauve," *Art News*, vol. 41 (December 15, 1942), 28.

Farber, M. "Chaim Gross, Milton Avery, and William Steig," *Magazine of Art*, vol. 36 (January, 1943), 10–15.

"Two Averys Grow; Exhibition at the Durand-Ruel Galleries; Theme, Growth, and Development of the Painter's Daughter," *Art Digest*, vol. 21 (February 15, 1946), 23.

Wight, Frederick S. *Milton Avery*. Baltimore: The Baltimore Museum of Art, 1952.

Greenberg, Clement. "Milton Avery," *Arts Magazine*, vol. 32 (December, 1957), 40–45.

Guest, B. "Avery and Gatch: Lonely Americans," *Art News*, vol. 59 (March, 1960), 42–45.

Kramer, Hilton. *Milton Avery: Paintings, 1930-1960.* New York: Thomas Yoseloff, 1962.

Judd, Don. "Exhibition at Borgenicht Gallery," *Arts Magazine*, vol. 38 (December, 1963), 61.

Milton Avery. Lincoln, Nebraska: Shelton Memorial Art Gallery, 1966.

Milton Avery 1893-1965. San Francisco: Reece Palley Gallery, 1968. (Contains essay by James Mellow and statements by Gottlieb and Rothko.)

Ashton, Dore. "Milton Avery: A Painter's Painter at Borgenicht," *Arts Magazine*, vol. 42 (May, 1968), 34–35.

ALEXANDER CALDER

On Calder:

Sweeney, J. J. *Mobiles by Calder.* Chicago: Arts Club of Chicago, 1935.

———. "Alexander Calder," *Axis*, vol. 1, no. 3 (July, 1935), 19–21.

Buffet-Picabia, Gabrielle. "Sandy Calder, Forgeron Lunaire," *Cahiers d'Art*, vol. 20-21 (1946), 324–333.

Sartre, Jean-Paul. *Alexander Calder: Mobiles, Stabiles, Constellations.* Paris: Louis Carré Galerie, 1946.

Soby, James Thrall. "Three Humorists: Klee, Miró, Calder," *Contemporary Painters.* New York: The Museum of Modern Art, 1948. Pp. 99–103.

Masson, André. "L'Atelier de Calder," *Cahiers d'Art*, vol. 24, no. 2 (1949).

"Calder," *Derrière le Miroir*, Paris, no. 31 (July, 1950).

Sweeney, J. J. *Alexander Calder.* New York: The Museum of Modern Art, 1951.

Sylvester, David. "Mobiles and Stabiles by Alexander Calder," *Art News and Review*, vol. 2, no. 26 (January 27, 1951), 4.

XXVI Biennale di Venezia, Venice, 1952, 371–378. Introduction by J. J. Sweeney.

Banham, Rayner. *"Eppur si mouve,"* *Art*, London, vol. 1, no. 7 (February 17, 1955), 4.

Calder. Basel: Kunsthalle, 1957.

Alexander Calder. Amsterdam: Stedelijk Museum, 1959.

Derrière le Miroir, Paris, no. 113 (1959). Issue devoted to Calder.

Restany, Pierre. "L'Autre Calder," *Art International*, vol. 3, nos. 5-6 (1959), 46–47.

Sweeney, J. J. *Alexander Calder.* London: The Arts Council of Great Britain, 1962.

Rickey, George. "Calder in London," *Arts Magazine*, vol. 36 (September, 1962), 22–27.

Agam. Y. "Calder en Pleine Nature," *XXᵉ Siècle* (December, 1962), 79–82 (Eng. trans.).

Derrière le Miroir, Paris, no. 141 (November, 1963). Issue devoted to Calder.

Alexander Calder: A Retrospective Exhibition. New York: The Solomon R. Guggenheim Museum, 1964. Introduction by Thomas Messer.

Anderson, Wayne V. "Calder at the Guggenheim," *Artforum*, vol. 3 (March, 1965), 37–41.

Arnason, H. H. *Alexander Calder.* Princeton: Van Nostrand, 1966.

Calder. Saint Paul, France: Fondation Maeght, 1969.

By Calder:

Statement in *Mobiles by Calder.* Andover, Mass.: Addison Gallery of American Art, 1943.

"The Ides of Art: 14 Sculptors Write," *The Tiger's Eye*, vol. 1, no. 4 (June 15, 1948), 74.

Giedion-Welker, Carola. *Contemporary Sculpture.* New York: Wittenborn, 1960. Pp. 92, 204–209, 212, 326.

Calder, An Autobiography with Pictures. New York: Pantheon, 1966.

JOHN CHAMBERLAIN

On Chamberlain:

Judd, D. "Exhibition at Castelli Gallery," *Arts Magazine*, vol. 38 (September, 1961), 71.

Creeley, Robert. "John Chamberlain," *Recent American Sculpture*. New York: The Jewish Museum, 1964. Pp. 17–18.

Judd, Donald. "Chamberlain: Another View," *Art International*, vol. 7, no. 10 (January, 1964), 38–39.

Rose, Barbara. "How to Look at Chamberlain's Sculpture," *Art International*, vol. 7, no. 10 (January, 1964), 38–39.

Lippard, Lucy. "New York Letter," *Art International*, vol. 9, no. 3 (April, 1965), 53.

Judd, Donald. "John Chamberlain," *7 Sculptors*. Philadelphia: Institute of Contemporary Art, University of Pennsylvania, 1966. Pp. 7–9.

JOSEPH CORNELL

On Cornell:

Tyler, Parker. *Exhibition of Objects by Joseph Cornell*. New York: Julien Levy Gallery, 1939.

Motherwell, Robert. "Preface to a Joseph Cornell Exhibition," A Statement on Cornell for a Proposed Catalogue for a Joseph Cornell Exhibition held at The Walker Art Center, Minneapolis, 1953. Unpublished.

Goosen, E. C. "The Plastic Poetry of Joseph Cornell," *Art International*, vol. 3, no. 10 (1959–60), 37–40.

Goldwater, Robert. "Joseph Cornell," *Dictionary of Modern Sculpture*, ed. Robert Maillard. New York: Tudor Publishing Co., 1960. Pp. 64–65.

Seitz, William. *Art of Assemblage*. New York: The Museum of Modern Art, 1961. Pp. 68–71, 72, 73, 85, 86.

Coplans, John. "Notes on the Nature of Joseph Cornell," *Artforum*, vol. 1 (February, 1963), 27–29.

Ashton, Dore. "New York Letter," *Das Kunstwerk*, Baden-Baden, vol. 16, no. 10 (April, 1963), 32.

Hopps, Walter. "Boxes," *Art International*, vol. 8, no. 2 (March, 1964), 38–41.

Waldman, Diane. "Cornell: The Compass of Boxing," *Art News*, vol. 64 (March, 1965), 42–45, 49–50.

Johnson, Ellen H. "Arcadia Enclosed: The Boxes of Joseph Cornell," *Arts Magazine*, vol. 39 (September–October, 1965), 35–37.

Hess, Thomas B. "Eccentric Propositions," *Art News Annual*, vol. 33 (1966), 9–27.

Joseph Cornell. Pasadena: Pasadena Art Museum, 1966. Introduction by Fairfield Porter.

Porter, Fairfield. "Joseph Cornell," *Art and Literature*, no. 8 (Spring, 1966), 120–130.

Waldman, Diane. *Joseph Cornell*. New York: The Solomon R. Guggenheim Museum, 1967.

Samaras, L. "Cornell's Size," *Arts Magazine*, vol. 41 (May, 1967), 45–47.

Rosenberg, Harold. "Object Poems," *The New Yorker* (June 3, 1967), 112, 114–118.

Ashbery, John. "Cornell: The Cube Root of Dreams." *Art News*, vol. 66 (Summer, 1967), 56–59.

STUART DAVIS

On Davis:

Gorky, Arshele. "Stuart Davis," *Creative Art*, vol. 9 (September, 1931), 12–17.

Jewell, Edward Alden. "Stuart Davis Offers a Penetrating Survey of the American Scene," *The New York Times* (May 10, 1932), 19.

Coates, Robert M. "Davis, Hartley and the River Seine," *The New Yorker*, vol. 18 (February 13, 1943), 58.

Wolf, Ben. "Stuart Davis: 30 Years of Evolution," *Art Digest*, vol. 20 (November 1, 1945), 10, 34.

Greenberg, Clement. "Art," *The Nation,* vol. 161 (November 17, 1945), 533–534.

Wight, Frederick S. "Stuart Davis," *Art Digest,* vol. 27 (May 15, 1953), 13, 23.

Stuart Davis. Minneapolis: The Walker Art Center, 1957.

de Kooning, Elaine. "Stuart Davis: True to Life," *Art News,* vol. 56 (April, 1957), 40–42, 54–55.

Woodruff, Hale A. "Stuart Davis, American Modern," *School Arts,* vol. 57 (October, 1957), 36–37.

Goosen, E. C. *Stuart Davis.* New York: George Braziller, 1959.

Blesh, Rudi. *Stuart Davis.* New York: Grove Press, 1960.

Stuart Davis Memorial Exhibition. Washington, D.C.: Smithsonian Institution, National Collection of Fine Arts, 1965.

By Davis:

"Self-Interview," *Creative Art,* vol. 9 (September, 1931), 208–211.

Introduction, *Abstract Painting in America.* New York: The Whitney Museum of American Art, 1935. Reprinted in *Art of Today,* vol. 6, no. 3 (April, 1935), 9–10; reprinted in part in Homer St. Gaudens, *The American Artist and His Times.* New York: Dodd, Mead, 1941. Pp. 224–225.

"Paintings by Salvadore Dali, Julien Levy Gallery," *Art Front,* vol. 1, no. 2 (January, 1935), 7.

"The New York American Scene in Art," *Art Front,* vol. 1, no. 3 (February, 1935), 6. Reprinted in part and with comment in *Art Digest,* vol. 9, no. 11 (March 1, 1935), 4, 21. Thomas Benton replies in *Art Digest,* vol. 9, no. 12 (March 12, 1935), 20–21, 25; reprinted in *Art Front,* vol. 1, no. 4 (April, 1935), 4, 8.

"American Artists and the American Dream," *New York World Telegram* (May 4, 1935), 14.

"Art at the Fair," *The Nation,* vol. 149 (July 22, 1939), 112.

"Abstraction," *The New York Times* (August 20, 1939), sec. 9, p. 7.

"Art and the Masses," *Art Digest,* vol. 14 (October 1, 1939), 13, 34.

"Abstract Art in the American Scene," *Parnassus,* vol. 13 (March, 1941), 100–103.

"Arshile Gorky in the 1930's: A Personal Recollection," *Magazine of Art,* vol. 44 (February, 1951), 56–58.

"What Abstract Art Means to Me," *Museum of Modern Art Bulletin,* vol. 18 (Spring, 1951), 14–15.

"Place of Painting in Contemporary Culture," *Art News,* vol. 56 (June, 1957), 29–30.

Statement in *Second Loan Exhibition.* New York: The Whitney Museum of American Art, 1959.

"Artists on Art and Reality, on Their Work and Values," *Daedalus,* vol. 89 (1960), 118–120.

WILLEM DE KOONING

On de Kooning:

"Spotlight on de Kooning," *Art News,* vol. 47 (April, 1948), 33.

Venice XXV Biennale, Catalogo, 1950, pp. 383–386.

de Kooning Retrospective. Boston: Boston Museum School, 1953. Foreword by Clement Greenberg.

Hess, Thomas B. "de Kooning Paints a Picture: *Woman,*" *Art News,* vol. 52 (March, 1953), 30–33, 64–67.

Fitzsimmons, J. "Review of Exhibition at Sidney Janis Gallery with Comments on 'de Kooning Paints a Picture: *Woman,*' by T. B. Hess," *Arts and Architecture,* vol. 70 (May, 1953), 4.

Steinberg, L. "de Kooning Shows Recent Painting in Woman Series at Janis Gallery," *Arts Magazine,* vol. 30 (November, 1955), 46–47.

Hess, Thomas. *Willem de Kooning.* New York: George Braziller, 1959.

Janis, Harriet, and Blesh, Rudi. *De Kooning.* New York: Grove Press, 1960.

Recent Painting by Willem de Kooning. New York: Sidney Janis Gallery, 1962. Introduction by T. B. Hess.

Hess, Thomas B. "Willem de Kooning," *Art News,* vol. 61 (March, 1962), 40–51, 60–61.

Porter, F. "Class Content in American Abstract Painting," *Art News,* vol. 61 (April, 1962), 26–28.

Fried, Michael. "New York Letter," *Art International,* vol. 6, no. 10 (December 20, 1962), 54–55, 57.

Denby, Edwin. "My Friend, de Kooning," *Art News Annual*, no. 29 (1964), 82–99.

Kozloff, Max. "The Impact of de Kooning," *Arts Yearbook*, no. 7 (1964), 77–88.

Rosenberg, Harold. "de Kooning," *The Anxious Object: Art Today and Its Audience*. New York: Horizon Press, 1964.

Within the Easel Convention: Sources of Abstract Expressionism. Cambridge, Mass.: Fogg Art Museum, 1964. Text on de Kooning by Rosalind Krauss.

Ashton, Dore, *Willem de Kooning*. Northampton, Mass.: Smith College Museum of Art, 1965.

Hess, Thomas B. "de Kooning's New Women," *Art News*, vol. 64 (March, 1965), 36–38, 63–65.

Kozloff, Max. "The Critical Reception of Abstract Expressionism," *Arts Magazine*, vol. 40 (December, 1965), 27–32.

Hess, Thomas B. *De Kooning: Recent Painting*. New York: Walter and Co., 1967.

———. *Willem de Kooning*. Amsterdam: Stedelijk Museum, 1968.

Krauss, Rosalind. "The New de Koonings," *Artforum*, vol. 6 (January, 1968), 44–47.

Hess, Thomas B. *Willem de Kooning*. New York: The Museum of Modern Art, 1969.

Bannard, Walter Darby. "Willem de Kooning's Retrospective at the Museum of Modern Art," *Artforum*, vol. 7 (April, 1969), 42–49.

By de Kooning:

Letter to the Editor (on Arshile Gorky), *Art News*, vol. 47 (January, 1949), 6. (Reprinted in *New American Painting*. New York: The Museum of Modern Art, 1958–59).

"Renaissance and Order," *Transformation*, vol. 1, no. 2 (1951), 85–87. (Reprinted in *Willem de Kooning*. Northampton, Mass.: Smith College Museum of Art, 1965.)

"Is Today's Artist with or Against the Past?" *Art News*, vol. 57 (Summer, 1958), 27, 56.

Sylvester, David. "de Kooning's Women," *Ramparts*, vol. 7, no. 11 (April, 1969), 20–24.

BURGOYNE DILLER

On Diller:

Ashton, Dore. "Exhibition Rose Fried Gallery," *Art Digest*, vol. 26 (November 15, 1951), 20.

de Kooning, Elaine. "Diller Paints a Picture: *Third Theme, 1946–1952*," *Art News*, vol. 51 (January, 1953), 26–29.

Tillim, Sidney. "What Happened to Geometry? An Inquiry into Geometrical Painting in America," *Arts Magazine*, vol. 33 (June, 1959), 38–44.

Campbell, Lawrence. "The Rule that Measures Emotion," *Art News*, vol. 60 (May, 1961), 34–35, 56–58.

Sandler, Irving H. "New York Letter," *Quadrum*, no. 14 (1963), 116.

Judd, Donald. "Exhibition at the Chalette Gallery," *Arts Magazine*, vol. 37 (January, 1963), 52.

Ashton, Dore. "Exhibition at Chalette Gallery," *Studio*, vol. 165 (March, 1963), 118.

Burgoyne Diller: 1906–1965. Trenton, N.J.: State Museum, 1966. (Contains a reprint of Campbell's 1961 article.)

Campbell, Lawrence. "Diller: The Ruling Passion," *Art News*, vol. 6 (October, 1968), 36–37.

MARK DI SUVERO

On Di Suvero:

Judd, Don. "Exhibition at the Green Gallery," *Arts Magazine*, vol. 35 (October, 1960), 60.

Geist, S. "New Sculptor: Mark di Suvero," *Arts Magazine*, vol. 35 (December, 1960), 40–43. Discussion, vol. 35 (March, 1961), 7.

Johnston, Jill. "Mark di Suvero," *Recent American Sculpture*. New York: The Jewish Museum, 1964.

Judd, Don. "Exhibition at 79 Park Place Gallery," *Arts Magazine*, vol. 38 (February, 1964), 23.

Kozloff, Max. "Further Adventures in American Sculpture," *Arts Magazine*, vol. 39 (February, 1965), 30.

Rosenstein, H. "Di Suvero: The Pressures of Reality," *Art News*, vol. 65 (February, 1967), 36–39.

Kozloff, Max. "Mark di Suvero," *Artforum*, vol. 5 (Summer, 1967), 41–46.

By Di Suvero:

McShine, Kynaston. Moderator for "New Sculpture," Symposium on Primary Structures Held at The Jewish Museum, New York, May 3, 1966, with Barbara Rose, Robert Morris, Don Judd, Mark di Suvero.

DAN FLAVIN

On Flavin:

Judd, Donald. "Black, White and Gray," *Arts Magazine*, vol. 38 (March, 1964), 38.

———. "New York Exhibition: In the Galleries, Dan Flavin," *Arts Magazine*, vol. 38 (April, 1964), 31.

Johnston, Jill. "Reviews and Previews: Dan Flavin," *Art News*, vol. 63 (January, 1965), 13.

Kozloff, Max. "Further Adventures of American Sculpture," *Arts Magazine*, vol. 39 (February, 1965), 26.

Lippard, Lucy R. "New York Letter: Off Color," *Art International*, vol. 10 (April 20, 1966), 73–75.

———. "Rejective Art," *Art International*, vol. 10 (October 20, 1966), 33–36.

Piene, N. R. "Light Art," *Art in America*, vol. 55, no. 3 (May, 1967), 38.

By Flavin:

"The Artists Say," *Art News*, vol. 4 (Summer, 1965), 72.

Statement in Barbara Rose, "ABC Art," *Art in America* (October, 1965), 68.

" '. . . In Daylight or Cool White,' An Autobiographical Sketch," *Artforum*, vol. 4 (December, 1965), 20–24.

"Some Remarks," *Artforum*, vol. 5 (December, 1966), 27–29.

Portfolio: 4 Sculptors, Recent Works and Statements by Four Young Americans," *Perspecta*, no. 11 (1967), 44.

Statement in *American Sculpture of the Sixties*. Los Angeles: Los Angeles County Museum of Art, 1967. P. 45.

"Some Other Comments . . . ," *Artforum*, vol. 6 (December, 1967), 20–25.

HELEN FRANKENTHALER

On Frankenthaler:

Coates, Robert M. "The Art Galleries," *The New Yorker*, vol. 27 (November 24, 1951), 89–91.

———. "The Art Galleries," *The New Yorker*, vol. 33 (March 9, 1957), 80, 83–84.

Rudikoff, Sonya. "Helen Frankenthaler's Painting," in B. H. Friedman, ed. *School of New York: Some Younger Artists*. New York: Grove Press, 1959.

O'Hara, Frank. *Helen Frankenthaler*. New York: The Jewish Museum, 1960.

Goosen, E. C. "Helen Frankenthaler," *Art International*, vol. 5 (October 20, 1961), 76–79.

Ashbery, John. "Paris Notes," *Art International*, vol. 5 (November 20, 1961), 48–50.

Judd, Don. "In the Galleries," *Arts Magazine*, vol. 36 (January, 1962), 38–39.

Fried, Michael. "New York Letter," *Art International*, vol. 7 (April 25, 1963), 54–56.

———. "New York Letter," *Art International*, vol. 7 (May 25, 1963), 69–72.

Kozloff, Max. "Art and the New York Avant-Garde," *Partisan Review*, vol. 31 (Fall, 1964), 535–554.

Berkson, William. "Poet of the Surface," *Arts Magazine*, vol. 39 (May–June, 1965), 44–50.

Ashton, Dore. "Helen Frankenthaler," *Studio,* vol. 170 (August, 1965), 52–55.

Baro, Gene. "The Achievement of Helen Frankenthaler," *Art International,* vol. 11, no. 7 (September 20, 1967), 33–38.

Goosen, E. C. *Helen Frankenthaler.* New York: The Whitney Museum of American Art, 1969.

Rosenstein, Harris. "The Colorful Gesture," *Art News,* vol. 68 (March, 1969), 29–31, 68.

Rose, Barbara. "Painting Within the Tradition, the Career of Helen Frankenthaler," *Artforum,* vol. 7 (April, 1969), 28–33.

By Frankenthaler

"New Talent in the U.S.," With Note by the Artist, *Art in America,* vol. 45 (March, 1957), 28–29.

"Discussion: Is There a New Academy?" *Art News,* vol. 58 (June, 1959), 34.

Quotations from an Interview for the B.B.C., London, by David Sylvester, 1962, in *Helen Frankenthaler.* Bennington, Vt.: Bennington College, 1962.

Geldzahler, Henry. "An Interview with Helen Frankenthaler," *Artforum,* vol. 4 (October, 1965), 36–38.

Cyr, Donald J. "A Conversation with Helen Frankenthaler," *School Arts,* vol. 67 (April, 1968), 30–32.

Transcript of a Tape-Recorded Interview by Barbara Rose (August, 1968). Archives of American Art.

ARSHILE GORKY

On Gorky:

An Exhibition of Work by 46 Painters and Sculptors under 35 Years of Age, ed. Dorothy C. Miller. New York: The Museum of Modern Art, 1930.

Kiesler, Frederick J. "Murals Without Walls: Relating to Gorky's Newark Project," *Art Front,* vol. 2 (December, 1936), 10–11.

Sweeney, J. J. "Five American Painters," *Harper's Bazaar* (April, 1944), 122, 124.

Greenberg, Clement. "Art: Arshile Gorky," *The Nation,* vol. 160 (March 24, 1945), 342–343; vol. 162 (May 4, 1946), 552–553; vol. 166 (March 6, 1948), 384–385; vol. 167 (December 11, 1948), 676.

———. "Art Chronicle," *Partisan Review,* vol. 15 (March, 1948), 369; vol. 17 (May–June, 1950), 512–513; vol. 22 (Spring, 1955), 179–196.

Crowley, Malcolm. "Arshile Gorky—A Note from a Friend," *New York Herald Tribune* (September 5, 1948), sec. 6, p. 3.

de Kooning, Willem. Letter to the Editor, *Art News,* vol. 47 (January, 1949), 6.

Barr, Alfred H., Jr. "Gorky, de Kooning, Pollock," *Art News,* vol. 49 (Summer, 1950), 22, 60.

Schwabacher, Ethel. *Arshile Gorky Memorial Exhibition.* New York: The Whitney Museum of American Art, 1951.

de Kooning, Elaine. "Gorky: Painter of His Own Legend," *Art News,* vol. 49 (January, 1951), 38–41, 63–66.

Davis, Stuart. "Arshile Gorky in the 1930's," *Magazine of Art,* vol. 44 (February, 1951), 56–58.

Goodenough, Robert. "Arshile Gorky," *Art News,* vol. 49 (February, 1951), 46.

Goodrich, Lloyd. "Notes on Eight Works by Arshile Gorky," *Magazine of Art,* vol. 44 (February, 1951), 59–61.

Arshile Gorky. Princeton: Princeton University Art Museum, 1952.

Seitz, William C. "A Gorky Exhibit," *Daily Princetonian,* vol. 76 (October 14, 1952), 2.

Fitzsimmons, James. "The Late Gorky," *Art Digest,* vol. 27 (May 1, 1953), 16.

Seitz, William. "Arshile Gorky's *The Plough and the Song,*" Oberlin College, *Allen Memorial Art Museum Bulletin,* vol. 12, no. 1 (1954), 4–15.

Porter, Fairfield. "Arshile Gorky," *Art News,* vol. 53 (April, 1954), 53.

Schwabacher, Ethel. *Arshile Gorky.* New York: Macmillan, 1957.

Shapiro, Meyer. "Gorky: The Creative Influence," *Art News,* vol. 56 (September, 1957), 28–31, 52.

Ashton, Dore. "Art: Gorky and Contemporary American Painting," *Art and Architecture,* vol. 75 (January, 1958), 6.

Rosenblum, Robert. "Arshile Gorky," *Arts Magazine*, vol. 32 (January, 1958), 30–33.

Rosenberg, Harold. *Gorky*. New York: Horizon Press, 1962.

Seitz, William. *Arshile Gorky: Paintings, Drawings, Studies*. New York: The Museum of Modern Art, 1962.

Rieff, R. "Late Works of Arshile Gorky," *Art Journal*, vol. 22 (Spring, 1963), 148–152.

Rubin, William. "Arshile Gorky, Surrealism, and the New American Painting," *Art International*, vol. 7, no. 2 (February 25, 1963), 27–38.

Roberts, K. "Major Retrospective Exhibition at the Tate," *Burlington Magazine*, vol. 107 (May, 1965), 270–271.

Mooradian, K. "Unknown Gorky," *Art News*, vol. 66 (September, 1967), 52–53.

Levy, Julien. *Arshile Gorky*. New York: Harry N. Abrams, 1968.

By Gorky:

Johnson, Malcolm. "Interview," *New York Sun* (August 22, 1941).

Statement about *Garden in Sochi*, Collections Archives, The Museum of Modern Art, June, 1942 (at request of Dorothy Miller).

"The WPA Murals at the Newark Airport" (included in H. Rosenberg, *Gorky*. New York: Horizon Press, 1962).

ADOLPH GOTTLIEB

On Gottlieb:

Newman, Barnett. *Adolph Gottlieb*. New York: Wakefield Gallery, 1944.

Frost, Rosamund. "Adolph Gottlieb," *Art News*, vol. 43 (February 15, 1944), 23.

Greenberg, Clement. "Art: Adolph Gottlieb," *The Nation*, vol. 165 (December 6, 1947), 629–630.

Kootz, Samuel M. *Adolph Gottlieb*. New York: Kootz Gallery, 1952.

Fitzsimmons, James. "Adolph Gottlieb," *Everyday Art Quarterly*, no. 25 (1953), 1–4.

Greenberg, Clement. *Adolph Gottlieb*. Bennington, Vt.: Bennington College, Williams College, 1954.

Rosenblum, Robert. "Adolph Gottlieb: New Murals," *Art Digest*, vol. 28 (April 15, 1954), 11.

Greenberg, Clement. *Adolph Gottlieb*. New York: The Jewish Museum, 1957.

Rubin, William. "Adolph Gottlieb," *Art International*, vol. 3, nos. 3–4 (1959), 34–37.

Sandler, Irving H. "Adolph Gottlieb," *Art News*, vol. 57 (February, 1959), 10.

Alloway, Lawrence. "Sign and Surface: Notes on Black and White Painting in New York," *Quadrum*, no. 9 (1960), 49–62.

Judd, Don. "Adolph Gottlieb," *Arts Magazine*, vol. 35 (December, 1960), 52–53.

Fried, Michael. "New York Letter," *Art International*, vol. 6 (October 25, 1962), 75–76.

Friedman, Martin. *Adolph Gottlieb*. Minneapolis: The Walker Art Center, 1963.

Rosenstein, Harris. "Gottlieb at the Summit," *Art News*, vol. 65 (April, 1966), 42–43.

Doty, Robert, and Waldman, Diane. *Adolph Gottlieb*. New York: The Whitney Museum of American Art, The Solomon R. Guggenheim Museum, 1968.

Waldman, D. "Gottlieb: Signs and Suns," *Art News*, vol. 66 (February, 1968), 26–29.

Ashton, Dore. "Adolph Gottlieb at the Guggenheim and Whitney Museums," *Studio*, vol. 175 (April, 1968), 201–202.

Hudson, Andrew. "Adolph Gottlieb's Paintings at the Whitney," *Art International*, vol. 12, no. 4 (April 20, 1968), 24–28.

By Gottlieb:

Gottlieb, Adolph, and Rothko, Mark, in "The Realism of Art: A New Platform: Globalism Pops into View," by Edward Alden Jewell. *The New York Times* (June 13, 1943), 9.

Letter to the Editor, *The New York Times* (June 13, 1943), sec. 2, p. 9 (with Rothko and Newman).

"The Portrait and the Modern Artist," mimeographed script of broadcast by Gottlieb and Rothko on "Art in New York," H. Stix, Director, WNYC, New York (October 13, 1943).

Statement in "The Ides of Art," *The Tiger's Eye*, vol. 1, no. 2 (December, 1947), 43.

"Unintelligibility," 1948 mimeographed script of talk given in forum: The Artist Speaks, The Museum of Modern Art, New York, May 5, 1948.

"My Painting," *Arts and Architecture*, vol. 68 (September, 1951), 21.

"The Artist and the Public," *Art in America*, vol. 42, no. 4 (December, 1954), 266–271.

"Artist and Society: A Brief Case History," *College Art Journal*, vol. 14 (Winter, 1955), 96–101.

"Adolph Gottlieb: An Interview with David Sylvester," *Living Arts*, no. 2 (1963), 2–10.

"Postcards from Adolph Gottlieb," *Location*, vol. 1 (Summer, 1964), 19–26.

"Jackson Pollock: An Artists' Symposium," *Art News*, vol. 66 (April, 1967), 31.

PHILIP GUSTON

On Guston:

Janson, H. W. "Philip Guston," *Magazine of Art*, vol. 40, no. 2 (February, 1947), 54–58.

Ashton, Dore. "Art: The Age of Lyricism," *Arts and Architecture*, vol. 73, no. 3 (March, 1956), 14–15, 43–44.

Creeley, Robert. "Philip Guston: A Note," *Black Mountain Review*, Black Mountain, N.C. (Spring, 1956).

Steinberg, Leo. "Fritz Glarner and Philip Guston Among '12 Americans' at the Museum of Modern Art," *Arts Magazine*, vol. 30 (June, 1956), 42–45.

Sandler, Irving. "Guston: A Long Voyage Home," *Art News*, vol. 58 (December, 1959), 36–39, 64–65.

Ashton, Dore. *Philip Guston*. New York: Grove Press, 1960.

Arnason, H. H. *Philip Guston*. New York: The Solomon R. Guggenheim Museum, 1962.

Hunter, Sam. "Philip Guston," *Art International*, vol. 6, no. 4 (May, 1962), 62–67.

O'Hara, Frank. "Growth and Guston," *Art News*, vol. 61 (May, 1962), 31–33.

Ashton, Dore. "Philip Guston," *Aujourd'hui*, vol. 6 (June, 1962), 28–29.

Alloway, Lawrence. "Notes on Guston," *Art Journal*, vol. 22, no. 1 (Fall, 1962), 8–11.

Sylvester, David. "London," *New Statesman*, vol. 65, no. 1666 (February 15, 1963), 247–248.

Feldman, Morton. "Philip Guston: The Last Painter," *Art News Annual*, no. 31 (1965), 97–100.

Berkson, Bill. "Dialogue with Philip Guston," *Art and Literature*, no. 7 (Winter, 1965), 56–59.

Philip Guston: Recent Paintings and Drawings. New York: The Jewish Museum, 1966. Introduction by Sam Hunter.

Berkson, W. "Philip Guston: A New Emphasis," *Arts Magazine*, vol. 40 (February, 1966), 15–18.

Ashton, Dore. "Exhibition at the Jewish Museum," *Arts and Architecture*, vol. 83 (April, 1966), 7.

By Guston:

Statement in *It Is*, no. 1 (Spring, 1958), 44.

Recorded Interview with H. H. Arnason in *Philip Guston*. New York: The Solomon R. Guggenheim Museum, 1962.

Statements (translated) in *Philip Guston*. Amsterdam: Stedelijk Museum, 1962.

Interview with David Sylvester, B.B.C., 1963 (typescript).

"Piero della Francesca: The Impossibility of Painting," *Art News*, vol. 64 (May, 1965), 38–39.

"Philip Guston's Object: A Dialogue with Harold Rosenberg," *Philip Guston: Recent Paintings and Drawings*. New York: The Jewish Museum, 1966.

HANS HOFMANN

On Hofmann

Matter, Mercedes. "Hans Hofmann," *Arts and Architecture*, vol. 63 (May, 1946), 26–28, 48.

de Kooning, Elaine. "Hans Hofmann Paints a Picture," *Art News*, vol. 48 (February, 1950), 38–41, 58–59.

Fitzsimmons, James. "Hans Hofmann," *Everyday Art Quarterly*, no. 28 (1953), 23–26.

Greenberg, Clement. *Hans Hofmann: A Retrospective Exhibition*. Bennington, Vt.: Bennington College, 1955.

Sawyer, Kenneth B. "Largely Hans Hofmann," *Baltimore Museum of Art News,* vol. 18, no. 3 (February, 1955), pp. 9–12.

Kaprow, Allan. "Hans Hofmann." New Brunswick, N.J.: Rutgers University, 1956.

Wight, Frederick S. *Hans Hofmann.* Berkeley: University of California Press, 1957. Published on the occasion of the Hofmann Retrospective at The Whitney Museum of American Art and the Art Galleries of the University of California.

Greenberg, Clement. "Hofmann's Early Abstract Paintings," *Hans Hofmann.* New York: Kootz Gallery, 1959

————. *Hofmann.* Paris: Georges Fall, 1961.

Hunter, Sam. *Hans Hofmann.* New York: Harry N. Abrams, 1963 (reprints of five texts by the artist).

Seitz, William, *Hans Hofmann.* New York: The Museum of Modern Art, 1963.

Fried, Michael. "New York Letter," *Art International,* vol. 1, no. 1 (April, 1963), 54–55.

Judd, Don. "Hofmann," *Arts,* vol. 37, no. 7 (April, 1963), 55.

Bultman, Fritz. "The Achievement of Hans Hofmann," *Art News,* vol. 62 (September, 1963), 43–45, 54–55.

Rosenberg, Harold. "Hans Hofmann and the Stability of the New," *The New Yorker,* vol. 39 (November 2, 1963), 100, 103–105, 108–110.

Fried, Michael. "New York Letter," *Art International,* vol. 7, no. 9 (December, 1963), 66.

Hans Hofmann. New York: Kootz Gallery, 1964.

Loran, Erle. *Hans Hofmann.* Berkeley: University of California Press, 1964.

Rosenberg, Harold. "Homage to Hans Hofmann," *Art News,* vol. 65 (January, 1967), 49.

Kootz, Sam. "Credibility of Color: Hans Hofmann, An Area of Optimism," *Arts Magazine,* vol. 41 (February, 1967), 37–39.

Bannard, Walter Darby. "Hofmann's Rectangles," *Artforum,* vol. 7 (Summer, 1969), 38–41.

By Hofmann:

"Painting and Culture," *Fortnightly,* Campbell, Calif., vol. 1, no. 1 (September 11, 1931), 5–7.

"On the Aims of Art," *Fortnightly,* Campbell, Calif. vol. 1, no. 13 (February 26, 1932), 7–11.

Statement in *Hans Hofmann.* New York: Art of This Century, 1944.

Search for the Real and Other Essays. Andover, Mass.: Addison Gallery of American Art, 1948. Republished by the M.I.T. Press, 1967.

"The Resurrection of the Plastic Art," *Hans Hofmann.* New York: Kootz Gallery, 1954.

"The Color Problem in Pure Painting: Its Creative Origin," *Hans Hofmann.* New York: Kootz Gallery, 1955. (Reprinted in *Hans Hofmann Retrospective Exhibition Catalogue.* Berkeley: University of California Press, 1957; and in San Hunter, *Hans Hofmann.* New York: Harry N. Abrams, 1963.)

Statement in *It Is,* no. 3 (Winter–Spring, 1959), 10.

Statement in *Hans Hofmann.* New York: Kootz Gallery, 1960.

"Hans Hofmann on Art," *Art Journal,* vol. 22, no. 3 (Spring, 1963), 180, 182.

EDWARD HOPPER

On Hopper:

Goodrich, Lloyd. "The Paintings of Edward Hopper," *The Arts,* vol. 11 (March, 1927), 134–138.

du Bois, Guy Pène. "The American Paintings of Edward Hopper," *Creative Art,* vol. 8 (March, 1931), 187–191.

Crowninshield, Frank. "A Series of American Artists, No. 3—Edward Hopper," *Vanity Fair,* vol. 38 (June, 1932), 11, 30.

Edward Hopper Retrospective. New York: The Museum of Modern Art, 1933. Articles by Alfred H. Barr, Jr., and Charles Burchfield.

Paintings, Watercolors and Etchings by Edward Hopper. Pittsburgh: Carnegie Institute, 1937.

Robert Henri and Five of His Pupils. New York: Century Association, 1946.

Brown, Milton. "The Early Realism of Hopper and Burchfield," *College Art Journal*, vol. 7 (Autumn, 1947), 3–11.

Goodrich, Lloyd. *Edward Hopper Retrospective Exhibition*. New York: The Whitney Museum of American Art, 1950.

Burchfield, Charles. "Hopper: Career of Silent Poetry," *Art News*, vol. 49 (March, 1950), 14–17.

Richardson, E. P. "Three American Painters: Sheeler, Hopper, Burchfield," *Perspectives U.S.A.*, vol. 16 (Summer, 1956), 111–119.

Tyler, Parker. "Hopper/Pollock," *Art News Annual*, no. 26 (1957), 86–107.

Geldzahler, Henry. "Edward Hopper," *Metropolitan Museum Bulletin*, vol. 21 (November, 1962), 113–117.

A Retrospective of Oils and Watercolors by Edward Hopper. Tucson: University of Arizona, 1963.

Goodrich, Lloyd. *Edward Hopper*. New York: The Whitney Museum of American Art, 1964.

Tillim, Sidney. "Edward Hopper and the Provincial Principle," *Arts Magazine*, vol. 39 (November, 1964), 24–31.

Edward Hopper. São Paulo IX, United States of America, 1967. Statements by B. O'Doherty, J. T. Soby, John Canaday; Essays by Lloyd Goodrich and William C. Seitz. Published by the Smithsonian Institution, Washington, D.C.

By Hopper:

Statement in *Edward Hopper*. New York: The Museum of Modern Art, 1933.

"Edward Hopper Objects" (Letter to Nathaniel Pousette-Dart), *The Art of Today*, vol. 6 (February, 1935), 11.

JASPER JOHNS

On Johns:

Heller, Ben. "Jasper Johns," *School of New York: Some Younger Painters*, ed. by B. H. Friedman. New York: Grove Press, 1959. Pp. 30–35.

16 Americans. New York: The Museum of Modern Art, 1959.

Restany, Pierre. "Jasper Johns and the Metaphysic of the Commonplace," *Cimaise*, Serie 8, no. 3 (September, 1961), 90–97.

Janis, Harriet, and Blesh, Rudi. *Collage*. Philadelphia: Chilton Co., 1962.

Jasper Johns Retrospective. Los Angeles: Everett Ellin Gallery, 1962.

Rosenblum, Robert. "Les Œuvres Recentes de Jasper Johns," *XXᵉ Siècle*, ns. 24, Supp. 19–20 (February, 1962).

Gottlieb, Carla. "The Pregnant Woman, The Flag, The Eye: Three New Themes in Twentieth Century Art," *The Journal of Aesthetics and Art Criticism* (Winter, 1962), 117–187.

Tono, Yoshiaki. "Jasper Johns, or the Metaphysics of Vulgarity," *Mizue*, Tokyo, no. 685 (April, 1962), 24–40.

Steinberg, Leo. *Jasper Johns*. New York: Wittenborn, 1963.

Fried, Michael. "New York Letter," *Art International*, vol. 7, no. 2 (February 25, 1963), 60–62.

Swenson, G. R. "Reviews and Previews: Jasper Johns," *Art News*, vol. 61 (February, 1963), 11–12.

Judd, Don. "Six Painters and the Object at the Guggenheim," *Arts Magazine*, vol. 37 (May, 1963), 108.

Jasper Johns. New York: The Jewish Museum, 1964. Essays by Alan Solomon and John Cage.

Porter, Fairfield. "The Education of Jasper Johns," *Art News*, vol. 62 (February, 1964), 44–45, 61–62.

Rosenberg, Harold. "Jasper Johns; Things the Mind Already Knows," *Vogue*, vol. 143, no. 3 (February, 1964), 74.

Tillim, Sidney. "Ten Years of Jasper Johns," *Arts Magazine*, vol. 38 (April, 1964), 22–26.

Ashbery, John. "Brooms and Prisms," *Art News,* vol. 65 (March, 1966), 58–59.

Kozloff, Max. "Jasper Johns: Colors, Maps, Devices," *Artforum,* vol. 6 (November, 1967), 26–31.

———— *Jasper Johns.* New York: Harry N. Abrams, 1969.

By Johns:

Statement in *16 Americans.* New York: The Museum of Modern Art, 1959. P. 22.

"Duchamp," *Scrap* (December 23, 1960).

Interview with Walter Hopps, *Artforum,* vol. 3 (March, 1965), 32–36.

DONALD JUDD

On Judd:

Hopps, Walter. "Donald Judd," United States of America, An Exhibition Organized by the Pasadena Art Museum for the VIII Bienal de São Paulo, Brazil, 1965.

Rose, Barbara. "Donald Judd," in U.S. Section VIII, San Paulo Bienal, 1965, *Artforum,* vol. 3 (June, 1965), 30–32.

Rose, Barbara. "ABC Art," *Art in America,* vol. 53 (October–November, 1965), 58–69.

Friedman, Martin. "Donald Judd," *Eight Sculptors: The Ambiguous Image.* Minneapolis: The Walker Art Center, 1966.

McShine, Kynaston. Introduction, *Primary Structures.* New York: The Jewish Museum, 1966.

Krauss, Rosalind. "Allusion and Illusion in Donald Judd," *Artforum,* vol. 4 (May, 1966), 24–26.

Bochner, M. "Primary Structures," *Arts Magazine,* vol. 40 (June, 1966), 32–35.

Rose, Barbara. *A New Aesthetic.* Washington: Washington Gallery of Modern Art, 1967. Pp. 8–20, 43–49.

Fried, Michael. "Art and Objecthood," *Artforum,* vol. 5 (June, 1967), 12–23.

Agee, William C. *Don Judd.* New York: The Whitney Museum of American Art, 1968.

By Judd:

Regular Reviewer for *Arts Magazine,* 1959–1965.

"Specific Objects," *Contemporary Sculpture, Arts Yearbook 8* (1965), 74–82.

Glaser, Bruce, moderator; Lucy Lippard, ed. "Questions to Stella and Judd," *Art News,* vol. 65 (September, 1966), 55–61.

ELLSWORTH KELLY

On Kelly:

Goosen, E. C. "Ellsworth Kelly," *Derrière le Miroir,* no. 110 (1958).

Tillim, S. "Profiles: Ellsworth Kelly," *Arts Yearbook 3* (1959), 148–155.

———— "Exhibition at Betty Parsons," *Arts Magazine,* vol. 34 (October, 1959), 48–50.

Alloway, Lawrence. "Heraldry and Sculpture," *Art International,* vol. 6, no. 3 (April, 1962), 52–53.

Rubin, William. "Ellsworth Kelly: The Big Form," *Art News,* vol. 62 (November, 1963), 32–35.

Fried, Michael. "New York Letter," *Art International,* vol. 7, no. 9 (Christmas–New Year, 1963–64), 54–55.

Ashton, Dore. "Exhibition at Janis Gallery," *Studio,* vol. 170 (July, 1965), 40–42.

"4 Drawings of 1965," *Artforum,* vol. 4 (February, 1966), 40–41.

Rose, Barbara. "Ellsworth Kelly as Sculptor," *Artforum,* vol. 5 (Summer, 1967), 51–55.

"*Spectrum II,* 1966–1967, A Painting by E. Kelly, American, Born 1923," *St. Louis Museum Bulletin,* vol. 3 (November, 1967), 4–5.

Waldman, D. "Kelly Color, New Show at Janis," *Art News*, vol. 67 (October, 1968), 40–41.

Coplans, John. "The Earlier Work of Ellsworth Kelly," *Artforum*, vol. 7 (Summer, 1969), 48–55.

By Kelly:

Geldzahler, Henry. "Kelly," Interview with Ellsworth Kelly, *Art International*, vol. 8, no. 1 (February 15, 1964), 47–48.

FRANZ KLINE

On Kline:

Hess, Thomas B. "Miracle at Schenby Park," *Art News*, vol. 51 (November, 1952), 28–30, 66–67.

Goodenough, Robert. "Kline Paints a Picture," *Art News*, vol. 51 (December, 1952), 36–39, 63–64.

Ashton, Dore. "Art," *Arts and Architecture*, vol. 73 (April, 1956), 3, 10–12; vol. 75 (July, 1958), 10, 31–33; vol. 76 (March, 1959), 8, 28–29.

Sawyer, Kenneth B. "Franz Kline," Venice XXX Biennale, United States Section, 1960, pp. 314–316.

Kline. New York: Sidney Janis Gallery, 1960, 1961, 1963.

Ashton, Dore. "Franz Kline," *Cimaise*, vol. 8 (May–June, 1961), 70–83.

de Kooning, Elaine. *Franz Kline Memorial Exhibition*. Washington: Washington Gallery of Modern Art, 1962.

Goldwater, Robert. "Art Chronicle: Masters of the New," *Partisan Review*, vol. 29 (Summer, 1962), 416–420.

Langsner, Jules. "Kline," *Artforum*, vol. 1 (July, 1962), 4–5.

de Kooning, Elaine. "Franz Kline: Painter of His Own Life," *Art News*, vol. 61 (November, 1962), 28–31, 64–69.

Franz Kline. Amsterdam: Stedelijk Museum, 1963. Introduction by Frank O'Hara.

Langsner, Jules. "Franz Kline Calligraphy and Information Theory," *Art International*, vol. 7, no. 3 (March, 1963), 25–29.

O'Hara, Frank, *Franz Kline*. London: Whitechapel Gallery, 1964.

Robbins, Daniel and Eugenia. "Franz Kline: Rough Impulsive Gesture," *Studio*, vol. 167 (May, 1964), 186–189.

Pavia, Philip. "Polemic on One-Eye Formats," *Art News*, vol. 65 (December, 1966), 28–31, 62–64.

Dawson, Fielding. *An Emotional Memoir of Franz Kline*. New York: Pantheon Books, 1967.

Franz Kline. New York: Marlborough-Gerson Gallery, 1967. (Introduction by Robert Goldwater.)

Gordon, John. *Franz Kline: 1910–1962*. New York: The Whitney Museum of American Art, 1968.

By Kline:

O'Hara, Frank. "Franz Kline Talking," *Evergreen Review*, vol. 2 (Autumn, 1958), 58–68.

"Franz Kline, 1910–1962: An Interview with David Sylvester," *Living Arts*, no. 1 (1963), 2–13.

GABRIEL KOHN

On Kohn:

Petersen, Valerie. "Gabriel Kohn Makes a Sculpture," *Art News*, vol. 60 (October, 1961), 48–51, 66–67.

"Gabriel Kohn," *Art News*, vol. 61 (January, 1963), 39, 49.

Tillim, Sidney. "Month in Review: Gabe Kohn," *Arts Magazine*, vol. 37 (February, 1963), 43–44.

Rose, Barbara. "New York Notes," *Art International*, vol. 7, no. 2 (February 25, 1963), 77–78.

Coplans, J. "Sculptors Meet at Long Beach," *Art News*, vol. 64 (December, 1965), 52, 61.

Wilson, W. "Four Defectors to L.A.," *Art in America*, vol. 56 (March, 1968), 102.

ROY LICHTENSTEIN

On Lichtenstein:

Swenson, G. R. "New American Sign Painters," *Art News*, vol. 61 (September, 1962), 44–47.

Tillim, Sidney. "Roy Lichtenstein and the Hudson River School at Mi Chou," *Arts Magazine*, vol. 37 (October, 1962), 55–56.

Rosenblum, Robert. "Roy Lichtenstein and the Realist Revolt," *Metro*, 8 (April, 1963), 38–46.

Loran, Erle. "Cézanne and Lichtenstein: Problem of Transformation," *Artforum*, vol. 2 (September, 1963), 34–35.

Judd, Don. "Exhibition at Castelli Gallery," *Arts Magazine*, vol. 38 (November, 1963), 32–33.

Kozloff, Max. "Art: Dissimulated Pop," *The Nation*, vol. 199 (November 30, 1964), 418.

Lichtenstein. Rome: Fantazaria, 1966. (Contains Alan Solomon, "Conversation with Lichtenstein"; Maurizio Calvesi, "Lichtenstein: A Global Painter"; Alberto Boatto, "The Comic Strip Under the Microscope"; Filiberta Menna, "The Organized Perception of Lichtenstein"; Max Kozloff, "Dissimulated Pop"; Ellen H. Johnson, "Lichtenstein and the Printed Image"; Robert Rosenblum, "Lichtenstein at the XXXIII Venice Biennale.")

Fry, Edward F. "Roy Lichtenstein's Recent Landscapes," *Art and Literature*, Lausanne, no. 8 (Spring, 1966), 111–119.

Beeren, Wim. *Roy Lichtenstein*. Amsterdam: Stedelijk Museum, 1967.

Coplans, John. *Roy Lichtenstein*. Pasadena: Pasadena Art Museum, 1967.

Alloway, Lawrence. "Roy Lichtenstein's Period Style: From the Thirties to the Sixties and Back," *Arts Magazine*, vol. 42 (September, 1967), 24–29.

Waldman, D. "Remarkable Commonplace," *Art News*, vol. 66 (October, 1967), 28–31.

Hamilton, R., and Alloway, L. "Roy Lichtenstein," *Studio*, vol. 175 (January, 1968), 20–31.

Baro, Gene. "Roy Lichtenstein: Technique as Style," *Art International*, vol. 12, no. 9 (November 20, 1968), 35–39.

Boime, Albert. "Roy Lichtenstein and the Comic Strip," *Art Journal*, vol. 28 (Winter, 1968–69), 155–159.

By Lichtenstein:

Coplans, John. Interview, *Artforum*, vol 2 (October, 1963), 31. (Reprinted in *Roy Lichtenstein*. Amsterdam: Stedelijk Museum, 1967.)

Swenson, Gene. "What Is Pop Art?" Interview, *Art News*, vol. 62 (November, 1963), 25, 62–63.

Glaser, B. "Lichtenstein, Oldenburg, Warhol: A Discussion," *Artforum*, vol. 4 (February, 1966), 20–24.

Coplans, John. "Talking with Roy Lichtenstein," *Artforum*, vol. 4 (May, 1967), 34–40.

MORRIS LOUIS

On Louis:

Berkowitz, Leon. "Statement on the Artist," *Morris Louis*. Washington, D.C.: Workshop Art Center, 1953.

Greenberg, Clement. Note, in Gallery Announcement, Emerging Talent. New York: Kootz Gallery, 1954.

Tapié de Céylèran, Michel. Introduction to Catalogue: *Morris Louis*. New York: Martha Jackson Gallery, 1957.

Sawin, Martica. "Morris Louis," *Arts Magazine*, vol. 33 (May, 1959), 58–59.

Greenberg, Clement. "Louis and Noland," *Art International*, vol. 4, no. 5 (May 25, 1960), 26–29.

Alloway, Lawrence. Introduction, *Morris Louis: 1912–1962*. New York: The Solomon R. Guggenheim Museum, 1963.

Greenberg, Clement. Introduction, in *Three New American Painters: Louis, Noland, Olitski*. Regina, Canada: Normal McKenzie Art Gallery, 1963. (Reprinted in *Canadian Art*, vol. 20 [May, 1963], 172–175 and excerpts reprinted in *Morris Louis*. London: Kasmin Ltd., 1963.)

Rosenblum, Robert. Note in *Towards a New Abstraction*. New York: The Solomon R. Guggenheim Museum, 1963.

Fried, Michael. "Some Notes on Morris Louis," *Arts Magazine*, vol. 38 (November, 1963), 22–27.

Rosenblum, Robert. "Morris Louis at the Guggenheim Museum," *Art International*, vol. 7, no. 9 (December 5, 1963), 24–27.

Fried, Michael. "The Confounding of Confusion," *Arts Yearbook*, no. 7 (1964), 36–45.

Tillim, Sidney. "Exhibition at Emmerich Gallery," *Arts Magazine*, vol. 39 (December, 1964), 66–67.

Robbins, Daniel. "Morris Louis at the Juncture of Two Traditions," *Quadrum*, no. 18 (1965), 41–54.

Rosenblum, Robert. Introduction, *Morris Louis*. Amsterdam: Stedelijk Museum, 1965.

Solomon, Alan. Introduction, *Morris Louis*. London: Whitechapel Gallery, 1965.

Greenberg, Clement. Letter to the Editor, *Art International*, vol. 9, no. 4 (May, 1965), 66.

Fried, Michael. *Morris Louis: 1912–1962*. Boston: Boston Museum of Fine Arts, 1967.

————. "The Achievement of Morris Louis," *Artforum*, vol. 5 (February, 1967), 34–40.

Goldin, A. "Morris Louis Thinking the Unwordable," *Art News*, vol. 67 (April, 1968), 48–49.

"Kenneth Noland, Morris Louis and Anthony Caro at the Metropolitan Museum," *Arts Magazine*, vol. 42 (Summer, 1968), 56.

Fried, Michael. *Morris Louis*. New York: Harry N. Abrams, 1969.

ROBERT MORRIS

On Morris:

Judd, Don. "Black, White and Gray," *Arts Magazine*, vol. 38 (March, 1964), 36–38.

————. "Exhibition at the Green Gallery," *Arts Magazine*, vol. 39 (February, 1965), 54.

Kozloff, Max. "Further Adventures in American Sculpture," *Arts Magazine*, vol. 39 (February, 1965), 27.

Rose, Barbara. "Looking at American Sculpture," *Artforum*, vol. 3 (February, 1965), 29–36.

————. "ABC Art," *Art in America*, vol. 53 (October–November, 1965), 58–69.

Friedman, Martin. *Eight Sculptors: The Ambiguous Image*. Minneapolis: The Walker Art Center, 1966. Pp. 18, 20–21.

Antin, David. "Art and Information. 1: Grey Paint, Robert Morris," *Art News*, vol. 65 (April, 1966), 22–24, 56–58.

Ranier, Y. "Don't Give the Game Away," *Arts Magazine*, vol. 41 (April, 1967), 44.

Battcock, Gregory. "Robert Morris: New Sculptures at Castelli," *Arts Magazine*, vol. 42 (May, 1968), 30–31.

Müller, Gregoire. "Robert Morris Presents Anti-Form," *Arts Magazine*, vol. 43 (February, 1969), 29–30.

By Morris:

"Notes on Dance," *Tulane Drama Review*, vol. 10 (Winter, 1965), 179–186.

"Notes on Sculpture," *Artforum*, vol. 4 (February, 1966), 42–44; Part II, vol. 5 (October, 1966), 20–23; Part III, vol. 5 (Summer, 1967), 24–29; Part IV, vol. 7 (April, 1969), 50–54.

McShine, Kynaston, moderator. "The New Sculpture," Symposium on Primary Structures Held at The Jewish Museum, New York, May 3, 1966, with Barbara Rose, Robert Morris, Don Judd, Mark di Suvero.

"Anti-Form," *Artforum*, vol. 6 (April, 1968), 33–35.

ROBERT MOTHERWELL

On Motherwell:

Greenberg, Clement. "Art," *The Nation*, vol. 159 (November 11, 1944), 598–599; vol. 164 (May 31, 1947), 664–665; vol. 166 (May 29, 1948), 612–614.

Kees, W. "Robert Motherwell," *Magazine of Art*, vol. 4 (March, 1948), 86–88.

Fitzsimmons, James. "Robert Motherwell," *Design Quarterly*, no. 29 (1954), 18–22.

Goosen, Eugene C. *Robert Motherwell: First Retrospective Exhibition*. Bennington, Vt.: Bennington College, 1959.

_____. "Robert Motherwell and the Seriousness of Subject," *Art International*, vol. 3, nos. 1–2 (1959), 33–35, 38, 51.

Robert Motherwell: A Retrospective Exhibition. Pasadena: Pasadena Art Museum, 1962. Texts by T. W. Leavitt, Frank O'Hara, Sam Hunter.

"Exhibition at the Sidney Janis Gallery," *Art News*, vol. 61 (January, 1963). Reply by E. Vicente, vol. 61 (February, 1963), 6; Rejoinder by Motherwell, vol. 62 (March, 1963), 6.

Tillim, Sidney. "Exhibition at the Sidney Janis Gallery," *Arts Magazine*, vol. 37 (January, 1963), 40–42.

Ashton, Dore. "Motherwell Loves and Believes," *Studio*, vol. 165 (March, 1963), 116–117.

_____. "Robert Motherwell: Passion and Transfiguration," *Studio*, vol. 167 (March, 1964), 100–105.

O'Hara, Frank. *Robert Motherwell*. New York: The Museum of Modern Art, 1965.

Robert Motherwell. Northampton, Mass.: Smith College Museum of Art, 1965 (Preface by the artist).

Edgar, N. "Satisfactions of Robert Motherwell," *Art News*, vol. 64 (October, 1965), 38–41. Reply by Motherwell, vol. 6 (December, 1965), 6.

O'Hara, Frank. "Robert Motherwell at the Museum of Modern Art," *Art in America*, vol. 53, no. 5 (October–November, 1965), 80–81.

Tillim, Sidney. "Motherwell: The Echo of Protest," *Artforum*, vol. 4 (December, 1965), 34–36.

Robertson, B. "From a Notebook on Robert Motherwell," *Studio*, vol. 171 (March, 1966), 89–93.

Banham, R. "Motherwell Retrospective at Whitechapel," *Architectural Review*, vol. 140 (July, 1966), 59–60.

Krauss, Rosalind. "Robert Motherwell's New Paintings," *Artforum*, vol. 7 (May, 1969), 26–28.

Arnason, H. H. "Motherwell and the Window," *Art News*, vol. 68 (Summer, 1969), 48–52.

By Motherwell:

"Painter's Objects," *Partisan Review*, vol. 11 (Winter, 1944), 93–97.

"The Modern Painter's World," *Dyn*, vol. 1, no. 6 (November, 1944), 9–14.

Editorial Statement in *Possibilities*, vol. 1, no. 1 (Winter, 1947–48), 1.

Statement in *Robert Motherwell: Collages 1943–1949*. New York: Kootz Gallery, 1949.

Modern Artists in America. New York: Wittenborn, Schultz, 1951 (co-editor with Ad Reinhardt).

The School of New York. Beverly Hills: Frank Perls Gallery, 1951.

"The Rise and Continuity of Abstract Art," *Arts and Architecture*, vol. 68 (September, 1951), 20–21, 41. (Lecture at the Fogg Art Museum, Cambridge, Mass.)

"Painting as Existence," *Metro*, 7 (1962), 94–97. Interview with David Sylvester, Recorded and Broadcast over B.B.C. (October 23, 1960).

Kozloff, Max. "Interview with Robert Motherwell," *Artforum*, vol. 4 (September, 1965), 33–37.

"David Smith: A Major American Sculptor; A Personal Appreciation," *Studio*, vol. 172 (August, 1966), 65–68.

BARNETT NEWMAN

On Newman:

Greenberg, Clement, "Art," *The Nation*, vol. 165 (December 6, 1947), 629–630.

Hess, Thomas B. "Newman," *Art News*, vol. 49 (March, 1950), 48.

_____. "Newman," *Art News*, vol. 50 (Summer, 1951), 47.

Greenberg, Clement. *Barnett Newman: First Retrospective Exhibition*. Bennington, Vt.: Bennington College, 1958.

_____. *Barnett Newman: A Selection, 1946–1952*. New York: French and Co., 1959 (reprinted from Bennington Catalogue, 1958).

Goosen, E. C. "The Philosophic Line of Barnett Newman," *Art News*, vol. 57 (Summer, 1958), 30–31, 62–63.

Crehan, Hubert. "Barnett Newman," *Art News*, vol. 58 (April, 1959), 12.

Ashton, Dore. "Art," *Arts and Architecture*, vol. 76 (May, 1959), 6, 7.

Hess, Thomas B. "Willem de Kooning and Barnett Newman," *Art News*, vol. 61 (December, 1962), 12.

Tillim, Sidney. "Paintings by William de Kooning and Barnett Newman at the Allan Stone Gallery," *Arts Magazine*, vol. 37 (December, 1962), 38–40.

Fried, Michael. "New York Letter," *Art International*, vol. 6, no. 10 (December 20, 1962), 54–57.

Rosenberg, Harold. "Barnett Newman: A Man of Controversy and Spiritual Grandeur," *Vogue*, vol. 141 (February 1, 1963), 134–135, 163, 166 (reprinted in *The Anxious Object*. New York: Horizon Press, 1964, pp. 169–174).

Alloway, Lawrence. "Barnett Newman," *Artforum*, vol. 3 (June, 1965), 20–22.

_____. *Stations of the Cross*. New York: The Solomon R. Guggenheim Museum, 1966.

Calas, Nicolas. "Subject Matter in the Work of Barnett Newman," *Arts Magazine*, vol. 42 (November, 1967), 38–40. (Reprinted in Calas, *Art in the Age of Risk*. New York: E. P. Dutton, 1968.)

Hess, Thomas B. *Barnett Newman*. New York: Walker and Co., 1969. (On occasion of Knoedler exhibition.)

Rosenberg, Harold. "The Art World: Icon Maker," *The New Yorker*, vol. 45 (April 19, 1969), 136, 138, 140, 142.

By Newman:

Adolph Gottlieb. New York: Wakefield Gallery, 1944.

Pre-Columbian Stone Sculpture. New York: Betty Parsons Gallery, 1944.

North West Coast Indian Painting. New York: Betty Parsons Gallery, 1946.

The Ideographic Picture. New York: Betty Parsons Gallery, 1947.

"The First Man Was an Artist," *The Tiger's Eye*, vol. 1 (October, 1947), 57–60.

"The Object and the Image," *The Tiger's Eye*, vol. 1, no. 3 (March, 1948), 111.

"The Sublime Is Now," *The Tiger's Eye*, vol. 1, no. 6 (December 15, 1948), 51–53.

Letter to the Editor, *Art News*, vol. 60 (May, 1961), 6 (first reply to Panofsky).

Letter to the Editor, *Art News*, vol. 60 (September, 1961), 6 (second reply to Panofsky).

18 Cantos 1963–64. Preface to a volume of lithographs by Barnett Newman. West Islip, N.Y.: 1964.

Statement in São Paulo Bienal VIII, São Paulo, Brazil: 1965.

"The Fourteen Stations of the Cross," *Art News*, vol. 65 (May, 1966), 26–28.

Letter to the Editor, *Art International*, vol. 11, no. 7 (September, 1967), 51 (first reply to Motherwell). Refers to Interview with Motherwell by Sidney Simon called "Concerning the Beginnings of the New York School," *Art International*, vol. 11, no. 6 (Summer, 1967), 20–23.

Letter to the Editor, *Art International*, vol. 11 (November, 1967), 24, 27 (second reply to Motherwell). Answers letter from Motherwell in the October, 1965, issue, p. 38.

"For Impassioned Criticism," *Art News*, vol. 67 (Summer, 1968), 26. *Discussion*, vol. 67 (September, 1968), 6.

ISAMU NOGUCHI

On Noguchi:

Levy, Julien. "Isamu Noguchi," *Creative Art*, vol. 12 (January, 1933), 29–35.

Hess, Thomas B. "Isamu Noguchi, '46," *Art News*, vol. 45 (September, 1946), 34–38, 47, 50–51.

Greenberg, Clement. "Art: Isamu Noguchi," *The Nation,* vol. 168 (March 19, 1949), 341–342.

Frankfurter, Alfred. "The Controversial Noguchi Sets for Lear," *Art News,* vol. 54 (December, 1955), 42–43.

Page, Addison Franklin. "Isamu Noguchi: The Evolution of a Style," *Art in America,* vol. 44 (Winter, 1956–57), 24–26, 64–66.

Ashton, Dore. "Isamu Noguchi," *Arts and Architecture,* vol. 46 (August, 1959), 14–15; vol. 80 (June, 1963), 6–7.

Raynor, Vivien. "In the Galleries: Isamu Noguchi," *Arts Magazine,* vol. 35 (September, 1961), 36–37.

Michelson, Annette. *Isamu Noguchi.* Paris: Galerie Claude Bernard, 1964 (text in English and French).

Jacobs, J. "Projects for Playgrounds, *Art in America,* vol. 55 (November, 1967), 44–47.

Gordon, John. *Isamu Noguchi.* New York: The Whitney Museum of American Art, 1968.

Edgar, N. "Noguchi, Master of Ceremony," *Art News,* vol. 67 (April, 1968), 50–52.

By Noguchi:

"Meanings in Modern Sculpture," *Art News,* vol. 48 (March, 1949), 12–15.

"Towards a Reintegration of the Arts," *College Art Journal,* vol. 9, no. 1 (Autumn, 1949), 59–60.

A Sculptor's World. New York: Harper and Row, 1968.

"Artist Speaks: Isamu Noguchi," *Art in America,* vol. 56 (March, 1968), 28–31.

KENNETH NOLAND

On Noland:

Greenberg, Clement. "Louis and Noland," *Art International,* vol. 4, no. 5 (May 25, 1960), 26–29.

Ashbery, John. "Paris Notes," *Art International,* vol. 5, nos. 5–6 (June–August, 1961), 42, 92.

Kenneth Noland. Zurich: Galerie Charles Lunhard AG, 1962. Introduction by E. C. Goosen.

Judd, Don. "Exhibition at Emmerich Gallery," *Arts Magazine,* vol. 36 (September, 1962), 49.

Greenberg, Clement. "After Abstract Expressionism," *Art International,* vol. 6 (October 25, 1962), 24–32.

————. Introduction, *Three New American Painters: Louis, Noland, Olitski.* Regina, Canada: Norman McKenzie Art Gallery, 1963. (Reprinted in *Canadian Art,* vol. 20 [May, 1963], 172–175.)

Fried, Michael. "New York Letter," *Art International,* vol. 7, no. 5 (May, 1963), 69–70.

Judd, Donald. "In the Galleries," *Arts Magazine,* vol. 37 (September, 1963), 53–54.

Solomon, Alan. XXXII International Biennial Exhibition of Art, Venice, 1964, United States of America, New York: The Jewish Museum, 1964.

Rose, Barbara. "Kenneth Noland," *Art International,* vol. 8, nos. 5–6 (Summer, 1964), 58–61.

Geldzahler, Henry. "Recent American Painting," *Cimaise,* nos. 69–70 (July–October, 1964), 42–47.

Fried, Michael. *Kenneth Noland.* New York: The Jewish Museum, 1965.

————. *Three American Painters* (Noland, Olitski, Stella). Cambridge, Mass.: Fogg Art Museum, 1965.

Nordland, Gerald. *The Washington Color Painters.* Washington: Washington Gallery of Modern Art, 1965.

Cone, Jane Harrison. "On Color in Kenneth Noland's Painting," *Art International,* vol. 9, no. 5 (June, 1965), 36–38.

————. "Kenneth Noland's New Paintings," *Artforum,* vol. 6 (November, 1967), 36–41.

Fried, Michael. "Recent Work by Kenneth Noland," *Artforum,* vol. 7 (Summer, 1969), 36–37.

By Noland:

Letter to the Editor, *Art News,* vol. 61 (November, 1962), 6 (on Louis).

CLAES OLDENBURG

On Oldenburg:

Tillim, Sidney. "Claes Oldenburg's 'The Store,'" *Arts Magazine*, vol. 36 (February, 1962), 35–37.

Kozloff, Max. "Art: New Works by Oldenburg," *The Nation*, vol. 198, no. 18 (April 27, 1964), 445–446.

Restany, Pierre. "Une Personalité Charnière de l'Art Americain: Claes Oldenburg Premieres Œuvres," *Metro*, 9 (April, 1965), 20–26.

Geldzahler, Henry. "Happenings: Theatre by Painters," *Hudson Review*, vol. 18, no. 4 (Winter, 1965–66), 581–586.

Claes Oldenburg: Skulpturer och Teckningar. Stockholm: Moderna Museet, 1966.

Rosenstein, Harris. "Climbing Mt. Oldenburg," *Art News*, vol. 64 (February, 1966), 21–25, 56.

Ashton, Dore. "Exhibition at the Sidney Janis Gallery," *Studio*, vol. 171 (May, 1966), 204–205.

Berkson, William. "In the Galleries: Claes Oldenburg," *Arts Magazine*, vol. 40 (May, 1966), 57–58.

Baro, Gene. "Claes Oldenburg or the Things of This World," *Art International*, vol. 10 (November 20, 1966), 40–43, 45–49.

Melville, R. "Exhibition at the Robert Frazer Gallery," *Architectural Review*, vol. 141 (February, 1967), 141–142.

"Take a Cigarette Butt and Make It Heroic: Projects for Colossal Civic Monuments in Capital Cities," *Art News*, vol. 66 (May, 1967), 30–31.

Rose, Barbara. "Claes Oldenburg's Soft Machines," *Artforum*, vol. 5 (Summer, 1967), 30–35.

_____. *Claes Oldenburg.* New York: The Museum of Modern Art, 1969.

By Oldenburg:

"Environments, Situations, Spaces." New York: Martha Jackson Gallery, 1961.

"From the Studio Notes by Claes Oldenburg," *New Work by Oldenburg*. New York: Sidney Janis Gallery, 1966.

Injun and Other Histories. New York: Something Else Press, 1966.

Statements in *Claes Oldenburg: Sculpturer och Techningar*. Stockholm: Moderna Museet, 1966.

Store Days. New York: Something Else Press, 1967.

JULES OLITSKI

On Olitski:

Greenburg, Clement. Introduction. *Three New American Painters: Louis, Noland, Olitski.* Regina, Canada: Norman McKenzie Art Gallery, 1963. (Reprinted in *Canadian Art*, vol. 20 [May, 1963], 172–175.)

Rose, Barbara. "New York Letter," *Art International*, vol. 7, no. 4 (April 25, 1963), 57, 58.

Kozloff, Max. "Frankenthaler and Olitski," *The Nation* (April, 1965), 374.

Fried, Michael. "Jules Olitski's New Paintings," *Artforum*, vol. 4 (November, 1965), 36–40.

_____. *Three American Painters* (Noland, Olitski, Stella). Cambridge, Mass.: Fogg Art Museum, 1966.

Lord, Barry. *Frankenthaler, Noland, Olitski.* New Brunswick, Canada: New Brunswick Museum, 1966.

Fried, Michael. *Jules Olitski: Paintings, 1963–1967.* Washington, D.C.: The Corcoran Gallery of Art, 1967.

_____. "Olitski and Shape," *Artforum*, vol. 5 (January, 1967), 20–21.

Champa, K. S. "Olitski: Nothing But Color," *Art News*, vol. 66 (May, 1967), 36–38, 74–76.

Krauss, Rosalind. *Jules Olitski: Recent Paintings.* Philadelphia: Institute of Contemporary Art, University of Pennsylvania, 1968.

Hudson, Andrew. "On Jules Olitski's Painting and Some Changes of View," *Art International*, vol. 12, no. 1 (January, 1968), 31–36.

Moffett, Kenworth. "The Sculpture of Jules Olitski," *Metropolitan Museum of Art Bulletin*, vol. 27 (April, 1969), 366–371. (Reprinted and revised in *Artforum*, vol. 7 [April, 1969], 55–58.)

By Olitski:

"Olitski on Color," *Artforum*, vol. 5 (January, 1967), 20. (Slightly revised and expanded version of Olitski's catalogue statement in Venice Biennale Catalogue, 1966.)

"On Sculpture," *Metropolitan Museum of Art Bulletin*, vol. 27 (April, 1969), 366. (Reprinted in *Artforum*, vol. 7 [April, 1969], 59.)

JACKSON POLLOCK

On Pollock:

Sweeney, J. J. *Jackson Pollock*. New York: Art of This Century, 1943.

Greenberg, Clement. "Art: Jackson Pollock," *The Nation*, vol. 157 (November 27, 1943), 621; vol. 160 (April 7, 1945), 397; vol. 162 (April 13, 1946), 445; vol. 164 (February 1, 1947), 137, 139; vol. 166 (January 24, 1948), 107–108; vol. 168 (February 19, 1949), 221.

"Jackson Pollock: Is He the Greatest Living Artist in the United States?" *Life*, vol. 27 (August 8, 1949), 42–45.

Tyler, Parker. "Jackson Pollock: The Infinite Labyrinth," *Magazine of Art*, vol. 43 (March, 1950), 92–93.

Ossorio, Alfonso. *Jackson Pollock*. New York: Betty Parsons Gallery, 1951.

Goodenough, Robert. "Pollock Paints a Picture," *Art News*, vol. 50 (May, 1951), 38–41.

Greenberg, Clement. Preface, *Retrospective Exhibition of Jackson Pollock*. Bennington, Vt.: Bennington College, 1952.

⸻. "Jackson Pollock's New Style," *Harper's Magazine*, vol. 85 (February, 1952), 174–175.

Friedman, B. H. "Profile: Jackson Pollock," *Art in America*, vol. 43 (December, 1955), 49.

Steinberg, L. "Fifteen Years of Work Shown at the Sidney Janis Gallery," *Arts Magazine*, vol. 30 (December, 1955), 43–44.

Hunter, Sam. "Jackson Pollock: The Maze and the Minotaur," *New World Writing*. New York: New American Library, 1956.

Shapiro, Meyer. "The Younger American Painters of Today," *The Listener* (January 26, 1956), 146.

Hess, Thomas B. "Jackson Pollock, 1912–1956," *Art News*, vol. 55 (September, 1956), 44–45.

Greenberg, Clement. "Jackson Pollock," *Evergreen Review*, vol. 1 (1957).

Tillim, Sidney. "Jackson Pollock: A Critical Evaluation," *College Art Journal*, vol. 16, no. 3 (Spring, 1957), 242–243.

Kaprow, Allan. "The Legacy of Jackson Pollock," *Art News*, vol. 57 (October, 1958), 24–26.

Alloway, Lawrence. "The Art of Jackson Pollock: 1912–1956," *The Listener*, vol. 60 (November 27, 1958), 888.

Kramer, Hilton. "Jackson Pollock and Nicholas de Staël, Two Painters and Their Myths," *Arts Yearbook*, no. 3 (1959), 53–60.

O'Hara, Frank. "Jackson Pollock, 1912–1956," in Peter Selz, *New Images of Man*. New York: The Museum of Modern Art, 1959. Pp. 123–128.

⸻. *Jackson Pollock*. New York: George Braziller, 1959.

Rubin, William. "Notes on Masson and Pollock," *Arts Magazine*, vol. 34 (November, 1959), 36–43; Correction: vol. 34 (December, 1959), 9.

Guggenheim, Peggy. "Art of This Century," in *Confessions of an Art Addict*. New York: Macmillan, 1960.

Robertson, Bryan. *Jackson Pollock*. New York: Harry N. Abrams, 1960.

Alloway, Lawrence. *Jackson Pollock: Paintings, Drawings and Watercolors from the Collection of Lee Krasner Pollock*. London: Marlborough Fine Art Ltd., 1961.

Tillim, Sidney. "Retrospective at the Marlborough-Gerson Gallery," *Arts Magazine*, vol. 38 (March, 1964), 55–56.

Fried, Michael. "New York Letter," *Art International*, vol. 8 (April, 1964), 57–58.

O'Connor, Francis V. "The Genesis of Jackson Pollock: 1912–1943." Unpublished Ph.D. dissertation, The Johns Hopkins University, Baltimore, 1965.

Fried, Michael. "Jackson Pollock," *Artforum*, vol. 4 (September, 1965), 14–17.

O'Connor, Francis V. *Jackson Pollock*. New York: The Museum of Modern Art, 1967.

Rubin, William. "Jackson Pollock and the Modern Tradition," *Artforum*, vol. 5 (February, 1967), 14–22; (March, 1967), 28–37; (April, 1967), 18–31; (May, 1967), 28–33. (April and May issues contain correspondence between Rubin and Rosenberg.)

"Jackson Pollock: An Artists' Symposium, Part I," *Art News*, vol. 66 (April, 1967), 29. (Statements by James Brooks, Elaine de Kooning, Adolph Gottlieb, Al Held, Allan Kaprow, Alex Katz, Robert Motherwell, Barnett Newman, Philip Pavia, Larry Rivers.)

Judd, Don. "Jackson Pollock," *Arts Magazine*, vol. 41 (April, 1967), 32–35.

"Jackson Pollock: An Artists' Symposium," Part II, *Art News*, vol. 66 (May, 1967), 27. (Statements by Al Brunelle, Jane Freilicher, David Lee, Joan Mitchell, Kenneth Noland, David Novros, Claes Oldenburg, George Segal.) Editorial on Symposium by T. B. Hess, vol. 66 (April, 1967), 27; Rejoinder by W. Rubin, vol. 66 (May, 1967), 6.

O'Connor, Francis V. "The Genesis of Jackson Pollock," *Artforum*, vol. 5 (May, 1967), 16–23.

Rosenberg, Harold. "The Mythic Act," *The New Yorker*, vol. 43 (May 6, 1967), 162, 164, 167–171.

By Pollock:

"Jackson Pollock Answers to a Questionnaire," *Arts and Architecture*, vol. 61 (February, 1944), 14.

"My Paintings," *Possibilities*, vol. 1 (Winter, 1947–48), 78–83.

Excerpts from an Interview. Taped by William Wright, The Springs, Long Island, 1950. *Art in America*, vol. 53 (August–September, 1965), 111; reprinted in Francis V. O'Connor, *Jackson Pollock*. New York: The Museum of Modern Art, 1967. Pp. 79–81.

Narration for the film, *Jackson Pollock*, made by Hans Namuth and Paul Falkenberg, 1951. Typescript in Library of The Museum of Modern Art, New York.

LARRY POONS

On Poons:

Tillim, Sidney. "Larry Poons: The Dotted Line," *Arts Magazine*, vol. 39 (February, 1965), 16–21.

Johnson, Ellen H. "Three Young Americans: Hinman, Poons and Williams," *Oberlin College Bulletin* (Spring, 1965), 83–100.

Kozloff, Max. "Larry Poons," *Artforum*, vol. 3 (April, 1965), 26–29.

Fry, E. F. "Poons: A Clean and Balanced World?" *Art News*, vol. 65 (February, 1967), 34–35.

Lippard, Lucy R. "Larry Poons: The Illusion of Disorder," *Art International*, vol. 11 (April 20, 1967), 22–26.

Champa, Kermit S. "New Paintings by Larry Poons," *Artforum*, vol. 6 (Summer, 1968), 39–42.

ROBERT RAUSCHENBERG

On Rauschenberg:

"Exhibition at the Stable," *Arts and Architecture*, vol. 70 (October, 1953), 33–34.

Meyers, David. "Robert Rauschenberg," in B. H. Friedman, ed., *School of New York: Some Younger Artists*. New York: Grove Press, 1959.

The United States Representation at Venice Biennale of The Museum of Modern Art, 1959. Introduction by Sam Hunter, published by Minneapolis Institute of Arts.

Ashton, Dore. "Rauschenberg's Thirty-Four Illustrations for Dante's Inferno," *Metro,* vol. 2 (1961), 51–62.

Cage, John. "On Robert Rauschenberg, Artist and His Work," *Metro,* vol. 2 (1961), 36–51.

Rauschenberg. Paris: Galerie Ileana Sonnabend, 1963. (Text by Lawrence Alloway, John Cage, Françoise Choay, Gillo Dorfles, Alain Jouffroy, André Parinaud, Michel Ragon.)

Solomon, Alan. *Robert Rauschenberg.* New York: The Jewish Museum, 1963.

Swenson, G. R. "Rauschenberg Paints a Picture," *Art News,* vol. 62 (April, 1963), 44–47.

Robert Rauschenberg. London: Whitechapel Gallery, 1964. (Articles by John Cage, Henry Geldzahler, Max Kozloff, Bryan Robertson.)

Swanson, Dean. *Robert Rauschenberg.* Minneapolis: The Walker Art Center, 1965.

Tomkins, Calvin. *The Bride and the Bachelors.* New York: Viking, 1965.

Johnson, E. H. "Image Duplicators: Lichtenstein, Rauschenberg, Warhol," *Canadian Art,* vol. 23 (January, 1966), 12–19.

Forge, Andrew. *Robert Rauschenberg.* Amsterdam: Stedelijk Museum, 1968.

——————. *Robert Rauschenberg.* New York: Harry N. Abrams. To be published.

By Rauschenberg:

"The Artist Speaks: Robert Rauschenberg," *Art in America,* vol. 54, no. 3 (May–June, 1966), 84.

AD REINHARDT

On Reinhardt:

"Reinhardt," *Arts and Architecture,* vol. 64 (January, 1947), 20, 27.

Hess, Thomas B. "Reinhardt: The Position and Perils of Purity," *Art News,* vol. 52 (December, 1953), 26–27.

de Kooning, Elaine. "Pure Paints a Picture," *Art News,* vol. 56 (Summer, 1957), 57, 86–87.

Tillim, Sidney. "What Happened to Geometry? An Inquiry into Geometrical Painting in America," *Arts Magazine,* vol. 33 (June, 1959), 38–44.

Ad Reinhardt: 25 Years of Abstract Painting. New York: Betty Parsons Gallery, 1960.

Kramer, Hilton. "Art," *The Nation,* vol. 196 (June 22, 1963), 533–534.

Colt, Priscilla. "Notes on Ad Reinhardt," *Art International,* vol. 8, no. 8 (October, 1964), 32–34.

Lippard, Lucy R. *Ad Reinhardt.* New York: The Jewish Museum, 1966.

Michelson, Annette. "Ad Reinhardt or the Artist as Artist," *Harper's Bazaar* (November, 1966), 176.

Rose, Barbara. "Reinhardt," *Vogue,* vol. 148 (November 1, 1966), 183.

McShine, Kynaston. "More than Black," *Arts Magazine,* vol. 41 (December, 1966), 49–50.

Sandler, Irving. "The Purist Backlash," *Arts Magazine,* (December, 1966), 40–47.

Ashton, Dore. "Notes on Reinhardt's Exhibition," *Arts and Architecture,* vol. 83 (January, 1967), 4–5.

By Reinhardt:

"Stuart Davis," *New Masses* (November 27, 1945), 15.

"Open Letter to Roland L. Redmond, President of the Metropolitan Museum of Art, Protesting the American Painting Exhibition There," *Art News,* vol. 49 (Summer, 1950), 15.

Modern Artists in America. New York: Wittenborn, Schultz, 1951. (Co-editor with Robert Motherwell.)

"Twelve Rules for a New Academy," *Art News,* vol. 56 (May, 1957), 37–38, 56. (Reprinted in *Ad Reinhardt: 25 Years of Abstract Painting.* New York: Betty Parsons Gallery, 1960.)

"44 Titles for Articles for Artists Under 45," *It Is,* no. 1 (Spring, 1958), 22–23.

"25 Lines of Words on Art," *It Is,* no. 1 (Spring, 1958), 42.

"Is Today's Artist With or Against the Past?" *Art News*, vol. 57 (Summer, 1958), 26–28, 56–58.

Sandler, Irving. "In the Art Galleries: Interview with Ad Reinhardt," *New York Post* (August 12, 1962), 12.

"Art as Art," *Art International*, vol. 6, no. 10 (December, 1962), 36–37.

"The Next Revolution in Art," *Art News*, vol. 62 (February, 1964), 48–49.

"The Next Revolution in Art: Art as Art Dogma," Part II, *Art International*, vol. 8, no. 2 (March, 1964), 57–58.

"Reinhardt Paints a Picture" (Auto-Interview), *Art News*, vol. 64 (March, 1965), 39–41, 66.

"Art vs. History" (Book Review of George Kubler's *The Shape of Time*), *Art News*, vol. 64 (January, 1966), 19, 61–62.

Glaser, Bruce. Interview with Ad Reinhardt, *Art International*, vol. 10, no. 10 (December, 1966), 18–21.

Kallick, P. Interview with Ad Reinhardt, *Studio*, vol. 174 (December, 1967), 269–273.

JAMES ROSENQUIST

On Rosenquist:

Seckler, Dorothy G. "Folklore of the Banal," *Art in America*, vol. 50, no. 4 (Winter, 1962), 56–61.

Lippard, Lucy. "James Rosenquist: Aspects of a Multiple Art," *Artforum*, vol. 4 (December, 1965), 41–44.

Irwin, D. "Pop Art and Surrealism," *Studio*, vol. 171 (May, 1966), 191.

"Les Images sans Passion de Rosenquist," *Aujourd'hui*, vol. 10 (January, 1967), 142–143.

James Rosenquist. Ottawa: National Gallery of Canada, 1968.

Geldzahler, Henry. "James Rosenquist's *F-111*," *Metropolitan Museum of Art Bulletin*, vol. 26 (March, 1968), 177–281.

By Rosenquist:

Statement in *Art in America*, vol. 51, no. 3 (1963), 48.

"What Is Pop Art?" Interview with G. R. Swenson, *Art News*, vol. 62 (February, 1964), 40–43.

Swenson, G. R. "The *F-111*: An Interview with James Rosenquist," *Partisan Review*, vol. 32 (Fall, 1965), 589–601.

MARK ROTHKO

On Rothko:

Collier, Oskar. "Mark Rothko," *Iconograph* (Fall, 1947), 40–44.

MacAgy, Douglas. "Mark Rothko," *Magazine of Art*, vol. 42 (January, 1949), 20–21.

Mark Rothko, Houston: Contemporary Arts Museum, 1957. Preface by Elaine de Kooning (reprinted in *Art News Annual*, 1957–58).

de Kooning, Elaine. "Two Americans in Action: Kline and Rothko," *Art News Annual*, vol. 27, Part II (1958), 86–97, 174–179.

Hunter, Sam. "Mark Rothko." New York: The Museum of Modern Art, Stati Uniti d'America, XXIX Biennale, Venice, 1958.

Ashton, Dore. "Art: Mark Rothko," *Arts and Architecture*, vol. 74, no. 8 (April, 1958), 8, 29, 32.

Butor, Michel. "Les Mosquées de New York ou l'Art de Mark Rothko," *Revue-Critique Editions de Minuit*, no. 173 (1961), 843–860.

Mark Rothko. London: Whitechapel Gallery, 1961. Preface by Bryan Robertson.

Selz, Peter. *Mark Rothko*. New York: The Museum of Modern Art, 1961.

Goosen, E. C. "Rothko: The Omnibus Image," *Art News*, vol. 59 (January, 1961), 38–40, 60–61.

Goldwater, Robert. "Reflections on the Rothko Exhibit," *Arts Magazine*, vol. 35 (March, 1961), 42–45.

Sandler, I. "New York Letter: Rothko," *Art International*, vol. 2 (March, 1961), 40–41.

Kozloff, Max. "Mark Rothko's New Retrospective," *Art Journal*, vol. 20 (Spring, 1961), 148–149.

Harrison, Jane. "Rothko," *Arts Review*, vol. 13 (October 21–November 4, 1961), 2, 18.

Alloway, Lawrence. "Notes on Rothko," *Art International*, vol. 6, nos. 5–6 (Summer, 1962), 90–94.

Fried, Michael. "New York Letter," *Art International*, vol. 7 (May 25, 1963), 70–72.

Judd, Don. "Mark Rothko," *Arts Magazine*, vol. 37 (September, 1963), 57–58.

"Recent Acquisitions," *St. Louis Museum Bulletin*, no. 2 (May, 1966), 2–3.

By Rothko:

Letter to the Editor, *The New York Times*, June 13, 1943. Quoted in Rudi Blesh, *Modern Art USA*. New York: Alfred A. Knopf, 1956. Pp. 226–227. Also in Thomas B. Hess, *Abstract Painting: Background and American Phase*. New York: Viking, 1951. P. 145.

"The Romantics Were Prompted," *Possibilities*, vol. 1, no. 1 (Winter, 1947–48), 84–86.

Ashton, Dore. "Art: Lecture by Rothko," *The New York Times* (October 31, 1958), p. 26, col. 2. Lecture from the Pratt Institute.

GEORGE SEGAL

On Segal:

Judd, Don. "Exhibition at the Green Gallery," *Arts Magazine*, vol. 36 (September, 1962), 55.

Segal. Paris: Galerie Ileana Sonnabend, 1963. (Introductory essays by Michel Courtouis and Allan Kaprow.)

Van der Marck, Jan. "George Segal," *Ten American Sculptors*. Organized by The Walker Art Center, Minneapolis, for United States Section of the VII Bienal de São Paulo, Brazil, 1963.

Geldzahler, Henry. "George Segal," *Recent American Sculpture*. New York: The Jewish Museum, 1964. (Reprinted in *Quadrum*, no. 19 [1965], 115–116.)

Solomon, Alan. *Amerikanst Pop-Konst*. Stockholm: Moderna Museet, 1964.

Kaprow, Allan. "Segal's Vital Mummies," *Art News*, vol. 62 (February, 1964), 30–33, 65.

Pincus-Witten, Robert. "George Segal as Realist," *Artforum*, vol. 5 (Summer, 1967), 84–87.

Tuchman, Phyllis. "George Segal," *Art International*, vol. 12, no. 7 (September 29, 1968), 51–53.

Perreault, John. "Plaster Caste," *Art News*, vol. 67 (November, 1968), 54–55, 75, 76.

By Segal:

Geldzahler, Henry. An Interview with George Segal, *Artforum*, vol. 3 (November, 1964), 26–29. (Reprinted in *Quadrum*, no. 19 [1965], 118–126.)

DAVID SMITH

On Smith:

Greenberg, Clement. "Art," *The Nation*, vol. 156 (January 23, 1943), 140–141; vol. 162 (January 26, 1946), 109–110; vol. 164 (April 19, 1947), 459–460.

Valentier, W. R. "Sculpture by David Smith," *Arts and Architecture*, vol. 65 (August, 1948), 22–23, 52.

Motherwell, Robert. "For David Smith," Foreword in *David Smith*. New York: Willard Gallery, 1950. Pp. 1–3.

de Kooning, Elaine. "David Smith Makes a Sculpture: Cathedral," *Art News*, vol. 50 (September, 1951), 38–41, 50–51.

Goosen, E. C. "David Smith," *Arts*, vol. 30 (March, 1956), 23–27.

Greenberg, Clement. "David Smith," *Art in America*, vol. 44, no. 5 (Winter, 1956–57), 30–33, 66. (Reprinted in *Art in America*, vol. 51, no. 4 [August, 1963], 112–117.)

Hunter, Sam. "David Smith" (with catalogue and bibliography), *Museum of Modern Art Bulletin*, vol. 25, no. 2 (1957), 3–36.

Porter, Fairfield. "David Smith: Steel into Sculpture," *Art News*, vol. 56 (September, 1957), 40–43, 54–55.

Kramer, Hilton. "Month in Review: Exhibition of Sculptures and Drawings at the Museum of Modern Art and Other Galleries," *Arts Magazine*, vol. 32 (October, 1957), 48–51.

———. "The Sculpture of David Smith," *Arts Magazine*, vol. 34 (February, 1960), 22–43. (Special David Smith issue.)

O'Hara, Frank. "David Smith: The Color of Steel," *Art News*, vol. 60 (December, 1961), 32–34, 69–70.

Rubin, William. "David Smith," *Art International*, vol. 7, no. 9 (December 5, 1963), 48–59.

Carandente, Giovanni. *Voltron*. Philadelphia: Institute of Contemporary Art, University of Pennsylvania, 1964.

Greenberg, Clement. *David Smith's New Sculpture*. Philadelphia: Institute of Contemporary Art, University of Pennsylvania, 1964. (Reprinted in *Art International*, vol. 8, no. 4 [May, 1964], 35–37.)

Judd, Don. "David Smith," *Arts Magazine*, vol. 39 (December, 1964), 62.

Baro, Gene. "Contemporary Sculpture: David Smith, 1906–1965," *Arts Yearbook*, no. 8 (1965), 100–105.

Motherwell, Robert. "David Smith: A Major American Sculptor," *Vogue*, vol. 145 (February 1, 1965), 134–139, 190–191. (Revised version in *Studio*, vol. 172 [August, 1966], 65–68.)

David Smith: A Retrospective Exhibition. Cambridge, Mass.: Fogg Art Museum, 1966. (Introduction by Jane Harrison Cone.)

Krauss, Rosalind. Introduction, *David Smith: Eight Early Works, 1935–1938*. New York: Marlborough-Gerson Gallery, 1967.

Cone, Jane Harrison. "David Smith," *Artforum*, vol. 5 (Summer, 1967), 72–78.

Krauss, Rosalind. Introduction, *David Smith, Small Sculptures of the Mid-Forties*. New York: Marlborough-Gerson Gallery, 1968.

Bannard, Darby Walter. "Cubism, Abstract Expressionism, David Smith," *Artforum*, vol. 6 (April, 1968), 22–32.

Fry, Edward. *David Smith*. New York: The Solomon R. Guggenheim Museum, 1969.

Kramer, Hilton. "A Critic Calls David Smith: Greatest of All American Artists," *The New York Times Magazine*, (February 16, 1969), 40–42, 44, 46, 49–52, 54, 59–60, 62.

Krauss, Rosalind. "The Essential David Smith," Part I, *Artforum*, vol. 7 (February, 1969), 43–49: Part II, vol. 7 (April, 1969), 34–41.

By Smith:

"David Smith," *The New Sculpture: A Symposium*. New York: The Museum of Modern Art, 1952. (Transcript in MOMA Library.)

"Hudson River Landscape," *Bennington Magazine*, vol. 3 (Spring, 1952), 16–17.

"Thoughts on Sculpture," *College Art Journal*, vol. 13, no. 2 (Winter, 1954), 96–100.

"Second Thoughts on Sculpture," *College Art Journal*, vol. 13, no. 3 (Spring, 1954), 203–207.

"Gonzalez: First Master of the Torch," *Art News*, vol. 54 (February, 1956), 34–37, 64–65.

"Sculpture and Architecture," *Arts Magazine*, vol. 31 (May, 1957), 20.

"The Secret Letter" (an interview with David Smith by Thomas B. Hess), June, 1964, in *David Smith*. New York: Marlborough-Gerson Gallery, 1964.

"David Smith Interviewed by David Sylvester," *Living Arts*, no. 3 (April, 1964), 4–13.

David Smith by David Smith, ed. by Cleve Gray. New York: Holt, Rinehart and Winston, 1968.

TONY SMITH

On Smith:

Judd, D. "Black, White and Gray," *Arts Magazine*, vol. 38 (March, 1964), 36–38.
Tony Smith: Two Exhibitions of Sculpture. Hartford, Conn.: Wadsworth Atheneum, 1966.
Burton, S. "Old Master at the New Frontier," *Art News*, vol. 65 (December, 1966), 52–55.
Baro, Gene. "Tony Smith: Toward Speculation in Pure Form," *Art International*, vol. 11, no. 6 (Summer, 1967), 27–30.
Lippard, Lucy R. "Tony Smith: The Ineluctable Modality of the Visible," *Art International*, vol. 11, no. 6 (Summer, 1967), 24–26.
Robbins, C. "New York: Public Sculpture in Public Places," *Arts Magazine*, vol. 41 (Summer, 1967), 50–51.
Chandler, John N. "Tony Smith and Sol Lewitt; Mutations and Permutations," *Art International*, vol. 12, no. 7 (September 20, 1968), 16–19.

By Smith:

"Remarks on Modules," *Tony Smith: Two Exhibitions of Sculpture.* Hartford, Conn.: Wadsworth Atheneum, 1966.
Wagstaff, Samuel, Jr. "Talking to Tony Smith," *Artforum*, vol. 5 (December, 1966), 14–19.

FRANK STELLA

On Stella:

"Three Young Americans," Oberlin College, *Allen Memorial Art Museum Bulletin*, vol. 17 (Fall, (1959), 18–19.
Judd, Donald. "Exhibition at Castelli Gallery," *Arts Magazine*, vol. 36 (September, 1962), 51.
Ashton, Dore. "Exhibition at the Castelli Gallery," *Das Kunstwerk*, Baden-Baden, vol. 16 (November–December, 1962), 69.
————. "Exhibition at the Leo Castelli Gallery," *Studio*, vol. 165 (February, 1963), 67.
Fried, Michael. *Three American Painters* (Noland, Olitski, Stella). Cambridge, Mass.: Fogg Art Museum, 1965.
Judd, Donald. "The Shaped Canvas," *Arts Magazine*, vol. 39 (February, 1965), 56.
Rosenblum, Robert. "Frank Stella," *Artforum*, vol. 3 (March, 1965), 20–27.
Kozloff, Max. "Art," *The Nation*, vol. 202 (March 28, 1966), 270–272.
Fried, Michael. *Frank Stella.* Pasadena: Pasadena Art Museum, 1966
Ashton, Dore. "Exhibition at Castelli Gallery," *Arts and Architecture*, vol. 83 (May, 1966), 5.
————. "New York at the Castelli Gallery," *Studio*, vol. 171 (May, 1966), 205.
Krauss, Rosalind. "Frank Stella, Castelli Gallery," *Artforum*, vol. 4 (May, 1966), 47–49.
Fried, Michael. "Shape as Form: Frank Stella's New Paintings," *Artforum*, vol. 5 (November, 1966), 18–27. (Reprinted from Pasadena Catalogue, 1966).
Cone, Jane Harrison. "Frank Stella's New Paintings," *Artforum*, vol. 6 (November, 1967), 34.
Kramer, Hilton. "Frank Stella: What You See Is What You See," *The New York Times*, sec. 2 (December 10, 1967), 39.

By Stella:

"Questions to Stella and Judd," B. Glaser, *Art News*, vol. 65 (September, 1966), 55–61.

CLYFFORD STILL

On Still:

Krasne, Belle. "Still's Non-Objective Cartography," *Art Digest*, vol. 24 (May 1, 1950), 22, 23.
Loran, Erle. "Art News from San Francisco . . . Clyfford Still," *Art News*, vol. 49 (October, 1950), 58–59.

Fitzsimmons, James. "Clyfford Still," *Art Digest*, vol. 25 (February 1, 1951), 17–18.
Paintings of Clyfford Still. Buffalo: Buffalo Fine Arts Academy and Albright Art Gallery, 1959.
Crehan, Hubert. "Clyfford Still: Black Angel in Buffalo," *Art News*, vol. 58 (December, 1959), 32, 58–60.
Goosen, E. C. "Painting as Confrontation: Clyfford Still," *Art International*, vol. 4 (1960), 39–43.
Sharpless, Ti-Grace. *Clyfford Still.* Philadelphia: Institute of Contemporary Art, University of Pennsylvania, 1963.
Kozloff, Max. "Art: Clyfford Still," *The Nation*, vol. 198 (January 6, 1964), 39–40.
Clyfford Still: Thirty-Three Paintings in the Albright-Knox Art Gallery. Buffalo: Albright-Knox Art Gallery, 1966. Introduction by Ti-Grace Sharpless.

By Still:

"Comment," *Albright-Knox Gallery Notes*, vol. 23, no. 2 (Summer, 1960).
Statements in *Clyfford Still.* Philadelphia: Institute of Contemporary Art, University of Pennsylvania, 1963. Pp. 9–10.
"An Open Letter to an Art Critic," *Artforum*, vol. 2 (December, 1963), 32.
Letter to the Editor, *Artforum*, vol. 2 (February, 1964), 2.

BRADLEY WALKER TOMLIN

On Tomlin:

Hess, Thomas B. "Bradley Walker Tomlin," *Art News*, vol. 49 (May, 1950), 52.
Krasne, Belle. "Of Time and Tomlin," *Art Digest*, vol. 24 (June 1, 1950), 18.
Baur, John I. H. *Bradley Walker Tomlin.* New York: The Whitney Museum of American Art, 1957.
Ashbery, John. "Tomlin: The Pleasures of Color," *Art News*, vol. 56 (October, 1957), 28–29, 54.
Sawin, Martica. "Bradley Walker Tomlin," *Arts Magazine*, vol. 32 (November, 1957), 22–25.
Ashton, Dore. "Art," *Arts and Architecture*, vol. 74 (December, 1957), 32–33.
Doty, B. "Trends and Traditions: Recent Acquisitions," *Albright-Knox Gallery Notes*, vol. 27 (Spring, 1964), 16–17.

By Tomlin:

Foreword, *Frank London.* Woodstock: Woodstock Art Association, 1948. Pp. 2–3.
Foreword, *Judson Smith Retrospective Exhibition.* Woodstock: Woodstock Art Association, 1952. Pp. 2–3.

ANDY WARHOL

On Warhol:

Fried, Michael. "New York Letter," *Art International*, vol. 6, no. 10 (December 20, 1962), 57.
Warhol. Paris: Galerie Ileana Sonnabend, 1964. Contains articles by John Ashbery, Alain Jouffroy, and Jean-Jacques Lebel.
Geldzahler, Henry. "Andy Warhol," *Art International*, vol. 8, no. 3 (April, 1964), 34–35.
Green, Samuel Adams. *Andy Warhol.* Philadelphia: Institute of Contemporary Art, University of Pennsylvania, 1965.
Solomon, Alan. *Andy Warhol.* Boston: I.C.A. Gallery, 1966.
Johnson, Ellen H. "Image Duplicators: Lichtenstein, Rauschenberg, Warhol," *Canadian Art*, vol. 23 (January, 1966), 12–19.
Antin, D. "Warhol: The Silver Tenement," *Art News*, vol. 65 (Summer, 1966), 47–49.
Andy Warhol. Stockholm: Moderna Museet, 1967–68.

By Warhol:

Andy Warhol's Index Book. New York: Random House, 1967.

481

GENERAL

Books:

Janis, Sidney. *Abstract and Surrealist Art in America.* New York: Reynal and Hitchcock, 1944.

Hess, Thomas B. *Abstract Painting: Background and American Phase.* New York: Viking Press, 1951.

Motherwell, Robert, and Reinhardt, Ad, eds. *Modern Artists in America.* New York: Wittenborn, Schultz, 1951.

Seitz, William. "Abstract Expressionist Painting in America." Princeton University, 1955. (Unpublished Ph.D. dissertation.)

Blesh, Rudi. *Modern Art USA.* New York: Alfred A. Knopf, 1956.

Rodman, Selden. *Conversations with Artists.* New York: Devin-Adair, 1957. Includes interviews with Calder, de Kooning, Gottlieb, Hopper, Kline, Pollock, Reinhardt, Rothko, D. Smith.

Hunter, Sam. "The United States," *Art Since 1945.* New York: Harry N. Abrams, 1958.

_____. *Modern American Painting and Sculpture.* New York: Dell, 1959.

Greenberg, Clement. *Art and Culture.* Boston: Beacon Press, 1961.

Ashton, Dore. *The Unknown Shore: A View of Contemporary Art.* Boston: Little, Brown and Co., 1962.

Kuh, Katherine. *The Artist's Voice.* New York: Harper and Row, 1962. Includes interviews with Albers, Calder, Davis, Hofmann, Hopper, Kline, Noguchi, D. Smith.

Rosenberg, Harold. *The Anxious Object: Art Today and Its Audience.* New York: Horizon Press, 1964. Includes chapters on de Kooning, Gorky, Hofmann, Newman, and Johns.

Geldzahler, Henry. *American Painting of the Twentieth Century.* New York: The Metropolitan Museum of Art, 1965.

Rublowsky, John. *Pop Art.* New York: Basic Books, Inc., 1965. Includes sections on Lichtenstein, Oldenburg, Rosenquist, and Warhol.

Battcock, Gregory, ed. *The New Art.* New York: E. P. Dutton, 1966.

Lippard, Lucy. *Pop Art.* New York: Frederick A. Praeger, 1966.

Art Criticism of the Sixties. New York: October House, 1967. Symposium at the Poses Institute of Fine Arts, Brandeis University, Waltham, Mass. Participants included Michael Fried, Max Kozloff, Barbara Rose, Sidney Tillim.

Rose, Barbara. *American Art Since 1900.* New York: Frederick A. Praeger, 1967.

Battcock, Gregory, ed. *Minimal Art.* New York: E. P. Dutton, 1968.

Rose, Barbara. *Readings in American Art Since 1900.* New York: Frederick A. Praeger, 1968.

Cavell, Stanley. *Must We Mean What We Say?* New York: Charles Scribner's Sons, 1969.

Exhibition Catalogues:

Fourteen Americans. New York: The Museum of Modern Art, 1946. Includes Gorky, Motherwell, Noguchi.

40 American Painters: 1940–1950. Minneapolis: University of Minnesota, The University Gallery, Department of Art, 1951. Includes Davis, Gottlieb, Guston, Hofmann, Hopper, Motherwell, Pollock, Reinhardt, Rothko, Tomlin. Contains statements by the artists.

Contemporary American Painting and Sculpture. Urbana: University of Illinois, 1948, 1949, 1950, 1951, 1952, 1953, 1955, 1957, 1959, 1961, 1963, 1965, 1967.

1948 includes Gottlieb, Guston, Hofmann, Hopper, Tomlin.

1949 includes Guston, Hofmann, Motherwell, Pollock, Tomlin.

1950 includes Avery, Davis, Gottlieb, Hofmann, Motherwell, Pollock, Rothko.

1951 includes Avery, Gottlieb, Hofmann, Motherwell, Pollock, Rothko, Tomlin.

1952 includes Avery, Davis, de Kooning, Gottlieb, Hofmann, Motherwell, Reinhardt.

1953 includes Albers, Davis, Gottlieb, Hofmann, Motherwell, Pollock, D. Smith.

1955 includes Albers, Avery, Davis, Gottlieb, Hofmann, Motherwell.

1957 includes Avery, Davis, Hofmann.

1959 includes Avery, Calder, Davis, Frankenthaler, Hofmann, Rauschenberg.

1961 includes Avery, Davis, Hofmann.

1963 includes Avery, Davis, Gottlieb, Hofmann, Kelly.

1965 includes Guston, Hofmann, Lichenstein, Motherwell.

15 Americans. New York: The Museum of Modern Art, 1952. Includes Pollock, Rothko, Still, Tomlin.

Younger American Painters. New York: The Solomon R. Guggenheim Museum, 1954. Includes de Kooning, Gottlieb, Guston, Kline, Motherwell, and Pollock.

The New Decade: 35 American Painters and Sculptors. New York: The Whitney Museum of American Art, 1955. Includes de Kooning, Gottlieb, Kline, Motherwell, Pollock, Reinhardt, Tomlin.

12 Americans. New York: The Museum of Modern Art, 1956. Includes Guston, Kline.

The New American Painting as Shown in Eight European Countries. New York: The Museum of Modern Art, International Council, 1958–59. Includes de Kooning, Gorky, Gottlieb, Guston, Kline, Motherwell, Newman, Pollock, Rothko, Still, Tomlin. Eight countries: Basel, Switzerland; Milan, Italy; Madrid, Spain; Berlin, Germany; Amsterdam, The Netherlands; Brussels, Belgium; Paris, France; London, England.

Sixteen Americans. New York: The Museum of Modern Art, 1959. Includes Johns, Kelly, Rauschenberg, Stella.

Arnason, H. H. *American Abstract Expressionists and Imagists.* New York: The Solomon R. Guggenheim Museum, 1961. Includes Albers, de Kooning, Frankenthaler, Gorky, Gottlieb, Guston, Hofmann, Johns, Kelly, Kline, Louis, Motherwell, Newman, Noland, Pollock, Rauschenberg, Reinhardt, Rothko, Stella, Still, Tomlin.

Seitz, William. *Art of Assemblage.* New York: The Museum of Modern Art, 1961. Includes Chamberlain, Cornell, de Kooning, Johns, Motherwell, Rauschenberg.

4 Amerikanare. Stockholm: Moderna Museet, 1962. Includes Johns, Rauschenberg.

Geometric Abstraction in America. New York: The Whitney Museum of American Art, 1962. Includes Albers, Calder, Davis, Diller, Gorky, Hofmann, Kelly, Noland, Reinhardt, D. Smith, Stella.

Americans 1963. New York: The Museum of Modern Art, 1963. Includes Kohn, Oldenburg, Reinhardt, and Rosenquist.

Toward a New Abstraction. New York: The Jewish Museum, 1963. Includes Kelly, Louis, Noland, Stella.

Amerikanst Pop-Konst. Stockholm: Moderna Museet, 1964. Includes Lichtenstein, Oldenburg, Segal, Warhol.

The New York School: The First Generation. Los Angeles: Los Angeles County Museum of Art, 1965. Includes de Kooning, Gorky, Gottlieb, Guston, Hofmann, Kline, Motherwell, Newman, Pollock, Reinhardt, Rothko, Still, Tomlin.

Alloway, Lawrence. *Systemic Painting.* New York: The Solomon R. Guggenheim Museum, 1966. Includes Kelly, Noland, Poons, and Stella.

McShine, Kynaston. *Primary Structures.* New York: The Jewish Museum, 1966. Includes Flavin, Judd, Morris, T. Smith.

Two Decades of American Painting. New York: The Museum of Modern Art, International Council, 1966. Exhibition traveled to Japan, India, Australia. Includes Albers, de Kooning, Frankenthaler, Gorky, Gottlieb, Guston, Hofmann, Johns, Kelly, Kline, Lichtenstein, Louis, Motherwell, Newman, Noland, Pollock, Poons, Rauschenberg, Reinhardt, Rosenquist, Rothko, Stella, Still, Tomlin, Warhol.

American Sculpture of the Sixties. Los Angeles: Los Angeles County Museum of Art, 1967. Includes Chamberlain, Cornell, Di Suvero, Flavin, Judd, Kelly, Kohn, Morris, Noguchi, Oldenburg, Rauschenberg, Segal, D. Smith, T. Smith.

14 Sculptors: The Industrial Edge. Minneapolis: The Walker Art Center, 1969. Includes Judd, Kelly, and Morris. Articles are by Barbara Rose, Christopher Finch, and Martin Friedman.

Russell, John and Gablik, Suzi. *Pop Art Redefined.* London, Thames and Hudson, 1969.

Solomon, Alan. *New York: The Second Breakthrough, 1959–1964.* Irvine: University of California at Irvine Art Gallery, 1969. Includes Johns, Lichtenstein, Louis, Noland, Oldenburg, Rauschenberg, Rosenquist, Stella, Warhol.

Photography Credits for Color Plates

Lee Boltin: 78
Dan Budnik: 107
Richard Nickel: 67, 73, 79, 85
M. Noguchi: 95
Eric Pollitzer: 68, 70, 71, 72, 75, 77, 83, 84, 86, 87, 88, 90, 91, 92, 94, 96, 97, 98, 99, 102, 103, 104, 105, 108, 109, 111, 112
Walter J. Russell: 74
Lois Steen: 66
F. J. Thomas: 69, 89
Malcolm Varon: 81
Courtesy Albright-Knox Art Gallery: 110
Courtesy Leo Castelli Gallery: 101
Courtesy The Cleveland Museum of Art: 93
Courtesy The Metropolitan Museum of Art: 76, 80
Courtesy The National Gallery of Canada, Ottawa: 106
Courtesy The Woodward Foundation: 65, 100
Courtesy Yale University Art Gallery: 82

Photography Credits for Black and White Illustrations

Oliver Baker: 217, 330
Lee Boltin: 169
Barbara Brown: 146
Rudolph Burckhardt: 124, 125, 145, 149 (top and bottom), 150, 152, 154, 155, 167, 185 (top), 187, 188 (top and bottom), 190, 191, 192 (top and bottom), 193, 194 (top and bottom), 196, 197, 198 (top), 217 (top and bottom), 218, 225, 228 (top), 230, 250, 251, 255, 256, 273 (top and bottom), 275, 276, 278, 279, 280, 281, 282, 283, 289, 291, 293 (bottom), 305 (top), 317, 318, 337
Barney Burstein: 138 (top), 308 (bottom)
Joe Cameron: 320 (top)
Ron Chamberlain: 137, 174, 176, 178, 302, 308 (top)
Geoffrey Clements: 126 (top), 127 (top), 129 (left), 130, 134, 161, 170, 171 (top), 199, 200 (bottom), 201, 202 (top and bottom), 206 (top left, top right, bottom), 207 (top left, top right, bottom), 208 (left and right), 213, 226, 246, 257 (top), 297 (bottom), 325, 326
Hollis Frampton: 294
Frank Lerner: 254 (bottom)
Robert E. Mates: 126 (bottom), 127 (bottom), 128 (left and right), 305 (bottom)
Ron Miyashiro: 228 (bottom)
O. E. Nelson: 120 (top), 169 (top), 235, 236 (top)
Richard Nickel: 153
M. Noguchi: 248
Eric Pollitzer: 119 (top), 132, 138 (bottom), 140, 151, 165 (top), 168, 173, 179, 189, 195, 209, 210 (top and bottom), 212 (bottom), 214 (top and bottom), 219 (top and bottom), 220, 221, 234, 236 (bottom), 239, 241, 247 (top and bottom), 254, 259, 260, 261, 262, 264, 265 (top), 274, 277, 284 (top and bottom), 285, 286, 287, 288, 292, 293 (top), 295, 297 (top), 298, 315, 316 (top and bottom), 320 (bottom), 321, 324
A. E. Princehorn: 160 (bottom)
Robert A. Propper: 306, 307 (top), 313
Nathan Rabin: 258
Walter K. Rosenblum: 135
Walter J. Russell: 147 (top), 240
Savage Studio: 301
John D. Schiff: 129, 143, 144 (top and bottom), 336
Lois Steen: 120 (bottom), 180, 252 (bottom), 253
Gregg Sterling: 123 (top and bottom)
Adolph Studly: 267
Joseph Szaszfai, Yale Art Gallery: 114 (top and bottom), 115, 116, 117 (top and bottom), 118
Frank J. Thomas Photography: 172, 290
Charles Uht: 249
Malcolm Varon: 181
Alfred J. Wyatt: 163, 266

Credit is also due the following museums, galleries, and institutions whose assistance provided photographs of works not necessarily within their domain at the time of this printing.

Harry N. Abrams, Inc.: 158 (top and bottom), 160 (top), 162
Albright-Knox Art Gallery: 319
Arts Magazine: 252 (top)
Irving Blum Gallery: 198 (bottom), 334
Leo Castelli Gallery: 185 (bottom), 186
André Emmerich Gallery: 223, 225 (top), 226, 227
Fischbach Gallery: 314 (top)
John Gibson Gallery: 146
The Solomon R. Guggenheim Museum: 126 (bottom), 127 (bottom), 128 (left and right)
Sidney Janis Gallery: 202 (top), 211, 257 (top), 258
M. Knoedler & Co., Inc.: 237 (top), 238, 240, 241, 242, 244 (left)
Kornblee Gallery: 147 (bottom)
Marlborough-Gerson Gallery: 235, 236 (top), 267, 273, 303, 304, 307 (bottom), 309
The Museum of Modern Art, New York: 133, 136, 231, 232, 268
Pasadena Art Museum: 172
Seattle Art Museum: 171 (bottom), 299

Otherwise it is understood that photographs were provided by those museums and galleries, etc., that are also credited with ownership of the works.

Photographic Credits

486

Index